Special Education Policies

Contributors

KAY A. BERTKEN is a graduate student and a research assistant in the School of Education, Stanford University.

GARRY D. BREWER is Professor, School of Organization and Management, Yale University.

JAY G. CHAMBERS is Associate Director and Senior Research Economist at the Institute for Research on Educational Finance and Governance, Stanford University.

JANE L. DAVID is President of the Bay Area Research Group, Palo Alto, California.

DAVID GREENE is Senior Associate, Active Learning Associates, Palo Alto, California.

WILLIAM T. HARTMAN is Associate Professor of Education, University of Oregon.

DAVID L. KIRP is Professor in the Graduate School of Public Policy, University of California, Berkeley.

MICHAEL W. KIRST is Professor of Education and Business Administration, Stanford University.

MARVIN LAZERSON is Professor of Education, University of British Columbia.

JACK TWEEDIE is Ph.D.-J.D. Candidate, Boalt School of Law, University of California, Berkeley.

Special Education Policies

THEIR HISTORY, IMPLEMENTATION, AND FINANCE

EDITED BY

*Jay G. Chambers and
William T. Hartman*

TEMPLE UNIVERSITY PRESS

PHILADELPHIA

Library of Congress Cataloging in Publication Data
Main entry under title:

Special education policies.

Includes index.
1. Handicapped children—Education—United States.
2. Handicapped children—Education—Great Britain.
   I. Chambers, Jay G.   II. Hartman, William T.
LC4031.S73   1983   371.9′0941   82-10515
                                ISBN 0-87722-280-0

Temple University Press, Philadelphia 19122
© 1983 by Temple University. All rights reserved
Published 1983
Printed in the United States of America

Contents

Contents

vi

Acknowledgments

The collection of papers in this volume arose out of a collaborative research project initiated by the Institute for Research on Educational Finance and Governance (IFG) at Stanford University as part of its overall research program for fiscal year 1980. The project was funded by a grant to the IFG by the National Institute of Education (NIE).

To foster interdisciplinary exchange, it was requested that each of the major discipline-based programs in existence in IFG at that time submit at least one research project or commissioned paper directed at special education policy and implementation, as part of their research program for fiscal year 1980. The major disciplines represented in this volume include: finance and economics, politics, organization, law, and history.

To further collaboration within IFG and within the field of special education, we decided to hold two conferences at Stanford—one in the spring of 1980 at the beginning phase of the project, and another in the fall. The spring conference, hosted by the editors of this volume, was confined primarily to the authors presented here plus two special outside participants, and it was designed to provide limited time for the authors to present their ideas and maximal time for discussion and interchange. At the fall conference, the authors presented drafts of papers prepared as part of the project, and results of their research, to a wider audience of policymakers and experts in special education from the federal, state, and local level. This conference also provided an opportunity for a special presentation of alternative views, by invited outsiders, on the issue of the federal role in special education policy.

We owe a debt of gratitude to the NIE for providing the support necessary to make this project possible and to the many individuals who participated in the endeavor. The two special participants at the first conference, invited because of their long-standing involvement in the development of special education policy and their recognized expertise in this area, were Mr. Frederick Weintraub, Assistant Executive Director of the Governmental Relations Unit for the Council for Exceptional Children; and Dr. Reginald Jones, Professor of Education at the University of California, Berkeley. All of the authors would agree that Dr. Jones and Mr. Weintraub contributed immeasurably to the success of the conference and to some of the final reformulations of the papers of this volume. We sincerely express our collective gratitude to them for their contribution. We would like to thank Mr. Weintraub additionally for his delivery of the keynote address at the second (fall) conference.

Our gratitude also goes to the outside participants at the second conference. These were: J. Myron Atkin, Dean of the Stanford School of Education; Ms. Nancy Barow, Legislative Analyst's Office, State of California; Dr. Robert Calfee, Professor, Stanford School of Education; Rep. Richard A. Flintrop, Assemblyman, State of Wisconsin; Mr. Jim Fox, Project Officer, NIE; Dr. David Greenberg, Director of Special Education, Indianapolis Public Schools; Ms. Theda Haber, Research Assistant, IFG; Dr. Ross Harrold, Visiting Scholar, IFG; Ms. Peggy Hartman, Special Education Consultant; Ms. Christine Hassell, Division of Higher Education Administration and Policy Analysis, University of California; Mrs. Elaine W. Hirsch, Member, Illinois State Advisory Council on the Handicapped; Ms. Kathy Hull, Research Assistant, IFG; Dr. Nancy Kaye, Director of Specialized Educational Services, Berkeley Unified School District (Berkeley, California); Ms. Ellen Kehoe, Research Associate, Division of Educational Policy and Management, University of Oregon; Ms. Meg Korpi, Research Assistant, Stanford School of Education; Rep. J. Kenneth Leithman, Chairman, Joint Subcommittee for Special Education Commission, State of Louisiana; Dr. Betsy Levin, General Counsel, U.S. Department of Education; Dr. Henry M. Levin, Director, IFG; Mr. Rudy Marshall, Legislative Analyst's Office, State of California; Dr. Robert Mattson, Associate Dean, Division of Educational Policy and Management, University of Oregon; David Neal, Center for Study of Law and Society, University of California, Berkeley; Dr. Arturo Pacheco, Associate Dean for Academic and Student Affairs, Stanford School of Education; Dr. Paul Peterson, visiting Professor, Stanford School of Education; Ms. Naomi Roth, Rand Corporation; Dr. Billy Ray Stokes, Executive Director of Special Education Programs, Louisiana State Department of Education; Dr. Al Sullivan, Associate Superintendent and Director of Special Education, Dallas Independent School District; Mrs. Katherine Tordoff, Director of Special Education Services, Milpitas Unified School District (Milpitas, California); Dr. Alvin Townsel, The Council of the Great City Schools; Ms. Lisa Walker, Coordinator, Education of the Handicapped Policy Project, Institute for Educational Leadership; Mr. Frederick Weintraub, Assistant Executive Director, Governmental Relations Unit, Council for Exceptional Children; Mr. Doug Wilms, Stanford School of Education; Ms. Linda Nelson, Assistant Director of Dissemination, IFG; Dr. Terry Wood, Assistant Superintendent, Special Education and Special Schools, Office of the Los Angeles County Superintendent of Schools. We wish to thank additionally, J. Myron Atkin, Betsy Levin, and Terry Wood, who gave the special presentations on alternative views of the federal role in special education at the fall conference.

We acknowledge the valuable assistance of several outside reviewers of the papers presented here. These include Dr. Richard A. Rossmiller, Dr. David B. Tyack, Dr. Paul Peterson, Dr. Dennis J. Encarnation, and Dr. John Meyer. Special thanks are extended to Kathy Hull for handling the organization of the fall conference, and to Theda Haber, Jo Zetler, and Linda Nelson, who assisted in the organization and coordination of the spring conference activities. Finally, thanks are due to Claudette Sprague for her typing of most of the final manuscripts, and to Marine Le Minor for her preparation of the index.

Introduction

CHAPTER 1/

Special Education Policies

JAY G. CHAMBERS and

WILLIAM T. HARTMAN

Special Education Policy Issues

One of the most fundamental effects of the Education for All Handicapped Children Act of 1975 (PL 94-142), state legislation, and successful judicial rulings was to raise the expectations of parents of handicapped children, special education advocacy groups, and others concerned with the welfare of handicapped children. This change was a sharp break with the history of special education in this country and the individual experiences of parents who had sought an education for their handicapped children. In his essay on the origins of special education, Marvin Lazerson identifies the two major historical incentives underlying special education as: (1) interest in controlling the non-normal population through removal from the "normal" school population; and (2) humanitarian concerns for the plight of handicapped children. Of the two, the protection of the nonhandicapped population has frequently been the more powerful motivator. This led to a tradition of exclusionary practices in public schools, second-class citizenship, stigmatization through labeling, and inadequate funding allocations.

Relatively quickly, a turnaround in the fortunes of special education occurred through the legislative and judicial breakthroughs just cited. This was not a chance happening, but rather was the result of a carefully constructed strategy formulated and carried out by advocates of the handicapped. Jack Tweedie's chapter, based on interviews with the principal federal policy actors associated with PL 94-142, describes this process in detail. Underlying the choice of tactics was the belief that school officials were reluctant to include all handicapped children in their programs, were unlikely to institute program reforms to develop

3

and provide appropriate educational programs and services, and were unable or unwilling to demand additional resources sufficient to fund the needed expansion of special education. Consequently, the activist strategy rejected the previous cooperation with school officials and embarked upon a coordinated confrontation approach. To gain sufficient power to obtain their demands, special education advocates used litigation and the threat of continued litigation to obtain concessions from local and state school officials. In turn, the school officials lobbied the congress for financial assistance to help support the new responsibilities and activities to which they had acquiesced.

The result was PL 94-142. Because of the careful use of an "alternative policy network"—outside the traditional, conservative congressional committee structure—to draft the legislation, the new law incorporated procedural safeguards for handicapped children and their parents. It was believed that parents, not school officials, were the best protectors of their children's interests. This fundamental approach accepted as inevitable conflicts at the district level over decisions concerning the appropriate education of handicapped children. Consequently, built in to the implementation process was the tension between parents and schools.

Parents and their allies successfully circumvented the public school system that had frustrated them for so long. Now, rather than having to ask, plead, or cajole for services for handicapped children, they approached schools armed with federal and state mandates legitimizing their claims. They could, and did, demand access to programs, participation in decisions previously made exclusively by educators, and new services. The tables were turned, and special education was placed in a favored position vis-à-vis regular education and many other public services.

While many special educators were strong allies of this movement, it did place the school systems in an adversary position with parents. As David Kirp points out, the use of the political process and the reliance on the legal system resulted in the establishment of legally enforceable rights to an appropriate education for handicapped children. The insistence on these rights led to conflict between parents seeking the accomplishment of legislative objectives and school authorities having to deal with the practical difficulties of implementation.

There can be an enormous gulf between the goals of the policy process and the actual results when translated through the implementation process. This is particularly true in situations, such as special education, where policy goals were formulated at the federal and state levels while implementation was largely the responsibility of local school districts. However, the special education case was somewhat unique in the extent of the detailed requirements established for the local school districts by the federal policy development process. PL 94-142 and its regulations placed many new specific programmatic and operating demands on school districts, which were monitored for compliance by state and federal officials.

The issues and problems facing school districts charged with implementing the new special education mandates are of a significantly different nature from those faced by the national and state level policymakers who established the mandates. School districts have to deal with the "how" of carrying out objectives decided upon by others. Importantly from an implementation standpoint, the policy objectives were established based upon the perceived needs of handicapped children (and the reluctance of school districts to serve them adequately), and deliberately did not consider existing school district and state education agency policies, procedure, and resources as constraints. PL 94-142 placed a significant real and perceived additional burden on school districts in a variety of ways. For example, the requirement for an "appropriate" education for all handicapped children has necessitated the creation of new instructional approaches, the offering of additional instructional programs and related services, and the provision and/or development of new instructional materials. These, in turn, have caused a demand for additional personnel, some with new skills. New procedures for locating all handicapped children and accurately diagnosing their educational needs have had to be established. Perhaps most burdensome of all was the requirement that every handicapped child have a written individual educational program (IEP) specifying current performance level, educational goals and objectives, special education programs and services to be provided, and a time schedule for carrying out the plan. Time is required from several different school personnel to prepare the information necessary to develop the IEP and to attend a conference with parents during which the IEP is specified. Additionally, record keeping and other paperwork activities have expanded to provide documentation of compliance with the new laws and regulations and to fulfill the increased reporting requirement.

These are not, however, insurmountable problems. The study by Jane

David and David Greene finds that school districts are largely in procedural compliance with PL 94-142. That is, school districts are meeting the legal requirements of the law and its regulations. These authors also find that the implementation activities, while technically correct, fall short of achieving the policy objectives that were the basis for the law. The response by school districts of procedural compliance was probably predictable from existing knowledge of public service bureaucracies; these typically deal with change through development of routine procedures incorporated into existing practices to minimize disruption to the system.

David and Greene identify three principal obstacles to full implementation of the intent of the law—the organizational characteristics of local education agencies, lack of adequate knowledge to specify accurately the components of an appropriate education for an individual handicapped child, and limited resources to carry out the mandates. Each has created tensions between policy intent and implementation.

Organizationally, special education has been somewhat isolated from other areas in education and from other (noneducation) agencies serving handicapped children. The traditional separation between regular and special education in the organizational structure of school districts (and state education agencies) hinders the mandated preference for placement of handicapped students in the least restrictive environment. Problems arise, such as overlapping and/or conflicting responsibilities for handicapped students placed in regular classrooms, supervision of special education staff assigned to regular schools, time required by regular classroom teachers to attend IEP conferences, lack of communication and coordination between regular and special education teachers. The existing tensions between regular and special education can be exacerbated by the changes imposed by new special education laws and regulations. On the one hand, regular education personnel now have greater demands placed upon them because of handicapped children. On the other hand, the special education organization and its staff have gained increased status and recognition with "their own" law and have benefited from whatever increased funding has been available. Special education has gained a priority position within education because of federal and state laws, a particularly enviable situation in a time of declining regular enrollments and budget pressures. However, this privileged status can also cause resentment and a backlash reaction among those now favored. The resulting organizational turmoil could prove very disruptive for the effective implementation of PL 94-142.

Another organizational boundary that has important implications for implementation is that between school districts and other public agencies providing services to handicapped children. Under PL 94-142, the education agencies are responsible for ensuring that all related services necessary for handicapped children to benefit from their education are provided, even if those services are available from another agency over which they have no jurisdiction. Further, the multitude of agencies that can become involved and the potential for buck-passing has often proven an overwhelming obstacle for parents seeking help for their handicapped children. Garry Brewer's chapter presents a response to this situation. In it, he describes the concept and implementation of "direction service"—an information-based activity intended to match the special needs of an individual handicapped child with the local service system's capabilities. Direction service cuts across organizational lines to collect and disseminate information about the variety of services from all agencies that are available for handicapped students—education, health, welfare, vocational and rehabilitation, and mental health and retardation. Efficient use of existing provider systems through improved information, coordination, referral and follow-up are frequently discussed as goals, but in the direction services experience they have been implemented and proven. The description of the translation of a concept into actual practice together with the lessons learned through this experience provide valuable insights into successful implementation efforts.

One of the major potential causes for conflict in the implementation of PL 94-142 is the provision for due process hearings. The law stipulates that parents can challenge school district decisions concerning the diagnosis, classification, or placement of their handicapped children, in a formal hearing process. Parents are given the power to question, disagree with, and request changes in areas that have heretofore been the prerogative of school personnel. Perhaps more than any other single provision, due process hearings raised the likelihood of conflict. School officials were concerned about the possibility for widespread use of the hearing process, the bitterness the hearings could create, the time required for them by school personnel, and the cost of hearings. The early experience in California with due process hearings is reported in the chapter by Michael Kirst and Kay Bertken. Their findings indicate that only a very small proportion (less than 1 percent) of children in special education in that state were involved in due process hearings and that the frequency of hearings decreased over time. However, those hearings that were held were time-consuming and costly to the district, both in

7

terms of the cost of the hearing process itself and in terms of the awards made by the hearing decisions. These outcomes resulted from a combination of factors: the bulk of the hearings requested school district payment for students placed in private schools and a strong bias favoring existing service arrangements emerged in the hearing decisions. As a consequence, districts that initiated new programs because of the new laws were frequently unable to recall children previously assigned to private schools and enroll them in their own programs.

The due process hearings also provide an example of a deviation between policymaker objectives and those of some parents of handicapped children (the beneficiaries of the policies). The concept of least restrictive environment is a cornerstone of PL 94-142; however, the hearing process, which was established in significant part to open public schools programs to handicapped children, was primarily used by parents to keep their children out of public schools and in a private and more restricted setting.

The final barrier to full implementation is the lack of adequate resources—not enough money. In his paper, William Hartman presents a conservative estimate of an *additional* $4.5 billion needed to provide an appropriate education to all school-aged handicapped children. This is on top of the very large increases in funding already provided, primarily from state and local levels. Due to the legislative mandates and the threat of litigation, special education budgets have generally risen faster than other sectors of education and other state-funded activities, and in some states substantially faster. This pattern has prevailed during good economic conditions as well as during poor ones (where a special education budget increase might be the exception to a general maintenance level budget or even cutbacks in other areas).

In addition to the programmatic and procedural requirements, PL 94-142 established the promise and expectation of a significant federal role in funding the new requirements. The federal authorization for PL 94-142 has a maximum level of $3.2 billion by 1982/83. This amount would make the federal government a much more equal partner in supporting special education and would provide funding for the bulk of the increased costs caused by the mandate. However, actual appropriations are expected to be less than one-third of the maximum permissible level. This represents a $2 billion shortfall in the federal commitment to special education. If this amount is not, or cannot be, made up by further increases in state and local funding, then changes in programmatic practices that reduce costs and/or changes in the extent of the commitment to the policy objectives of the mandates are likely to occur.

In his analysis, Hartman also indicates particular aspects of implementation under the control or influence of policymakers that can have a significant influence on special education costs. These include: eligibility standards that limit or encourage special education enrollments; standards or guidelines for class size and caseloads; placement pattern choices—the least restrictive alternative; and use of related services. Manipulation of programmatic standards such as these can be utilized by both policymakers and policy implementers. However, in either case, the tradeoffs involved represent a complex balancing act among perceived program quality, individual student needs, district capabilities, and available funds.

In addition to the amount of funds for special education, the allocation of those funds is an important policy issue having direct impact on implementation. This is particularly true for state funds, which comprise the largest source of funding for special education. Approaches to special education funding are varied across states and are not necessarily related to the costs incurred by districts in providing special education programs. Jay G. Chambers and William T. Hartman propose a new funding approach to be applied to special education—the resource-cost model. This model specifically incorporates into the funding mechanism systematic differences among districts in the type and severity of student needs, patterns of student placement in instructional programs and related services, levels of support and administrative services, and the prices of similar resources. The attempt is to provide an equitable allocation of funds among districts based on the comparable costs of each district for providing an appropriate education to all of its handicapped students. This approach can also be used as a planning tool to require an explicit designation of the programs, services, resources, and other programmatic specifications that constitute an appropriate education for the range of handicapped students to be served. This process can be used to bring together policymakers and policy implementers to discuss and reach some consensus on the components of an overall special education that fulfills the policy goals and objectives, represents an obtainable level of service, and meets funding availability.

9

Some Lessons Learned

The implementation of federal policy is, ultimately, a process involving inherent conflicts of objectives. In general, the necessity of establishing a particular change in federal policy derives from the fact that some larger or higher-order set of goals and objectives are not being achieved under present arrangements for state or local government provision. Some additional assurance is required then by the federal authority to ensure that an "appropriate" level of service is forthcoming and that comparable services are accessible to all who require them.

The conflict described above is indeed always a natural tension between higher and lower levels of government, resulting from differences in objectives and goals. It derives from the effort of the higher level of government to achieve the "greater social good," which is in some degree external to the interests of the lower governmental authority. The result is that the lower governmental authority exhibits natural resistance to the implementation of some of these policies because they are disruptive to the normal course of activities within the local agency. They involve additional, and often different, kinds of services than those presently provided, and they involve the establishment of certain procedures to ensure that the mandated services are provided. The establishment of those procedures will almost inevitably result in additional administrative costs for the local agency.

To ensure compliance of the local agencies involves various combinations of incentive mechanisms, enforcement procedures, and additional resources from the higher governmental authority. To the extent that there are substantial conflicts in objectives, only limited additional resources, and ineffective enforcement procedures, local organizations are likely to incorporate only procedural compliance into existing practices or routines. In essence, they meet the letter, but perhaps not the spirit, of the law.

The alteration of particular social goals and objectives of local governmental agencies to meet federal objectives has implications for social services and hence the composition of personnel employed by these agencies to support the new services. These changes in employment patterns change the nature of the labor markets by redirecting the emphasis among different categories of personnel. This creates additional obstacles for compliance by the local agency because it pits different groups of workers against one another due to the change in relative status and security of one group over the others. It may also change bargaining strategies of both the agency and the employee organizations and even alter the very structure and support of these organizations for such changes in policy. Bargaining issues and concerns raised by the employee organizations will differ in different locales, depending on the extent of the impact of the new federal objectives and the relevance of the new services for the particular agency clientele.

These sudden changes in services also have implications for the provision of training and retraining services in different locales as local agencies charged with implementation begin to feel the impact of the increased demand for new sets of skills to meet the new objectives. Existing personnel might have to be retrained, while new programs might have to be developed to train potential new entrants into the labor market. To the extent that these kinds of short-run adjustments are not taken explicitly into account in the mandates for new services, and to the extent that other institutions (e.g., training institutions) are involved in the adjustment process, another obstacle to implementation over which the local agency has perhaps little or no control is created.

Often one of the most prominent features of policy failure can be found in the lack of recognition of the secondary and tertiary effects of particular changes in policy. Not only are there profound effects on the agencies directly affected, but also on the organizations representing employees, on the individual employees conducting their day-to-day work activities, on training institutions, on agencies providing related services, and on individuals who are entitled to what might be described as competing services. Procedural compliance may be achieved in one area at the expense of services in another. The activities of other institutions and agencies may be disrupted. Increased services for one client group may be achieved at the sacrifice of services for other client groups originally served by the local agency. This last is particularly likely when the additional resources provided are insufficient to accomplish the new objectives and a reallocation of existing resources away from other client groups is required. This shift may cause a backlash from groups disadvantaged by the new policies and result in further resistance to implementation efforts at the local level. All of these factors must be recognized and addressed in the consideration of policy changes and their effects on overall goals and objectives.

The intention of this book is to offer some insights into this policy process from a variety of perspectives and provide both researchers and policy-makers with a set of alternative frameworks from which the issues of policy implementation might be evaluated and considered.

PART II/

Development of Special Education Policies

CHAPTER 2

The Origins of Special Education

MARVIN LAZERSON

These sightless eyes, deaf ears, mute tongues and vacant minds are a per-
petual witness against us; hereafter we cannot escape our responsibility by
pleading ignorance of the fact.

> New Jersey Commission on the Deaf and Dumb, Blind and
> Feebleminded, 1873

You can't put my Tony in the dumb-bell school.

> "Slavonian" woman in Los Angeles, mid-1930s

There is nothing more repulsive to me and nothing more unwarranted than
to single out little tots, under 12, put them in a separate room and label
them. . . . Before you give the child the Binet test, be sure to give him
first the Borden and Sheffield test, and for the benefit of out-of-towners, by
the Borden and Sheffield test, I mean find out if they get enough milk—
just plain cow's milk.

> New York City Mayor Fiorello LaGuardia
> to a conference of special educators, 1929

In general, crippled children in Boston are not allowed to attend school.
As a regular practice, school officials make no distinction between those
crippled children who doctors say are able to take part in normal school
activities, and those who are not. Except for isolated instances, they are
prevented from attending school altogether.[1]

> Task Force on Children Out of School, 1970

The history of special education is beset with contradictions. Benevolence and humanitarian concerns for the handicapped have coexisted
and often been outweighed by neglect, racist assumptions, and harsh
practices. Aid to the handicapped has often been most willingly given

15

when it could be justified as protecting "normals" from the deviant. Potential benefits of this aid have been undermined by labeling. Desperately fighting to become an accepted part of the educational system, special education has nonetheless always remained an outsider, subject to second-class citizenship. Part of the process of making public education truly universal, it has never provided access to all who might benefit, and has been used to exclude some youth from full participation with others.

Determining who was handicapped and who needed special education has itself been a torturous process. Was it someone who needed aid to survive physically or economically? Or was it someone who had a learning disability, couldn't "get along" in school, failed to keep up to grade level, or scored low on an IQ test? From its inception, some have condemned special education for not being available to enough children, and some, especially parents of handicapped children, have demanded more as well as better programs. Yet others have condemned special education for too readily identifying children as handicapped, and too readily placing them in segregated special classes. All, from within and outside the educational system, have acknowledged that special education has been the least accepted of our public school programs. To paraphrase John Dewey, if a society ought to provide for its children that which the best parent would provide, special education stands out as a measure of the failure of public responsibility.

Special Education and the Progressive Era

Although physically and mentally handicapped children received some attention in the nineteenth-century, primarily through the establishment of philanthropic and state institutions for the blind and deaf and for the mentally subnormal, most handicapped youth did not receive public attention. On the whole, the handicapped child was treated as a case of individual deviance, a "private trouble" for members of an individual family to handle in its own way. The dispersed population of nineteenth-century America, the limited apparatus of state government, the strength of individualism, and the ethic of private responsibility for child rearing kept most individuals, handicapped or otherwise, within their families and communities. Institutions for the handicapped remained few in number and limited in clientele. Placement in them was largely determined by two events: when individuals were identified as threats to themselves or to others (usually through transgressions of the law or because parents were deemed incapable of caring for their children), or when parents decided to place in institutions children they could not control or who were of no use at home. In essence, responsibility for handicapped children was private and familial. Only when parents were perceived, or perceived themselves, as incapable of caring for their child was he or she likely to become an object of public attention.[2]

At the turn of the century many of these assumptions changed, in part as a result of complaints about the custodial and retrogressive nature of public residential institutions, but more as a result of the creation of a mass public educational system and the expansion of notions of public responsibility. It is hard to overestimate the impact of an expanding, ultimately compulsory, system of schooling on the origins of special education. Schools that all were compelled to attend converted the problem of how to educate dependent and deviant children from a familial, to a school, concern. Baltimore's superintendent of public schools, James Van Sickle, made the point explicit in 1909: "Before attendance laws were effectively enforced there were as many of these special cases in the community as there are now; few of them, however, remained long enough in school to attract serious attention or to hinder the instruction of the more tractable and capable."[3] A decade and a half later, Ellwood Cubberley reaffirmed Van Sickle's understanding:

During the past quarter century our States have enacted a large amount of compulsory-education and child-welfare legislation, and one of the results of the enforcement of these laws has been to throw a new burden on the public schools. Not only have the truant and the incorrigible been brought into the schools in consequence, but also many children suffering from physical defects and disorders as well as those of low mentality. As a result our schools have experienced great difficulty in handling such children, and an educational problem has been created with which we formerly did not have to deal to any such extent as at present. Another result of such legislation which has brought into the school children who are crippled, deaf, suffering from speech or visual defects, the mentally deficient, the feebleminded, the mentally disordered, and the moral delinquent, has been to awaken public expectations which it has been hard for the school to fulfill.[4]

Cubberley was right: the enforcement of compulsory attendance laws was a new phenomenon. While a number of states had compulsory laws before 1900, their enforcement had been sporadic, the laws essentially symbolic statements that all children ought to be in school and that parents were responsible for seeing to their children's attendance. At the turn of the century, expectations shifted: children out of school were too threatening and the benefits of schooling too numerous for attendance to be left to chance. "As part of the broader concern for child welfare during the Progressive Era," David Tyack and Michael Berkowitz have noted, "the conception of attendance work changed substantially. Reformers and school people tried earnestly to attract or push all children into school and created elaborate organizational machinery to do so." Compulsory attendance was an attempt to take the idea of universal schooling seriously.[5]

Partly as a result of compulsory attendance laws, enrollment in the public schools expanded enormously. Between 1890 and 1915, public day school enrollment increased by 55 percent, from 12.7 million to 19.7 million. Average daily attendance went up by 84 percent; the average length of the school year went from 134.7 days to 159.4 days, an increase of 18 percent, while average number of days attended went from 86.3 to 121.2, a 40 percent increase. Total school expenditures climbed by 329 percent, from $141 million to $605 million, and per capita school expenditures from $2.24 to $6.03. In a number of cities, the expansion threatened to overwhelm school systems. Rarely were there enough desks to fill the demand; class size jumped under the burden of insufficient space and too few teachers. The result was a dramatic reordering of the way schools were organized: the introduction and elaboration of bureaucratic and hierarchical modes of operating, an emphasis on efficient use of resources, and the creation of specialized classes for those previously excluded because they were rebellious or deviant.[6]

The problem, educators claimed, was not simply numbers but the nature of the clientele. In a series of "retardation" studies early in the century, dealing with cases in which youth were overage for their grades, the dilemma of schooling seemed to be how poorly large numbers of youth were doing in school. Although there was some variation in the studies, the most prominent and influential, Leonard Ayres's *Laggards in the Schools* (1909), reported that 33.7 percent of all elementary school children were "retarded" with respect to their grade, i.e., more than two years older than the expected age for each grade. Most were in the first two or three grades.

If the lower grades of our schools contain many children who are not going ahead at the normal rate, this means that there are large numbers of pupils who are doing the work of the grades they are in for the second or third time. These children are repeaters . . . in the country as a whole about one-sixth of all of the children are repeating and we are annually spending about $27,000,000 in this wasteful process of repetition in our cities alone.

Ayres was uncertain about why the levels of retardation were so high: illness, irregular attendance, late entrance, loosely enforced or nonexistent compulsory attendance laws all played a part. Other writers were less cautious. For the U.S. Immigration Commission, retardation data were taken as evidence that some foreign groups showed little capacity to adjust to American life.[7]

However the problem of retardation was defined, its links to special education were direct. Writing in 1915, as part of a study of Cleveland's schools, Ayres found 22 percent of the city's elementary school children overaged and making slow progress. "The presence of such children," he wrote, "produces some of the most difficult problems of school administration. They need a different kind of teaching and a different sort of treatment from the other children, and their presence renders the teacher's work harder and its results poorer."[8] Michigan's superintendent of public instruction was even more explicit in 1914:

Schoolmen throughout the country are now beginning to manifest a marked interest in the education of backward and defective children. One factor which has been potent in arousing them to see that something must be done has been the series of investigations made by Thorndike, Ayres, Strayer, Goddard, and others.

Testing these backward children made clear that many of them were feeble-minded; coming to grips with the "retardation" problem thus meant coming to grips with the problem of the feeble-minded. A year later, Superintendent Fred Keeler ordered an investigation of special education in Michigan; this was soon followed by that state's first special education legislation.[9]

The relationship between retardation studies and special education was similar in New Jersey, where state legislation in 1911 authorized the following:

Each board of education in this state shall ascertain what children, if any, there are in the public schools who are three years or more below the normal. In each school district in this state in which there are ten or more children, three years or more below the normal, the board of education thereof, shall establish a special class or classes for their instruction, no class however, to contain more than fifteen children.[10]

Special education thus received its impetus from the enforcement of compulsory attendance legislation, the retardation studies which showed large numbers of children overage for their classes, and the association of retardation with the foreign born, truants, and the mentally deficient. Having fought to bring all children into the schools, educators were now obligated to make special provision for them. As one speaker before the National Education Association put it in 1908: "Public school men may say, 'This is not our problem.' To say this means nothing. The children are here; they are present in the public school in large numbers. They cannot be turned out." [11] Special classes were necessary for the physically handicapped, but more especially, for the "willfully and habitually absent," or those "who could not be controlled by the regular school discipline." [12] Elizabeth Farrell, the first director of ungraded classes in New York City, described her classes as follows:

The special classes in the public schools of the city of New York had their beginning in Public School 1, Manhattan, in 1899. It is interesting to know that this class, which was to demonstrate the need for further classification of children in public schools, was not the result of any theory. It grew out of conditions in a neighborhood which furnished many and serious problems in truancy and discipline. This first class was made up of the odds and ends of a large school. There were over-age children, so-called naughty children, and the dull and stupid children.[13]

The extension of schooling to ever larger numbers and to a more varied clientele for longer periods of time provided the raw material out of which special education and a host of other progressive era educational reforms emerged. But, in addition, the extension of public responsibility for the handicapped incorporated an even larger change: the belief that government intervention would have positive outcomes. This belief was crucial to the growth of social welfare legislation before World War I. The state was beneficent, its agents experts. When parents were negligent, or simply overwhelmed by their social conditions, the state had an obligation to respond. To progressive era reformers, "the old doctrines of laissez-faire and rugged individualism were excuses for cheating children of their birthright." [14] Schools incorporated this view, as a host of social welfare concerns were added on to them—health care, visiting nurses and social workers, Americanization classes, vocational preparation, counseling, kindergartens. [15] Special education was part of that expansion, and like so much else in the progressive era, it combined both optimism and fear, humanitarian concerns for children and the deprived and coercive practices to control deviant behavior. On the one hand, it was humanitarian and socially efficient to place responsibility for the handicapped in the single most important community institution—the public school—rather than placing such youth in residential schools or leaving them exclusively as a private responsibility of parents. On the other hand, while special education provided places for the physically handicapped, its impetus came from fear that the "morally" and "socially" deviant, usually immigrants and the poor, represented social threats. The two concerns—humanitarian and controlling—were always in tension with one another, but because they were so often class-based, the latter tended to overwhelm the former, as the humanitarian concerns of special education became secondary to the desire to segregate all those the educational system found disruptive. [16]

Assumptions and Practices

The arguments in support of special education reveal the conflicting tensions between humanitarian and controlling aims, between concern to enhance the lives of the handicapped and to protect "normals" from the handicapped. Efforts to gain public support for special education did not readily bring positive responses. The first issue was simply to legitimate the idea that the handicapped belonged in the public schools. Here approaches differed. The physically handicapped were the most obviously excluded; deaf, blind, and crippled children were simply kept out of school. They were considered difficult to accommodate in regular schools, they were very costly to provide facilities for, and they could turn to existing residential schools. On the whole they were expected to be a family concern. When placed under public school auspices, they were likely to be put in separate special schools. Less physically handicapped could enter available speech, reading, and hearing classes. Although public support for these children was always limited, and controversies over pedagogy flourished, the basic issues for the physically handicapped seemed relatively straightforward: to provide places for such children and an education that would allow them to participate as much as possible in their communities. Efforts on their behalf were largely centered in a small number of philanthropic and parental groups that battled to establish special programs.

The mentally handicapped in contrast were treated as a much larger, more serious, and more threatening problem, and it was toward this group that most of the attention was directed. "It is impossible and also undesirable," Wyoming's director of special education wrote in 1925, "to build state institutions large enough for the maintenance and special training of all feeble-minded children."

> It is undesirable to take large numbers of children away from their homes. All who can with propriety and without offense remain in their homes and be trained in the community school should find, provided by that school, the special training facilities demanded by their mental handicaps. . . . The mentally handicapped child, as such, constitutes a part of the proper work of the public school—training children for community life.[17]

Three kinds of benefits would come with special education programs—those to the handicapped themselves, those to the regular students and teachers, and those to the society at large. By being brought into the schools, the handicapped would cease to be hidden away or poorly cared for, their health and discipline neglected by parents who all too often were poor and undisciplined. Upon receiving their first handicapped students, teachers in Washington, D.C. reported that "lack of care seems a general cause of defect. The classes include children with badly-shaped limbs, peculiar teeth, badly-shaped mouths, speech impediments, abnormal heads, defective hearing and eyesight, partial paralysis of the throat, most are bad with tendency to be very disobedient and want to do as they please . . . parents are as a rule very poor and seem to be ignorant of the essentials pertaining to the proper care of children."[18] But the handicapped could not just be brought into the schools; they had to be segregated from the other children so that, in Wallace Wallin's words, "they are relieved of the disheartening, cruel, and unjust competition with their superior fellows . . . and from the

22

feeling of inferiority which inevitably ensues." [19] In special classrooms or special schools, the handicapped would be given specially trained teachers, curriculum better suited to their needs and abilities, classroom environments suited to their handicaps, and the vocational training that would allow them to become economically self-sufficient.

Even more prominently argued than the benefits the handicapped would receive from special education were the presumed benefits to the "normals."

> In the regular grades the feeble-minded and subnormal represent, as it were, an unassimilable accumulation of human clinkers, ballast, driftwood, or derelicts which seriously retards the rate of progress of the entire class and which often constitutes a positive irritant to the teacher and other pupils. [20]

Over and over the argument that it was absolutely necessary to get the handicapped out of regular classrooms was emphasized. Washington, D.C.'s supervisor of ungraded schools found "these atypical pupils were not only a detriment to the normal children with whom they were placed, but a great trial to the teachers," a constant source of distraction and anxiety. [21] Special education would receive no support, Baltimore's superintendent of schools claimed, if it were not for the retrogressive effects of the handicapped on the "normals."

> If it were not for the fact that the presence of mentally defective children in a school room interfered with the proper training of the capable children, their education would appeal less powerfully to boards of education and the tax-paying public. It is manifestly more expensive to maintain small classes for backward and refractory children, who will profit relatively little by the instruction they receive, than to maintain large classes for children of normal powers. But the presence in a class of one or two mentally or morally defective children so absorbs the energies of the teacher and makes so imperative a claim upon her attention that she cannot under these circumstances properly instruct the number commonly enrolled in a class. [22]

Special education would also produce numerous social benefits. The individual, flexible, and vocationally oriented teaching of special education would spill over and inform regular classroom teaching. Gone would be the waste of human resources and the costs of supporting dependent adults who could have become self-supporting with the proper education and training.[23] By attracting handicapped youth and keeping them in school, special education would cut down truancy and neglect, and thereby reduce criminal behavior. The majority of the mentally defective, the New Jersey Commission on the Care of Mental Defectives reported in 1914, "are troublesome. . . . Outside of school they are in mischief and crave a notoriety accompanied by wrong doing. They are oversexed and practice indecencies or worse. They become the big, awkward, misunderstood, pitiable and dangerous companions of little children."[24]

Indeed, no argument associated with special education received greater attention in the first three decades of the twentieth-century than the fear that the unattended or uneducated feeble-minded were the carriers of social malignancy. No individuals did more to propagate that view than Henry C. Goddard and Lewis M. Terman.

Director of the Vineland [New Jersey] Training School for the Feeble-minded, Goddard was the first American to use intelligence tests on a large scale. Goddard assumed that mental defectives needed special training, and he began using a translated version of Binet's scale in 1910. Quickly finding that its classifications neatly accorded with the Training School's evaluations of its children, Goddard concluded that "experience with these tests has continually reassured us as to their amazing accuracy; their usefulness as a means of understanding the mental development of children is beyond question." Turning to the testing of public school children, he found that at least two percent of the school population were mentally defective, unable to achieve in the traditional classrooms, and ignored by the schools. At the same time, Goddard claimed that the results of his and his assistant Elizabeth Kite's research into a family of degenerates—the Kallikaks—confirmed that mental deficiency was a hereditary characteristic subject to Mendelian laws. Armed with this knowledge, Goddard embarked on a career to warn the public against the menace of social degeneracy, attacking what he considered excessively laissez faire approaches to social policy and the educational system's archaic attachment to equality.[25]

Goddard's missionary zeal attracted considerable attention, but even more influential in tying special education to mental testing and the threat of the feeble-minded, was Stanford's Lewis Terman. With the publication of *The Measurement of Intelligence* (1916), Terman introduced the concept of IQ, gave step-by-step administrative and scoring instructions, and argued that all levels of intelligence could be measured. Over the next decade, Terman became America's most influential psychologist, his revision of the Binet scale became the bible of mental testing, and IQ became synonymous with intelligence. And Terman, like Goddard, was an indefatigable propagandist for his views.

Terman initially tried his revised Binet scale on "mentally deficient" children in San Luis Obispo, California, in 1912, and found all 24 children tested had low IQs. He recommended that the results of the tests be used to provide special classes, and claimed that they "provided good argument for the introduction of manual training, domestic science" into the schools. At the same time, he began to pose larger uses for school-based intelligence tests: to identify the feeble-minded, to help choose the methods for educating each child, to allow for promotions on the basis of intellectual ability, to develop vocational guidance through which "it would then be possible to lay before each child at the end of his school course an array of occupations in which (as far as intelligence is concerned) he might reasonably be expected to succeed," and to promote the segregation of the feeble-minded to prevent their corrupting normals. Like Goddard, he concluded that intelligence was largely hereditary, that IQ test scores were an accurate and relatively constant measure of intelligence, that the scores could predict future development, and that poor test performance was due to inferior mental endowment.[26]

Terman spelled out the implications of both his test findings and his assumptions about intelligence in 1917.

> Feeble-mindedness has always existed, but only recently have we begun to recognize how serious a menace it is to the social, economic and moral welfare of the state. Extensive and careful investigations in large numbers and in diverse parts of the United States have furnished indisputable evidence that it is responsible for at least one fourth of the commitments to state penitentiaries and reform schools, for the majority of cases of chronic and semi-chronic pauperism, and for much of our alcoholism, prostitution and venereal disease.

In California alone, Terman wrote, the feeble-minded were costing in excess of $5 million a year, and they were multiplying at an "undiminished rate." Survey after survey showed 1 to 4 percent of all children were feeble-minded; Terman's data indicated a population consistently above 2 percent, and that of these, at least half should be institutionalized.

> Feeble-minded children are present everywhere. They linger in the third, fourth, fifth and sixth grades. They consume a disproportionate amount of the teacher's time, they drag down the standards of achievement for normal children, they tend to become incorrigible and to feed the never-ending stream of juvenile court cases. . . . Feeble-minded children in the regular classes not only interfere with instruction, they are also likely to be a source of moral contagion. We have known a feeble-minded girl of fifteen years, eight years old mentally and so in the third grade with little girls eight to nine years, to teach her little classmates the grossest sexual practices.

The situation was bad and deteriorating. At least 1 percent of all school children should be segregated in residential custodial institutions, and preferably sterilized. Another 2.5 percent belonged in special classes, and an additional 15 percent should be provided with the kind of manually and vocationally oriented education that would prevent them from becoming burdens to the society.[27]

Goddard's and Terman's views did not go uncontested, but the association they drew between intelligence and moral and social behavior dominated debates in the 1920s, and, along with the tremendous faith placed in the measurement of intelligence through individual and group tests, they provided a powerful impetus to the special education movement.[28] So strong was the view that special education classes were a means of reducing delinquency, that New Jersey's Democratic boss, Frank Hague, supported a bureau of special service in the Jersey City public schools during the early 1930s to diagnose physical and mental problems, improve special education facilities, and expand recreational activities on school grounds in order to cut down the number of referrals to reform schools. Within a few years, the bureau claimed that it had reduced the number of Jersey City youth committed to state reformatories by 90 percent.[29]

The arguments for special education thus blended a multiplicity of assumptions, from optimism about the possibilities to pessimism that segregation in special settings was a minimal means of protecting the normals from the handicapped—especially from the mentally handicapped, since the humanitarian arguments for providing for the physically handicapped never carried the same political weight as the fear of neglecting the mentally subnormal. Special education was appealing, moreover, because it was an apparently logical extension of the organizational, curricular, and pedagogical reforms of progressive education. Not surprisingly then, in the decades before 1930, special education went from virtually nonexistent to being a subsystem within most large city school systems. New Jersey (1911), New York (1917), and Massachusetts (1920) passed legislation making it mandatory for local boards of education to determine the number of handicapped children in their districts, and to provide special classes where 10 or more mentally retarded children were found. Minnesota (1915), as well as New York and New Jersey, provided state subsidies of up to $100 or $200 for each special education child. Pennsylvania (1919) facilitated local school district cooperation in special education. Wyoming (1919), Missouri (1919), Connecticut (1921), Washington (1921), and Oregon (1923) enacted permissive legislation. California (1920) offered financial aid for deaf, blind, and crippled children in public school classes, of up to $700 for every nine children, then changed the funding in 1927 to one-half the excess cost for educating the physically handicapped, and added children with speech defects to the eligible list in 1931. Wisconsin (1921), Louisiana (1921), and Ohio (1921) authorized state aid; and between 1925 and 1928, Minnesota, New Jersey, Missouri, Connecticut, New York, Illinois, Ohio, and Michigan either introduced state aid or expanded the amount available. Maryland, whose compulsory education act in 1902 excluded handicapped children, called, in 1914, for special classes for "defective children" at each county's discretion and then provided state funds in 1930.[30]

The new concern at the state level reflected the growth of special education classes in urban school systems. Outside of a few large cities (New York, Chicago, Cleveland, Providence), almost no special segregated classes existed before 1900; those that did simply lumped together children unacceptable in regular graded classes, essentially truants and disciplinary problem children—this during an era when many of these same children could easily avoid coming to school. Exactly how many cities added special classes in the decades after 1900 is hard to determine. An unreliable U.S. Bureau of Education survey in 1911 found that 373 of the 898 city school systems that replied to a questionnaire had special classes for the mentally exceptional (54 city systems had classes for the exceptionally gifted); 91 of the cities had special classes for the physically handicapped. The data are quite suspect, but they suggest that as early as 1910, city superintendents felt it necessary to claim that they were responding to handicapped children. A 1924 Bureau of Education survey, apparently much more accurate, found that the number of city school systems providing special classes or day school programs for the mentally subnormal increased from 54 in 1914 to 133 in 1922. A 1919 survey by the National Committee for Mental Hygiene reported that 108 of 155 cities it polled had special classes for mentally defective children. By 1919, the six cities with the largest public school populations (New York, Chicago, Philadelphia, Boston, Cleveland, and St. Louis) all had special education classes, with the number of pupils enrolled in them varying from 0.5 percent of the total student population in St. Louis to 1.0 percent in Boston and 1.2 percent in Cleveland. By the end of the 1920s, the figures were even higher. In 1929, at the state level, Wisconsin, the lowest state, had 0.31 percent of its school population in special education classes; Massachusetts and Minnesota had about 1.5 percent, the highest in the nation. That same year, Detroit had 2.1 percent of its elementary school students in special education; Los Angeles, 3 percent; and Philadelphia, 3.2 percent. Cleveland went from 1.9 percent in 1913 to 5.4 percent in 1925 to a whopping 6.3 percent in 1929. Nationally, between 1922 and 1932, the number of students enrolled in special education programs provided by public schools went from 26 thousand to 162 thousand, from 0.1 percent to 0.6 percent of the total kindergarten through grade 12 public school enrollment, a larger proportionate increase than was to occur in any subsequent decade.[31]

Case Studies

The raw data tell us that special education had become a feature of urban public schooling by the mid-1920s. To understand how that happened, and what the limits of the process were, it is necessary to look at particular cities and states. Three will serve as illustrative examples: Oakland, California; Philadelphia, Pennsylvania; and the state of California.

In the decade around World War I, Oakland became a leader in introducing mental tests to groups of students in its public schools. Enthusiasm for the tests was part of a series of educational reforms designed to cope with the city's mushrooming school population, which grew a phenomenal 132 percent between 1910 and 1917. As early as 1901, the school system had introduced flexible promotions and some ungraded classes so that elementary school teachers could divide their classes according to the ability of their pupils, and then promote each group as it accomplished the grade's work. In 1911, a psychological clinic was established to use intelligence tests to examine "abnormal" children. The goal was to isolate the subnormal—"the absent, the tardy, the sickly, the unruly, the liars, thieves and cowards"—so that teachers could work with the normal children. Within a few years, special classes were created for those children found subnormal by the clinic.[32]

At the same time, Oakland responded to a survey of its schools by Ellwood Cubberley, then head of Stanford's Department of Education, by centralizing authority and by expanding the scientific assessment of student abilities and accomplishments. The latter task was undertaken in the fall of 1917 by Virgil Dickson, a student of Lewis Terman at Stanford. Dickson began with the by then standard study of student progress, and found less than half of Oakland's elementary school pupils making normal progress, with the highest rates of retardation and school failure concentrated in the immigrant districts. Over the next two years, Dickson tested 6,600 students (almost 45 percent of whom were in the first grade), about 15 percent of the city's school enrollment, and concluded that many students were failing because they "had inherent mental tendencies that make the ordinary course of study either impossible or impractical of attainment." These students had to be placed in special classes, otherwise they faced "loss of interest, a loss of self-respect or a resort to subterfuge," with the consequences being "social unrest, sham, and the I.W.W. spirit."

Dickson's analysis and recommendations were strongly supported by Oakland's administrators and teachers. Principals and teachers in the two elementary schools with the heaviest concentrations of immigrant children reported that ability grouping reduced discipline problems, dropouts, and made teachers and pupils "happier." Support from within the system led Dickson to expand his efforts; in 1919/20, he processed 20 thousand students through group intelligence tests, nearly half the total enrollment. The results affirmed previous findings: recent immigrants from Southern and Eastern Europe scored below average on the tests, and the highest percentage of "border zone" or "dull normal" pupils were in the immigrant schools. By the middle of the 1920s, the adoption of intelligence testing for ability grouping in Oakland was virtually complete. The city had become a pioneer in testing.

Developments in Oakland are striking in what they reveal about the growth of special education. First, the use of intelligence tests was crucial to the rapid expansion of special education, a phenomenon true throughout the country. In Wallace Wallin's words, "The widespread employment of these [IQ] tests . . . whatever their imperfections and virtues may be, had indubitably done more than anything else to promote the organization for special classes and the introduction of differentiated courses of instruction in the public schools." [33] Second, the tests, special education, and ability grouping were part of a broader series of reforms designed to make the schools more flexible and progressive, reforms that reflected the common educational wisdom of the day. Third, the major justification for the special classes was to isolate the "subnormal" in order to free teachers to work with normal children. Fourth, the problem of poor school progress was considered primarily an immigrant problem. Fifth, insofar as it was recorded, principals and teachers were enthusiastic about ability grouping in their schools. Finally, Oakland's experiment with intelligence tests and special classes was heavily influenced by Lewis Terman and carried out by his students. More broadly, special education was profoundly shaped by the heightened influence and prestige of the emerging profession of psychology, and by certain key psychologists.

In contrast to Oakland's early involvement with testing, grouping, and special education, Philadelphia was chastised early in the 1920s for failing to test and classify students by ability and for having special classes only for the "orthogenic backward," those children two to three years overage for their grades. The city was urged to appoint a citywide director of special education, to establish a psychological clinic to diagnose backward children, and to provide special training and higher salaries to attract competent special education teachers. The rationales were exactly those articulated in Oakland and elsewhere:

> Special classes not only offer opportunity to exceptional children but, by removing them from the regular grade classes, make the latter more homogeneous and thereby increase the efficacy of the teaching process in them. The main warrant for their existence and the additional expenditure of school funds necessary lies in this fact, though the advantages they offer to exceptionally handicapped children cannot be ignored. [34]

The Pennsylvania survey was part of a larger attack on the mismanagement of Philadelphia's schools, an attack that, as occurred in Oakland, urged the standard progressive education reforms. The problem of the handicapped was only one aspect of the reform movement. Yet between 1920 and 1930, Philadelphia's public school authorities moved to make the city an exemplar of special education. By mid-decade there were 325 special education classes with more than 6 thousand pupils in them; almost 60 percent of the pupils were in classes for the mentally deficient; most of the others were in classes for the sight-, speech-, or hearing-impaired. The newly created Division of Special Education included a director, a psychological clinic, a speech clinic, supervisors of classroom instruction, eight principals of special schools or special programs, as well as classroom teachers. The city's superintendent of schools called special education one of the "high spots in our school system," and claimed, "Probably no city in America is doing more for the various types of children who cannot profit by the regular class instruction than the City of Philadelphia." [35]

The superintendent was engaging in hyperbole, but the statistics on growth reveal that special education was indeed attracting a good deal of attention. By 1931, the number of special education classes was 546, with over 10,600 pupils. The rate of growth (at least 300 percent) surpassed that of the general school population, which grew by about 28 percent during the 1920s. Moreover, throughout the decade, annual school reports gave extra attention to special education, and the report of the director of special education was given prominent space. What began in the early twenties as a few paragraphs became by the end of the decade a 150-page monograph, discussing how backward children were recommended for special classes, describing the psychological clinic's work, expressing the determination to test as many school children as possible, and justifying the high cost of special education. [36]

These trends were not unique to Oakland and Philadelphia. In New Jersey, the classes for mental defectives during the 1920s were called "Binet classes" and were overwhelmingly populated by immigrant and behavior problem children. As part of its commitment to differentiate the curriculum and to establish special education classes between 1922 and 1924, Wyoming's Department of Education gave intelligence tests to 34 percent of the state's 50,580 public school students. San Jose initiated a testing program stressing concern about immigrant retardation and immigrant mental deficiency, using intelligence tests to place "backward" children in special classes, and organized by Terman's students. Throughout the country, special education received its major impetus from the application of testing to the immigrant and the poor. In Cleveland, "congested districts of the city furnish the greater number of subnormal children," the superintendent of schools reported in 1930. "The majority of these children come from homes of day-laborers and factory workers, from homes where a foreign language is the medium of conversation, where educational standards are low, where means of learning are meager and the desire is limited by low mentality." Occasionally, the relationships between testing and the poor were altered. Upper middle class Palo Alto altered the common pattern by using intelligence tests primarily at the high school level for program placement and vocational guidance, revealing how closely linked testing and special education were to social class and ethnicity.[37] So powerful had the IQ ideology become that one mother of a truant child told Lillian Wald in New York, "I should worry. Ain't his IQ O.K.?"[38]

As in Oakland and Philadelphia, developments statewide in California reveal the growth of special education and the assumptions behind it. Before 1900, California had established two residential institutions for the physically and mentally handicapped. But between 1900 and 1920, concern escalated, especially over the mentally deficient. In 1915, the state legislature appointed a committee to investigate "Mental Deficiency and the Proposed Institution for the Care of Feebleminded and Epileptic Persons." Chaired by the superintendent of a state reform school and heavily influenced by Terman and Henry Goddard, the committee declared the feeble-minded (especially feeble-minded women) a social menace, called for their permanent custodial care and sterilization and recommended that mental examinations be given to all children in public schools "to early discover those who are so deficient mentally that they must ever remain children in mind."[39] Two years later the state legislation revealed what had come to be commonly accepted assumptions about the feeble-minded: their low intelligence was inherited and immutable; it caused crime and immorality; it was widespread and hidden until discovered by the intelligence tests; and it was increasing and threatened to overwhelm society unless controlled through segregation and sterilization. In 1919, a new state school law called for separate classes for "backward children or those who are irregular in work," wherein school boards could "substitute for regular course of study other types of school work . . . better adapted to the

32

mental needs of the pupils enrolled." The legislation institutionalized classes for "misfits"—examples of which were already operating in a number of cities—calling for their expansion, and offering no objection to the current understanding that the special classes would enroll primarily behavior problems and children from foreign born homes.[40]

By the 1920s, California had enshrined public school classes for backward children in its educational statutes, classes largely occupied by children of the poor and foreign born. There were public school classes for the deaf, blind, and speech handicapped; but in terms of numbers and concern these were insignificant when compared to the special classes for the mentally deficient. In the words of State Superintendent of Public Instruction Will C. Wood (1921), "The problem of providing for mental defectives is a far greater one than that of providing for the education of the deaf and the blind . . . it is a conservative estimate that two percent of the children enrolled in the public schools of California are definitely feebleminded."[41]

While the larger cities had special classes, rural areas do not seem to have had them. But perhaps most important, the expansion of special education in California as a public responsibility did not seem to touch the mentally subnormal children of middle-class and wealthy parents. The expectation remained that the well-off would do pretty much what they had always done: where parents did not want to institutionalize their children, they could band together to establish a private program or they could keep their children at home with no or little support services available. Since middle-class children were not regarded as a social menace, they were treated, Mercer and Richardson conclude, as "individual deviants whose welfare was of no particular concern to the larger society. As long as they did not become involved in delinquent acts, [middle-class] feebleminded children were treated as individual deviants for parents to handle as best they could."[42] In California, special education originated and remained a class and racially based system; it was not to change.

The 1930s: Raising Questions

The enthusiasm which greeted special education during the 1920s was deceiving. Growth and claims about beneficence hid a different reality. Most handicapped children remained the responsibility of their parents and received little special education. But even more telling, special education itself was providing questionable benefits. Occasionally questions about what special education actually did were raised in the 1920s, but they were invariably overwhelmed by the belief that special education's problem was quantitative: there simply was not enough of it. In the early 1930s, more serious questions began to be raised. Philadelphia's superintendent of schools noted in his 1931 report that economic conditions were forcing a slowdown in special education's growth and he suggested, "Perhaps it is well that we are compelled for economic reasons to move slowly, because any treatment of children which requires segregation, either of the dull or the brilliant, may cause errors of judgment which a lifetime will not correct." [43] Doubts about special education also emerged as the early findings on IQ tests were challenged, raising questions about the most commonly used mechanisms for entering children into special classes. [44] But despite these questions, special education remained a "good thing" marred only by faulty implementation. Nowhere was this view more apparent than in the 1930 White House Conference on Child Health and Protection.

Claiming that its data were "the most complete and searching which have been brought together," the Committee on Special Classes of the conference presented "a study of conditions [that] so obviously needed improvement that there should be no hesitation in effecting the recommendations of the various sub-committees." The committee's report was thorough, its tone frustrated and angry. The committee acknowledged that special education was accepted in many urban school systems, that it had grown substantially since early in the century, and that a number of states provided financial aid for special education classes. Nonetheless, the vast majority of handicapped children were still not receiving special education; many were simply excluded from school altogether. The committee estimated that there were 10 million maladjusted children of whom only 1 million were receiving special education. And opposition to a further expansion of special programs was strong. Even where special education was available, conditions were often deplorable—classes in basement rooms and former closets with the least trained teachers, children with different handicaps lumped together and no real effort made to teach them. Where adequate attention was being paid to any particular handicap, it was largely determined by the "influence of the organization interested in that particular type of child. On the other hand, special education for those types of handi-

34

capped children not sponsored by outside organizations is very frequently neglected." "Unfortunately," the committee concluded, "it is true that the vast majority of the people do not believe that the handicapped child is worth educating. . . . The majority of principals of elementary schools have little interest in the handicapped child," and the classroom teacher's only interest was "to get him out of her room where he is making unusual demands on her time and patience." [45]

The White House committee had little to offer on how to move from neglect to care. Indeed its tone was not optimistic. Admitting that the financial costs of educating handicapped children were high—two and a half to four and a half times the cost of regular elementary school classes, depending on the handicap—the committee concluded:

> It would seem almost unnecessary to have to justify, in these United States, the cost of the education of any child who is educable. Humanitarianism alone would seem a sufficient justification. Yet it must be remembered that the state is responsible to the taxpayers for the use of public moneys and that in consequence the state tends to look upon all education as an investment that will pay justifiable dividends.

To gain those dividends, the Committee on Special Classes resorted to what had become the common wisdom, in effect summarizing three decades of agitation for special education: extend special education to more handicapped children; make greater efforts at early diagnosis, treatment, and training; coordinate services; modify the curriculum so that it conforms to abilities; increase the vocational orientation and oversee job placement and follow-up; establish a national council for handicapped children and state advisory councils; and engage in more active campaigns to publicize the need and advantages of special education. [46]

The White House committee was not the first to criticize the state of special education. Right from the beginning, supporters as well as opponents complained that the classes were being used as dumping grounds where the "most helpless of our school population" were placed in "small, poorly lighted, poorly heated, and poorly ventilated rooms with meager equipment" and untrained teachers. [47] But more important, the committee's complaints were not rectified over the next decade. Hostility to special education continued, funds were cut. Special educators bitterly complained about the "type of school administrator who does

35

not consider that the handicapped child possesses any rights; who tolerates him in school merely because of the mandate of the compulsory attendance statute, and who would exclude him from school altogether if the laws so permitted." [48] And, we might add, did effectively exclude such children. [49] Efforts to overcome parents' hostility to placing their children in the "dumb" classes led to name changes—"opportunity classes," programs for "exceptional children"—and to a new emphasis on the "gifted" child as a responsibility of special educators. In 1941, the National Education Association took the obvious step, changing the name of its Department of Special Education to the International Council for Exceptional Children. [50]

The 1930s, then, were not good times for special education. The classes were, in the words of a Chicago survey:

> so regarded that they cast a stigma on anyone who is assigned to them. They are frequently used as a club over children who are not otherwise amenable in order to admonish them to renewed efforts in their studies. Similarly, return to the regular class (and thus escape from the stigma of the special class) is often held out as a prize to children who have been assigned to the special class, in order to stimulate them to learn facts which otherwise can mean little to them. If this attitude of mind were confined to teachers and principals alone it would be bad enough, but it inevitably spreads to the entire school community. Pupils are inevitably trained to look upon the more unfortunate members of the school community as persons to be avoided, ridiculed, or maliciously tormented. . . . It is small wonder that parents often object strenuously to having their children placed in such classes. Any parent would be unintelligent, indeed, who did not object to treatment which automatically labels his child as incompetent, little fit to associate with normal persons. [51]

Special education was thus the setting for those the schools could not or did not want to educate, and just as often served as the transmission belt to exclude handicapped youth and behavior problems from the schools. Humanitarian and instrumental pleas to bring the physically handicapped into the schools were virtually ignored. The problems were not simply economic, but were rooted in the very origins of special education. Rather than a response to those roots, a kind of disassociation set in. What had been prominently discussed as a public issue became limited to the specialized professional organizations that assumed responsibility for educating the handicapped. Two examples of these trends are illustrative: Philadelphia, which, in the 1920s, had prominently featured special education as a centerpiece of its school system, virtually ceased to acknowledge the existence of special education by the mid-1930s; and New Jersey and California, states that were extremely active in passing special education legislation between 1910 and 1929, did almost nothing for the next decade. Save for interest generated by provisions for handicapped children in the Social Security Act, special education had had its day. Its humanitarian thrust had always been secondary to the fear generated by the mentally subnormal. Once the current of fear had declined, replaced by other concerns, once a structure had been established to place and thus control the deviants, special education seemed to have little to offer.[52]

The Post-War Reassessment

As Americans moved out of the Depression and World War II, the shape of special education was clear, and there was little reason aside from the chance of more funds, to think that much would change. Special education was both part of, and peripheral to, most urban school systems. Little political or public support existed. Although below-the-surface frustration on the part of parents whose children were excluded from the schools or were being mistreated while in school was mushrooming, few predicted the impending outburst of political agitation. The decline of the "social menace" fears of the 1920s, and doubts about the immutability of IQ or the inherent relationship of intelligence to criminality, had seemingly diminished interest in placing as many as possible in special classes. Educators, special and otherwise, continued to assume that many handicapped children did not belong in public schools, and that the removal of the handicapped from regular classrooms was essential if the normals were to receive adequate schooling. A few special educators did argue, however, that more attention should be paid to keeping the handicapped in regular classrooms. More and more, where special education was available, it was justified for its potential economic returns: providing the handicapped with vocational training and job placement. Meanwhile, the field itself had become professionalized, and attention shifted decisively away from the social issues that had generated the special education movement in the first place to technical problems of assessment, pedagogy, classroom management, and curriculum. But it was also clear that many special education programs existed only because groups outside the system had mounted effective political campaigns, and that if special education was going to change, it would come from a combination of parent organizations and some special educators.[53]

The sense of stability in the early postwar period was misleading, however, for two developments were dramatically altering the place of special education in the educational system: extraordinary growth of the student population, and tremendous conflicts over the presumed benefits of special education and the procedures for placing children in special classes. Between 1948 and 1968, the number of children in public school education programs went from 357 thousand to 2,252,000, from 1.2 percent to 4.5 percent of the total kindergarten through grade 12 enrollment. By 1976, the total had become 3,837,000 handicapped children in special education programs, amounting to 7.7 percent of total school enrollment. In 1948, 12 percent of the handicapped children were in special education; in 1963, 21 percent, and in 1968, 38 percent. That still left large numbers of handicapped receiving no formal schooling at all, perhaps a million plus during the 1960s.[54]

In part, the expansion was due to simple demographics. The postwar baby boom increased the number of handicapped children born, while improved medical technologies kept more alive or limited the severity of the handicap. At the same time, new concerns—speech impairment, reaction to the polio epidemic of the 1950s, the "discovery" of learning disabilities—generated still more potential clients for special education, especially among white middle-class families. Numbers severely strained the system, but perhaps most strikingly, they created a discrepancy between the number of available spaces and the desire of parents to have their handicapped children in public schools and adequately taught.

It is hard to overestimate the impact of parental organizations on special education in the 1950s and 1960s: they were the successful agitators for the expansion of the system. Often in uneasy alliance with professional special educators, through letter writing campaigns, through lobbying pressures in state legislatures and departments of education, and through the development of national coordinating groups, they forced the transfer of larger portions of educational funds to special education. In important ways, parent and professional lobbying groups simply continued activities that had been effective earlier; commentators on special education prior to World War II had openly admitted that without such pressure groups, special education programs, especially for the physically handicapped, would hardly have existed.[55] Even so, the prominence of these groups after World War II was extraordinary. To take one example: in California in 1963, a coalition of parents and professionals in support of programs for the neurologically handicapped (the funds for which were cut in 1960) joined with supporters of programs for behavioral problem youth to successfully lobby for a new state program for the "educationally handicapped," that is, youth neither physically nor mentally retarded but who, by reason of marked learning and/or behavioral problems, cannot reasonably benefit from ordinary education facilities. In state after state, similar processes worked as parents and professional lobbying organizations convinced key legislators to support more special education, fought the apathy or hostility of departments of education, and often wrote the legislation itself. Indeed, it was the 15 to 20 prior years of such activity that provided much of the political muscle for the federal legislation of the 1970s.[56]

The dramatic increase in the public and political presence of parents in the special education movement meant, inevitably, that along with an expansion of places and an end to exclusion would come agitation for better programs. Each time parents posed the possibility of public responsibility for their handicapped children, they found school systems that wanted nothing to do with them or programs so dreadful that only the least concerned would not be appalled.[57] As one Boston school official put it, "Crippled children don't belong here; this school is for normal kids," or another more gently, "Our schools aren't built to accommodate handicapped children."[58] Attacks on quality proliferated. A group of Boston school teachers told an investigating team from the Massachusetts Institute of Technology that "special classes are used as a 'dumping ground' for children who are trouble-makers in their regular classes. These children often do not have low I.Q.'s. Results of the Stanford-Binet tests are sometimes deliberately rigged."[59] Even more startling, a highly placed official in the California State Department of Public Instruction admitted that the *intent* of that state's classes for the educable mentally retarded (EMR) from the late 1940s to the mid-1970s was *not* to provide intensive services and education so that a child could return to regular classes. The expectation and the practice was permanent placement in the EMR class until the youth "dropped out" of school.[60] The expansion, then, of special education involved a simultaneous process of increased public criticism of special education. By the late 1960s, special education was both larger than it had ever been and subjected to greater criticism and hostility than ever before.

Part of that hostility emerged from the civil rights movement. Again, it would be hard to overestimate the impact of civil rights agitation on the movement to enhance educational and social opportunities for the handicapped. The latter movement was often closely connected to the former in the 1970s, and drew upon many of the organizational politics and legal justifications of the early civil rights movement. But the issue of race raised more serious questions than simply the right of access to and the qualify of, special education programs: the ways in which special education and race intersected raised doubts about the more general workings of the educational system and about the beneficence of special education in the first place.[61]

From its origins, special education was tied to views of racial inferiority; without the ethnic and racial antagonisms of the World War I years, special education would have received only the most minimal attention. The racial biases that made minorities the most likely candidates for placement in inadequate special education classes continued into the post–World War II period. Indeed, the biases played much the same role they had before: public education and special education expanded simultaneously, in the 1950s and 1960s, allowing school systems both to incorporate large numbers of nonwhite pupils into the schools while simultaneously segregating them within the schools. Two events in California, in 1947, which had their parallels throughout the country, reveal these associations. In that year, the California state legislature, reacting to a suit on behalf of Mexican-American children excluded from white public schools, repealed a clause in its education code that required racially segregated schools. That same year, the legislature created programs for educable retarded children. The two actions were independent of one another, but they soon came to be closely intertwined. As California's nonwhite and Chicano children began attending public schools in greater numbers, they also began to appear in EMR classes at a rate higher than their general enrollment levels, and as noted above, under the assumption that they would remain there until they dropped out of school.[62] Special education thus became disproportionately populated by nonwhites and foreign language children. Even as criticism mounted that the intelligence tests used were racially and culturally biased, that many of the youth placed in special education classes functioned quite well in nonschool settings and in some school activities, and that there was little educational benefit to be gained from such placement, special education remained a segregated, second-class (at best) feature of the educational system.[63]

By the early 1970s, then, a remarkable coalition had come together to challenge the assumptions, practices, and in some cases the existence, of special education. Middle-class white parents of handicapped children led the attack on exclusion from the educational system. They demanded, and they partially got, the right to have the education of their handicapped children recognized as a public responsibility. Schools could no longer exclude their children just because they did not belong, and, once admitted, the children had the right to an adequate education, sufficiently funded and staffed. Nonwhite and non-English-speaking parents joined the coalition, in part with the same ends in mind as the whites, but more often under a different incentive: too many of their children were being classified as handicapped and were being channeled into special education programs with little pretense that they would be educated. Whatever special education might be, these parents agitated against an organizational structure and procedures that looked remarkably similar to those that kept schools segregated and their children segregated within supposedly integrated schools.

Professional special educators found themselves caught in a particular dilemma. Some joined the coalition, others stayed out, many drifted in and out depending on the issue and the locale. For those acutely aware of and angry over the fact that special education programs were the second-class citizens of the educational system, underfunded and neglected, the coalitions of the 1960s and early 1970s were greeted enthusiastically. Only organized parents could develop the local muscle to improve local conditions. As the director of Boston's Department of Special Classes put it in 1969, when asked why he had changed a rule that prohibited special education from field trips, "I gave the parents what they yelled about."[64] But where condemnations of special education touched them, or where, as was increasingly to occur in the 1970s, criticisms suggested that much of what passed for special education ought to be eliminated altogether, many special educators became uncertain and even hostile. Parent participation might be politically necessary, but it was also dangerous.

41

These were the contexts of the emerging revolution in special education: an extraordinary expansion in the size and cost of special education; parents demanding access to and adequacy in special education; the spillover of the civil rights movement determined to prevent segregation, stigmatization, and de facto second-class citizenship through improper classification; and special educators and related professionals willing to join parental lobbies on behalf of handicapped children. Added to these was a special civil rights movement located among the handicapped themselves, able to organize and gain greater attention in the wake of the Vietnam War, and profiting from the gains of the larger civil rights movement. In a series of well-publicized legal cases, especially in Pennsylvania and Washington, D.C., courts established that children could not be excluded from school by reason of handicap, that individual handicapped children deserved individual and suitable educational programs, and that all things being equal, it was in the interests of equality of educational opportunity for handicapped children to spend as much time as possible with the nonhandicapped. In the early and mid-1970s, states and the federal government responded to these pressures; between 1970 and 1975, Congress passed 50 pieces of legislation on the handicapped. Especially significant was the Vocational Rehabilitation Act of 1973, which prohibited exclusion from vocational programs by reason of handicap, and the 1975 Education for All Handicapped Children Act (PL 94-142), which required an active search to locate all handicapped children excluded from public education, nondiscriminatory diagnostic procedures, individualized education programs, adequate due process procedures for all handicapped children, and placement in the least restrictive environment for learning.[65]

The legislation and court decisions of the early and mid-1970s were thus a frontal attack on many of the assumptions and practices which had pervaded special education from its origins—on race and ethnicity as a key determiner of who was handicapped, on the efficacy of segregated facilities, on the "outsider" classification of special education itself. Yet there were also important continuities—the dilemma of deciding who was handicapped and how might he or she be best educated, for example. But most of all was the continuity of a universal educational system: how could all be brought in and adequately educated? That question was posed by the progressive era. One of its answers was special education. The same question was asked in the 1970s, and one of its answers was PL 94-142, the Education for All Handicapped Children Act. Whether the latter answer would more effectively resolve the dilemmas of access and equity posed by an earlier generation remains to be seen.

Notes

1. The New Jersey Commission quote is taken from James Leiby, *Charity and Corrections in New Jersey: A History of State Welfare Institutions* (New Brunswick, N.J.: Rutgers University Press, 1967), p. 98; the "Slavonian" woman is quoted in *Journal of Exceptional Children* 4 (October 1937), 20–21; LaGuardia is quoted *ibid.* 6 (January 1940), 1958; Task Force on Children Out of School, *The Way We Go To School: The Exclusion of Children in Boston* (Boston: Beacon, 1970), p. 27.

2. Jane R. Mercer and John G. Richardson, "Mental Retardation as a Social Problem," *Issues in the Classification of Children*, ed. Nicholas Hobbs (San Francisco: Jossey-Bass, 1975), vol. 2. See also David Rothman, *The Discovery of the Asylum: Social Order and Disorder in the New Republic* (Boston: Little, Brown & Co., 1971); Michael Katz, "Origins of the Institutional State," *Marxist Perspectives* (Winter 1978): 6–21; Peter Tyor and Jamil Zainaldin, "Asylum and Society: An Approach to Institutional Change," *Journal of Social History* (Fall 1979): 23–48; Robert Bremner, John Barnard, Tamara Hareven, and Robert Mennel, eds., *Children and Youth in America* (Cambridge, Mass.: Harvard University Press, 1970/71), 1: 769–772; 2: 850.

3. Seymour B. Sarason and John Doris, *Educational Handicap, Public Policy, and Social History: A Broadened Perspective on Mental Retardation* (New York: The Free Press, 1979), pp. 262–263.

4. J. E. W. Wallin, *The Education of Handicapped Children* (Boston: Houghton Mifflin, 1924), intro.

5. David B. Tyack and Michael Berkowitz, "The Man Nobody Liked: Toward a Social History of the Truant Officer, 1840–1940," *American Quarterly* 29 (Spring 1977): 31–54.

6. The data are drawn from Paul Chapman, "Schools as Sorters: Lewis M. Terman and the Intelligence Testing Movement, 1890–1930" (Ph.D. diss., Stanford University, 1979), pp. 47–49.

7. Leonard P. Ayres, *Laggards in the Schools: A Study of Retardation and Elimination in City School Systems* (New York: Charities Publication Committee, 1909). U.S. Immigration Commission, *The Children of Immigrants in Schools* (Washington, D.C.: Government Printing Office, 1911.

8. Leonard P. Ayres, *Child Accounting in the Public Schools* (Cleveland: Cleveland Education Survey, 1915), pp. 39–48.

9. Jack D. Oatley, "A Study of the History of State Financing for Special Education in the State of Michigan with a Recommended Model for the Financing of Special Education in the State of Michigan" (Ph.D. diss., Michigan State University, 1975), pp. 56–58.

10. Shirley T. Staub, "Developments in Special Education in New Jersey Since 1900" (Ph.D. diss., Lehigh University, 1978), p. 214. The same legislation authorized that special classes be organized where 10 or more blind or deaf children not cared for in an institution were found in the school district.

11. Quoted in Sarason and Doris, *Educational Handicap*, p. 266.

12. The phrases were used in the authorization of special classes in Washington, D.C. Mamie Holloway Lindo, "A History of Special Education in the District of Columbia Public Schools Prior to the Waddy Decree of August 2, 1972" (Ph.D. diss., George Washington University, 1974), pp. 23–27.

13. Quoted in Sarason and Doris, *Educational Handicap*, pp. 288–309. For a brief biography of Farrell, see *Journal of Exceptional Children* 1 (February 1935): 73–76. On her work in New York, see Lillian Wald, *Windows on Henry Street* (Boston: Little, Brown & Co., 1934). Farrell lived at the Henry Street Settlement on New York's East Side for 25 years.

14. Tyack and Berkowitz, "The Man Nobody Liked," pp. 31–54. See also David Rothman, "The State as Parent: Social Policy in the Progressive Era," *Doing Good: The Limits of Benevolence*, ed. Willard Gaylin, Ira Glasser, Steven Marcus, and David Rothman (New York: Pantheon, 1978).

15. David B. Tyack, *The One-Best System* (Cambridge, Mass.: Harvard University Press, 1974); Marvin Lazerson, *Origins of the Urban School: Public Education in Massachusetts, 1870–1915* (Cambridge, Mass.: Harvard University Press, 1971).

16. Mercer and Richardson, "Mental Retardation," label the period between 1850 and 1940 "The Public Menace Cycle."

17. Beatrice McLeod, "Special Education in Wyoming," *School and Society* 22 (July 1925): 109–113.

18. Quoted in Lindo, "A History of Special Education," p. 25.

19. Wallin, *The Education of Handicapped Children*, p. 94.

20. Ibid., pp. 92–94.

21. Quoted in Lindo, "A History of Special Education," p. 26.

22. Quoted in Sarason and Doris, *Educational Handicap*, p. 263. See also McLeod, "Special Education in Wyoming," pp. 109–113.

23. The economic returns argument has continued into the present. In 1968, Hugh L. Carey, then representative from New York, argued in support of the Handicapped Children's Early Education Assistance Act, that the cost of maintaining a handicapped individual in institutions for 60 years would be $150 thousand, but if that person was educated and could thus be employed, he or she would contribute $60 thousand (at $1,500 per year for 40 years) (Frederick Weintraub, "Special Education and the Government—A History," *Encyclopedia of Education* [New York: Macmillan Co., 1971]: 350–351).

24. Quoted in Staub, "Developments in Special Education," p. 72.

25. Stephen Jay Gould, *The Mismeasure of Man* (New York: W. W. Norton, 1981). On Goddard and the Vineland Training School, see Mark H. Haller, *Eugenics: Hereditarian Attitudes in American Thought* (New Brunswick, N.J.: Rutgers University Press, 1963); Leiby, *Charity and Corrections*, pp. 102–109, 237–241. Two of Goddard's most famous papers on classifying the feebleminded (1910) and on the limited improvement to be expected from the feebleminded (1913) are reprinted in Marvin Rosen, Gerald R. Clark, and Marvin S. Kivitz, eds., *The History of Mental Retardation: Collected Papers* (Baltimore: University Park Press, 1976) 2: 355–376.

Collected Papers (Baltimore: University Park Press, 1976) 2: 355–376.

26. On Terman, see Chapman, "Schools as Sorters," pp. 47–49.

27. Lewis M. Terman, "Feeble-Minded Children in the Public Schools of California," *School and Society* 5 (February 1917): 161–165.

28. Attempting to justify educating the mentally subnormal on grounds other than protecting the society from the social menace, Wallace Wallin devoted three of 12 chapters of his 1924 book to criticizing the view that the mentally deficient were all moral delinquents. But even Wallin wound up concluding that special education would reduce tru-

ancy, juvenile delinquency, and adult crime (Wallin, *The Education of Handicapped Children*, pp. 265–329). On objections to early IQ interpretations, see the documents in Rosen et al., *The History of Mental Retardation*, 2: 51–96.

29. Leiby, *Charity and Corrections*, pp. 263–265.

30. Data drawn from Wallin, *The Education of Handicapped Children*, pp. 41–43; U.S. Bureau of Education, *Bulletin, no. 11* (1930); Weintraub, "Special Education and the Government," p. 351; Mercer and Richardson, "Mental Retardation"; Pauline P. Washington, "The Development of Special Education in Montgomery County, Maryland Public Schools From 1949 to 1975" (Ph.D. diss., American University, 1976) pp. 49–50.

31. The data are summarized in Sarason and Doris, *Educational Handicap*, pp. 275–279, 309–313; Wallin, *The Education of Handicapped Children*, pp. 37–38; William T. Hartman, "Estimating the Costs of Educating Handicapped Children: A Resource-Cost Model Approach" (Ph.D. diss., Stanford University, 1979), p. 15. Suffice it to say, the data are *very* inexact.

32. Unless otherwise noted, the material on Oakland is drawn from Chapman, "Schools as Sorters," pp. 64–73.

33. Wallin, *The Education of Handicapped Children*, p. 46.

34. Pennsylvania Department of Public Instruction, *Report of the Survey of the Public Schools of Philadelphia* (Philadelphia: The Public Education and Child Labor Association of Pennsylvania, 1922) 2: 285–291; 3: 11–45.

35. The quotations are from Philadelphia School District, *Annual Report of the Superintendent of Schools, 1925*, p. 17, and *1927*, p. 14.

36. Data are compiled from the city's annual school reports and should be treated with caution since there were often discrepancies and at least some of the counting is suspect. The magnitudes, however, are probably not too far off. It is also worth noting that there were always twice as many boys in special education as girls.

37. Staub, "Developments in Special Education," p. 156; McLeod, "Special Education in Wyoming," pp. 109–113; Cleveland, School District, *Annual Report of the Superintendent of Schools, 1929–30*, pp. 37–52; Chapman, "Schools as Sorters," pp. 64–73.

38. Quoted in *Journal of Exceptional Children* 1 (February 1935): 82.

39. James Allan Simmons, "A Historical Perspective on Special Education in California" (Ph.D. diss., University of Southern California, 1973), pp. 10–67; Mercer and Richardson "Mental Retardation."

40. A 1906 description of children placed in Los Angeles' ungraded classes said the children were there because of "deficiencies of prior education, slowness of mind, nervousness of temperament, imperfect knowledge of the English language, or similar cause" (quoted in Simmons, "A Historical Perspective on Special Education," p. 34).

41. Ibid., p. 48. The sections on the handicapped from Wood's report are reprinted on pp. 47–52.

42. Mercer and Richardson "Mental Retardation"; John G. Richardson, "The Case of Special Education and Minority Misclassification in California," *Educational Research Quarterly* 4 (Spring 1979): 25–40. For a similar conclusion outside of California, see Sarason and Doris, *Educational Handicap*, pp. 334–354.

43. Philadelphia School District, *Annual Report of the Board of Public Education, 1931*, p. 196.

44. On the challenges to early IQ interpretations, see Rosen et al., *The History of Mental Retardation*, pp. 51–96; N. J. Block and Gerald Dworkin, eds., *The IQ Controversy* (New York: Pantheon, 1976), pp. 4–44.

45. White House Conference on Child Health and Protection, *Special Education* (New

York: The Century Co., 1931), pp. 3, 8–9, 13. See also White House Conference on Child Health and Protection, *The Handicapped Child* (New York: The Century Co., 1933).

46. White House Conference, *Special Education*, p. 211, and passim.

47. Supervisor of defective classes, Trenton, New Jersey, quoted in Staub, "Developments in Special Education," p. 71.

48. J. E. W. Wallin in *Journal of Exceptional Children* 3 (October 1936): 26.

49. The Task Force on Children Out of School, *The Way We Go to School.*

50. These developments are clear from an examination of the *Journal of Exceptional Children* during the 1930s. Wallace Wallin had earlier expressed concern about labeling and had proposed that special education classes or schools be called "special schools for individual instruction, opportunity classes, developmental classes, orthogenic classes, or by some other designations which will not wound the sensibilities of the parents" (Wallin, *The Education of Handicapped Children*, p. 130).

51. Chicago Public Schools, *Report of the Survey of the Schools of Chicago, Illinois* (New York: Teachers College, Columbia University, 1932) 2: 100–101 and, more generally, 73–106.

52. Two examples further illuminate this argument. During the 1930s, special educators began to express hostility towards "progressive educators," once their allies, for turning their efforts elsewhere. At the same time, special educators began to talk more and more about the need to work with exceptional children in regular classrooms; such children later became known as special needs children. See for example, Charles S. Berry, "The Exceptional Child in Regular Classes," *Journal of Exceptional Children* 3 (October 1936): 15–17.

53. These themes all appear in the *Journal of Exceptional Children* and in discussions of special education at the National Education Association meetings during the early and mid-1940s. See also the evaluation of the District of Columbia Teachers College in 1948, summarized in Lindo, "A History of Special Education," pp. 87–104.

54. Hartman, "Estimating the Costs," pp. 16–23; Weintraub, "Special Education and the Government," pp. 351–352; John Gliedman and William Roth, *The Unexpected Minority: Handicapped Children in America* (New York: Harcourt Brace Jovanovich, 1980), p. 173.

55. In its section on crippled children, the White House Committee on Special Classes reported that "outside agencies are participating in the programs of these schools to an extent unprecedented in the history of public education in this country. In many instances the organization of a special class has been due to the activities of outside groups which, in the beginning, have provided the rooms or buildings, and the funds for special equipment and services" (White House Conference, *Special Education*, p. 82).

56. Examples can be found in Staub, "Developments in Special Education," pp. 179–213 and Leiby, *Charity and Corrections*, pp. 324–330 (New Jersey); and Mercer and Richardson, "Mental Retardation," (California); *Larry P.* v. *Riles*, U.S. District Court, Northern District of California, daily transcript, pp. 3333–3337 (California).

57. See for example the description of what parents of handicapped children in Paramus, New Jersey, discovered in the 1950s when they examined special education there, in Staub, "Developments in Special Education," pp. 196–202.

58. Task Force on Children Out of School, *The Way We Go to School*, p. 28.

59. Ibid., p. 41.

60. *Larry P.*, daily transcript, pp. 3328–3331.

61. See Gliedman and Roth, *The Unexpected Minority*, Sarason and Doris, *Educational Handicap*, pp. 321–354, and the voluminous testimony and decision in Larry P. case.

62. Richardson, "The Case of Special Education," pp. 25–40.

63. Jane R. Mercer, *Labeling the Mentally Retarded: Clinical and Social System Perspectives on Mental Retardation* (Berkeley: University of California Press, 1973).

64. Task Force on Children Out of School, *The Way We Go to School*.

65. Gliedman and Roth, *The Unexpected Minority*, pp. 173–237.

CHAPTER 3

The Politics of Legalization in Special Education Reform

JACK TWEEDIE

Exclusion: The Roots of Change

The history of special education has been a tale of exclusion—the exclusion of the handicapped from schools and the exclusion of their representatives from participation in education policymaking. The severely handicapped were viewed as something less than human creatures, to be treated as decently as limited charity would allow, not as persons with rights. As one parent recalled, "I was told, 'Put him in an institution. Forget you ever had him. His condition is hopeless. He will never talk. He will never be able to do anything.'"[1] The handicapped were to be kept separate from the normal world. Ironically, that separation was thought to benefit both the handicapped who were unable to cope and the nonhandicapped, who would not be exposed to handicapped persons. Parents and other advocates for the handicapped could not muster sufficient political strength to enter the education policymaking arena. One frustrated educator explained, "Under tough budgets, special [education] programs go down the drain, and our parents of the handicapped, though organized, are not always strong enough to fight for their rights."[2] Since parents of the handicapped were excluded from policymaking processes, the interests of handicapped children were continually neglected. As an advocate put it, "The handicapped were the last ones down the road to be considered. If there was money left over after other people were served, then handicapped were brought in."[3]

This dual exclusion of the handicapped is reflected in their limited

48

legal entitlements, even as recently as a quarter-century ago. While some states authorized special education programs, these programs remained " 'permissive' undertakings at the discretion of local school officials."[4] Many other states' compulsory attendance laws provided for the exclusion of the handicapped. With some exceptions, the special education programs that did exist involved largely a caretaking approach. Those handicapped children fortunate enough to gain entry to the public schools often faced continued isolation and minimal services. "Slow but determined growth," in the face of overwhelming need, marked this period.[5]

The role of special education professionals in these programs illustrates the schools' limited commitment. Education programs have generally been left to the expert discretion of professional educators who were held loosely accountable by local school boards. Special educators also generally controlled the content of the programs they offered and the assignment of students within these programs. The price for these professionals' control over special education was a rigid demarcation of the school program into two distinct spheres, regular and special education. Additionally, school policies included little money for special education and turned away many handicapped students.[6]

This pattern of exclusion and acquiescence began to change in the 1960s. Spurred by the claim of other minorities, advocates for the handicapped began to speak in terms of rights. Professionals contributed to this transformation by reassessing their appraisal of the handicapped, concluding that all children were educable.

Before this development, education for the handicapped had depended on the generosity of private charity and the largesse of state and local governments. Advocates for the handicapped were excluded from political bargaining for funds and programs; they possessed no special political leverage with which to compete against interest groups that could command the attention of education and government authorities. They could only appeal to the humanity of government and encourage its acceptance of responsibility for the handicapped. Lacking effective representation, handicapped children faced widespread neglect and abuse from schools.

Amid growing distrust of school officials' ability and willingness to provide adequate programs, special education advocates altered their strategy of cooperation with political officials. They undertook litigation to force comprehensive reform of special education. Coupled with specific demands for programs was a strategy to pressure the powerful education lobbies into supporting federal special education reforms. Right-to-education lawsuits, orchestrated by advocates for the handicapped, threatened school districts with the possibility of disruption, expensive litigation, and the complexity of implementing subsequent court-ordered programs. Afraid that litigation and court-ordered programs would cut into existing programs, and unable to provide needed reforms on their own, schools sought financial assistance from the Congress.

Those policymakers who were sympathetic to the handicapped tied guarantees of appropriate education to the financial relief that Congress provided to the schools. In the Education for All Handicapped Children Act of 1975 (PL 94-142),[7] Congress adopted the policy proposals of reformers—free appropriate public education, individualized education planning, education in the least restrictive environment, and procedures to safeguard children's rights to education. Congress also provided substantial federal funding to supplement increased state special education spending. During the consideration and implementation of PL 94-142, special education advocates took on significant policymaking roles in the expanded programs.

Representatives for the handicapped gained entry into the educational governance system through their strategic use of litigation. In PL 94-142, they created a parallel base of power within schools by establishing procedural safeguards. By insisting upon hearings, parents were empowered to threaten schools with disruption when requested services were denied. PL 94-142 also explicitly provided for continued access to litigation. Strategic use of these legal options gave advocates for the handicapped power within the educational system to effect comprehensive reform of special education within the open-ended mandates of PL 94-142.

PL 94-142 precipitated great improvements in education for the handicapped. Millions of handicapped children have been brought into the schools or given new special programs in the last six years. Much of this can be attributed to the continuing politics of litigation, though the efforts of educators and policymakers should also be given credit.

The special education movement chose a legal strategy to overcome exclusion from schools and from politics. Reliance on litigation and adversarial hearings, not political cooperation, produced far-reaching reforms. Advocates used litigation as a political tactic to gain congressional reforms and then incorporated the legal strategy into the reforms in order to retain effective leverage.[8] This paper presents the story of this political use of litigation to protect the rights of handicapped children.

The Politics of Litigation

Frustrated with the insufficient programs available through professional efforts within the constraints school officials imposed, advocates for the handicapped studied alternative strategies. Confronting the powerlessness of the handicapped in school politics, they found that one option was to sue schools for the equal opportunity education constitutionally guaranteed, in the context of racial discrimination, in *Brown* v. *Board of Education*.[9] In adopting that option, advocates also used the litigation as part of a political strategy. Widespread right-to-education litigation, and the threat of even more, generated a "quiet revolution" in school boards, state legislatures, and the Congress.[10] Litigation supplied the political leverage needed to gain comprehensive special education reforms. Faced with expensive litigation and court-ordered programs drawing from already limited budgets, local and state school officials changed their own policies and supported state and federal reform legislation. The capstone of the movement's efforts was the Education for All Handicapped Children Act of 1975.

The Problem of the Powerless

Advocates for the handicapped became frustrated with the continuing exclusion of handicapped children and the inadequate education given those allowed in schools. They grew further disenchanted with their traditional limited participation in education policymaking. These advocates—special educators, representatives of handicap groups, and parents—had achieved few gains through cooperation with school and state officials. They also feared budget cuts might erode these gains. They did not trust school officials, whom they regarded as uncomfortable with handicapped children and hostile to the children's presence in schools.

Special education activists drew inspiration from the civil rights and poor people's movements. Like blacks and the poor, the handicapped were a minority excluded from participation in politics and their share in society's affluence. Civil rights attorneys became directly involved when they noticed that a disproportionate number of racial minorities were classified as handicapped. Discussions between these lawyers, disgruntled parents, and academic professionals who disagreed with special education practices led to the development of a legal attack on exclusion and inadequate programs.[11]

Like those involved in the civil rights and poverty movements, the handicapped confront the problem of powerlessness. Disadvantage in society and politics often come hand in hand. Groups such as the poor or the handicapped, while needing government assistance in their quest for social and economic opportunity, fare badly in the political competition for government programs. In political bargaining, the excluded group has nothing to offer the other participants.[12]

Our political system is not readily accessible or responsive to these powerless interests.[13] Usual forms of political participation prove futile. Collective political actions, such as electoral campaigns or lobbying, are often inhibited by the problem of organizing diffuse interests for diffuse gains.[14] The equity of the disadvantaged group's claims seldom assures an adequate response. Within the norms of cooperation in the political system, the disadvantaged have little political recourse for their complaints.[15] Special education history testifies to that. Advocates decided a new strategy was needed.

Litigation Strategy

As it became clear that cooperating with school officials did not work, advocates considered alternative approaches designed to shift resources to the handicapped and end their exclusion from schools. Special educators, handicap groups, and the U.S. Bureau of Education for the Handicapped launched a campaign to publicize the educational needs of the handicapped. Activists organized extensive lobbying efforts at state legislatures and education agencies. This effort promised more than continued frustration because advocates decided to make an end run around the political process, relying on the courts to mandate "appropriate" education for the handicapped.

Lawsuits endangered ongoing programs managed by organizations for the handicapped. But lawyers convinced the organizations that litigation provided the only route to effective reform.[16] Movement leaders adopted an assertive stance. They saw special education, along with habilitation and fair treatment for those in institutions, as rights owed to handicapped children. Tales of maltreatment at such institutions as Pennhurst and Willowbrook sharpened the image of deprivation and pitched the issue in an emotional tone.[17] The issues were tartly characterized by one strategist—"The power is in the local district. Litigation was a political strategy. School superintendents were very much against it. It challenged their power. They held the power to turn handicapped kids away. This threatened to take away that arbitrary and capricious power. [We were challenging] the way of government in this country."

This pattern of strategy decisions was established when the Pennsylvania Association of Retarded Citizens (PARC) decided to challenge the state's failure to provide education programs for all retarded children. PARC rejected cooperative strategies and went to court to claim a constitutional right to education for all handicapped children. They argued that exclusion of severely retarded children is a denial of equal protection and that assignment of children to special programs without notice and a hearing violates due process. The PARC strategy included extensive professional testimony showing that education benefits all handicapped children. Those experts insisted that education be seen as individuals learning to cope and function within their environment.[18]

The PARC suit led to a consent agreement. Pennsylvania education officials, many of whom were sympathetic to the PARC claims, agreed to identify handicapped children, provide them with a suitable education, integrate them with normal children when possible, and provide due process hearings to resolve parental complaints.[19]

In a second major suit, *Mills* v. *Board of Education*, the court concluded that as a matter of constitutional right, all handicapped children were entitled to a "suitable" education and to an equal, publicly supported, education. The court also established procedural safeguards for handicapped students in instances of disputes over suitability.[20]

PARC and *Mills* served as models for the movement's strategy of litigation. Court actions quickly proliferated as activists throughout the country escalated pressure on the schools for reform. By 1973, 27 right-to-education lawsuits in 21 states were pending or recently completed.[21] Movement strategists used this litigation in two ways to gain needed political resources. Winning the lawsuits directly secured special education programs for handicapped children who had previously been excluded. The ongoing litigation gave special education advocates resources to use in political bargaining for changes in school policies and, more importantly, for legislative reforms. Movement strategists planned to "cook the school districts until they came to Congress demanding the funds that we [need] to provide appropriate programs."

Advocates for the handicapped based their litigation strategy on recent legal developments establishing new protections for disadvantaged groups unable to compete in politics. Procedural protections, implied conditions on agreements, and new substantive rights had been extended to members of these groups.[22] The right to equal educational opportunity established in *Brown* v. *Board of Education* and the procedural protections set out in *Goldberg* v. *Kelly*, a case involving public assistance, supplied the key precedents for special education litigation.[23]

The barrage of litigation led to several court orders requiring schools to provide special programs for all handicapped children, special efforts to identify children, and procedural requirements to protect children during evaluation, classification, and placement.[24] However, strategists viewed court actions, standing alone, as an insufficient basis for reform.

For one thing, they were not confident that appellate courts would uphold the constitutional right to education, so they did not want to base reforms solely on that right. They particularly feared that an increasingly conservative U.S. Supreme Court would reject a constitutional right to education for the handicapped. They chose their judges carefully and avoided appellate resolution of the issue. Conclusive rejection of the right would have emasculated their litigation strategy.

For another, litigation also consumed considerable resources. Supportive lawyers and educators could contribute only limited amounts of time. Financial resources were meager. And, after suits were settled, reformers faced continued resistance. Litigation left unchanged the ability and willingness of the schools to offer special programs. Judges could not easily enforce the special program orders because this would entail penetrating the organization of the school, and perhaps the state school authority, to effect changes in classroom behavior. Court orders could effectively end the exclusion of severely handicapped children, but to affect the program that a child received was often beyond their competence.[25]

Finally, constraints on school resources posed a barrier to reform. Costs of educating handicapped children ranged from two to seven times more than the costs of educating normal children.[26] Even sharply cutting back regular education programs would not provide the needed money. Courts could not order new resources, though in *Mills* v. *Board of Education*, they did require that handicapped children and normal children share the deprivation of limited funds.[27] Only legislative action could assure the funds. Advocates for the handicapped looked to Congress for this funding because the finances of many states and school districts were shrinking. It was also more practical to have one target rather than 50.

The political strength of the handicapped depended on the political resources gained through the litigation strategy. The right-to-education lawsuits constituted negative sanctions that advocates could withhold in return for the schools' active support of special education reform. The litigation imposed substantial costs on schools. They spent money on lawyers and experts in preparing their defense. Victories for the handicapped meant expensive court-ordered special education programs. Advocates threatened continued disruption of schools through litigation unless Congress and state legislatures adopted reforms. This threat was used explicitly: in Tennessee the dropping of a lawsuit was traded for new state legislation. In Kentucky, lawsuits were filed only after the frustration of legislative and administrative efforts.[28]

Despite the school representatives' fear of federal intervention in schools, the impact of the litigation strategy was widely felt. As one strategist put it, "They were getting hit in the courts. We said we'd stop going to court if they would accept rational standards. School officials hate judges even more than they do bureaucrats, even federal bureaucrats."

Reform and Legalization: The Education for All Handicapped Children Act

Litigation by special education advocates drew congressional attention to reform and turned powerful education interests into supporters of federal legislation. Policymakers sympathetic to the claims of the handicapped used the consensus supporting reform to incorporate the policies advocated by the special education movement. They also adopted strong procedural safeguards to enforce these policy changes. This legislation ensured representation of the handicapped. Advocates for the handicapped incorporated their legal strategy into the schools. They could use the statutory right to appropriate education and access to hearings just as they had used the constitutional right to education and resort to litigation in the special education movement. These entitlements could be pursued directly or used in a political strategy to influence the administrative and professional discretion normally exercised in the schools.

The Policy Frame: The Legal-Professional Perspective

The legal and political experience of special education reform shaped congressional policymaking. Activists developed their conception of needed federal policies during efforts in the courts and state legislatures. They derived the reform agenda from the civil rights origins of the movement: ending exclusion of handicapped children from public schools and developing means of classification that did not discriminate on the basis of race or ethnicity. Reform also developed from the legal perspective: a right to education suitable to the needs of each handicapped child and due process protections of that right.

The legal perspective reinforced the individual focus of those special educators who led the reform movement and participated in congressional policymaking. The special educators believed that education programs should meet "the unique needs of each child."[29] Professional disagreement over the correct educational response to certain handicaps and reactions to the pernicious effects of labeling precluded the specification of substantive education prescriptions for each kind of handicap.[30] Rather, both the professional and legal perspectives included a specified procedure for evaluation and placement focused on the individual. The educational value placed on integrating handicapped children with other children reflected legal-political concerns over exclusion and isolation. Similarities between the legal and professional perspectives aided cooperation between lawyers and special educators. Reforms developed by special educators fit smoothly into the legal frame; in turn, the legal frame strengthened the role of special educators in the schools.[31]

Political and administrative concerns constrained policymaking but actually served to strengthen the procedural and individual focuses of the legal-professional perspective. Respect for local school autonomy, necessitated by the schools' political clout, strictly limited the extent and means of federal intervention. This respect precluded a significant federal presence at the local level. However, schools did not object as strongly to federally mandated *procedures* presided over by local and state officials. Also, recognition of the limits of hierarchical program control over local programs indicated a nonregulatory enforcement approach that the legal-professional procedural safeguards could provide.

Distrust of school officials that had developed during the years of frustration influenced the attitude of reformers. Advocates for the handicapped doubted the school officials' willingness and ability to effect reforms. Advocates expected that many schools would have to be forced to comply. Even school officials acting in good faith had to operate on limited budgets; they might balk at the expensive services needed by some severely handicapped children. Advocates felt effective implementation of the reforms required an enforcement mechanism controlled by the handicapped: "We need to hold a stick, a big stick, in our hands."

The Reform Character of Policymaking

Congress readily adopted the legal-professional policy frame in consideration of special education reform. The way Congress considered the issue predisposed it to the sort of reforms sought by the special education movement. A policy network, outside the more conservative committee structure and linked with special education groups, did the primary work on the legislation. Established groups, which might have objected to the scope of the law, limited their participation to securing federal funding and preventing direct federal intervention in state and local school programs. The court cases exposing the abuse of handicapped children led to a demand for far-reaching federal reform of special education.

The alternative policy network. Legislation is normally drafted and evaluated under the direction of the relevant subcommittee staffs in the House and Senate—in this instance, the House Subcommittee on Select Education and the Senate Subcommittee on the Handicapped. Other members of Congress who have a special interest in the legislation participate with the assistance of their personal staffs, but the subcommittee staffs do most of the work developing the legislation. The legislation is strongly shaped by the policy perspective of the chair, through the staff, and the agencies and interests that develop working relationships with the subcommittee.[32] In the consideration of special education reform, however, the development of an alternative policy network circumvented these usual influences.

Senator Harrison Williams—chairman of the parent Committee on Labor and Public Welfare—had a particular interest in special education reform. Because the Senate subcommittee staff was seen as supporting a limited federal role in education, and this had been rejected as inadequate for special education, an alternative policy network developed around Senator Williams's staff. Lobbyists for special education interests, particularly the Council for Exceptional Children (CEC), were central to this network. This group, together with a few like-minded House staff members, drafted the legislation and organized the hearings.

The alternative policy network consisted primarily of a "progressive cohort" of personally and politically compatible legislative staff members and lobbyists. The common ground of this group included a belief in the social responsibility to remedy the denial of social rights to disadvantaged groups, a belief in a strong federal role in social policy through substantial resources tied to substantive standards, and perception of the need for local participation in managing federal programs.

These policymakers shared a strong commitment to handicapped children. They felt the handicapped had been "treated unfairly in schools and society and wanted to do whatever [they] could to make it up to them." This commitment limited the policymakers' openness to concerns that might be opposed to the interests of handicapped children, particularly complaints from school officials. Their perspective as advocates strongly influenced their attitude toward school officials. They saw the primary problem as officials being swayed by administrative and political concerns that should not interfere with the educational rights of handicapped children. Discounting claims of schools' inability to provide programs as disguised resistance, they saw implementation of reforms as largely an enforcement problem.

The participation of several interested legislators outside the network somewhat dampened the network's reform orientation. However, legislative and agency staff who were normally influential in special education legislation remained largely outside the alternative network. The Senate subcommittee staff did not participate actively in policy discussions. The White House barred the Bureau of Education for the Handicapped (BEH) from participating beyond helping with technical details. Under administration instructions, the Department of Health, Education, and Welfare (HEW) officially opposed the legislation.[33] The BEH staff provided some backstage support and consultation, but they resisted a large expansion of the federal role. The limited involvement of the Senate subcommittee staff and the BEH closed off most of the channels for participation by state and local school representatives.

Focused participation of education interests. Local school representatives such as the National School Boards Association and the American Association of School Administrators, and national teacher organizations, the National Education Association and the United Federation of Teachers, possess powerful political clout on education issues.[34] Pressure from special education litigation led these interests to petition Congress for special education funding and reform. But these interests played a limited role in shaping the reforms. The efforts of local school representatives focused on obtaining the needed funds and limiting federal intervention in school programs.

School representatives were convinced that comprehensive reforms were inevitable. The basic set of reforms had been routinely included in court orders establishing a right to education and were incorporated in the federal Education Amendments of 1974. In many states, the "quiet revolution" had already taken place: state legislatures had removed barriers to handicapped children's attendance in public schools and had set up some programs. These states had accepted the burden but could not pay for it. After legislating a right to education, a Maryland state official noted that "unless the State of Maryland receives additional federal support, [we] will be unable to meet [our] mandates and responsibilities to the handicapped."[35]

State and local education agencies were spending only $3 billion for special education compared to the estimated $7 billion needed to provide all handicapped children with an appropriate education.[36] School districts, facing a surge of tax levy defeats, pleaded poverty. States, while willing to accept some extra burden, claimed not to have the necessary revenues.[37] The federal government seemed a logical source of aid. School interests would have been satisfied with no-strings aid measures, but knew they had to accept substantive reforms in order to secure money. As one lobbyist observed, "The states and the schools wanted the money; we said you have to have strings."

School representatives' scrutiny of the legislation was keyed to obtaining money and limiting the federal presence in schools. One school representative explained, "We were not going to have to spend a lot of our own money and we were not going to have the feds hanging around telling us what to do. We would live anything else, and probably we're going to have to." School district representatives fought to eliminate burdensome administrative requirements and secured local entitlement funding as a way of limiting state oversight of local programs.

Demand for extensive federal reform. The special education movement's activities, particularly the publicity campaign and the court actions, gave the issue an emotional and political urgency. State and school officials, unable to fund the programs they had adopted under court orders, also pressed for funding. Witnesses at congressional hearings related stories of exclusion and neglect and told of the promise of new special programs unavailable to most handicapped children because of limited funds. Witnesses rejected the federal government's capacity-building role and called for substantial federal funding and the specification of day-to-day education programs.

The right to an appropriate education had been established politically, if not constitutionally, but only comprehensive reform at the federal level could effect the systemic change needed. This urgent demand freed policymakers from established policies and commissioned them to develop a new federal regime in special education subject to only slight political constraints.[38]

The Substance of Reforms

The basis of special education reform was the establishment of the handicapped child's right to education, ending his exclusion from public schools. Other policy reforms worked from this foundation. The definition of appropriate education was rooted in consideration of the child's individual needs. Rather than defining the substance of an appropriate education, PL 94-142 provided for an individualized education program developed at a conference among school administrators, teachers, and parents. Parents were to serve as advocates for their children. They were given the right to participate in the individual planning process and access to procedural safeguards under which an impartial officer would hear parental complaints. One substantive standard was included in the conception of appropriate education—education in the least restrictive environment appropriate to the needs of the child.

Right to a free appropriate public education. Reformers wanted a free, appropriate, public education for all handicapped children: no children would be turned away from schools, no fees would be charged, and the child's expenses at a private school would be paid by the public school if the latter did not offer a suitable program; and the child's education program would be tailored to the child's unique needs. Many special education programs classified and served children according to their primary handicapped condition (e.g., mildly retarded, physically handicapped, blind). An education appropriate to each child's needs encompassed the reformers' dissatisfaction with gross classifications, poor testing procedures, and inadequate programs not responsive to individual children's potentials. This perspective was related to professional norms of individualized education planning and education in the least restrictive environment. The statute opts for a procedural definition—an appropriate education "means . . . services . . . provided in conformity with the individualized education program." No attempt was made to include any substantive content other than that of the least restrictive environment.[39].

Individualized education program. The requirement for an individualized education program (the IEP) specifies a procedure for preparing an education plan for each handicapped child. The IEP states the child's level of educational performance, long range educational goals, intermediate objectives, the specific services to be provided, when services are to begin, their duration, and objective criteria and evaluation procedures to determine whether the objectives are achieved. The IEP was defined as "a written statement for each handicapped child developed in any meeting between a [special educator], the classroom teacher, and the parents." No further specification was provided.[40]

Parents as advocates. The value of individualized planning depends on including an effective advocate for the child in the planning process and enforcing the child's plan. Policymakers recognized the potentially adversary relationship between the school and the child so they empowered parents to act in the child's interest. Parents would represent the child in the IEP meeting. An impartial hearing would resolve disagreements between school officials and the parents. Parents could request an independent education evaluation. The parent's advocate role follows traditional conceptions of parental authority, and policymakers presumed that parents would be effective advocates. Policymakers ignored the problems of parents being intimidated, unconcerned, inarticulate, or ignorant about their child's needs.[41]

Education in the least restrictive environment. The least restrictive environment provision reflected the value placed on teaching the handicapped child along with the other children—"mainstreaming." The handicapped child had to be educated with nonhandicapped children "to the maximum extent appropriate," and schools had to provide supplementary aids and services to facilitate the child's integration. The requirement was stated in vague terms that, in effect, required schools to do what they could. Procedural safeguards protected this value; parents could complain that their child was segregated from other children without educational justification.[42]

Procedural Safeguards: Litigation in the Schools

The special education reforms contained in PL 94-142 are made effective by the procedural safeguards. Like litigation during the special education movement, they enforce legal entitlements and also provide political leverage within the school. In considering enforcement mechanisms, policymakers faced a choice parallel to the one faced by special education activists when they adopted the litigation strategy. The handicapped gained entry into schools through litigation, but once inside they could expect to face continued resistance. Depending on schools to implement the reforms was like relying on schools to respond to claims of equity: even school officials acting in good faith had other responsibilities and scarce resources.

The policymakers considered several administrative and participatory strategies before settling on a legal approach. Just as before, advocates for the handicapped were torn between cooperation with school officials and the inevitable adversariness of the legal strategy. Advocates for the handicapped, parents in this case, could use the procedural safeguards to secure the appropriate education that their child was entitled to. Advocates could also threaten to demand a hearing to overcome the resistance of school officials. The procedural safeguards were more accessible to parents than was litigation, increasing the potential for enforcement and political uses of hearings. Finally, the authors of PL 94-142 specifically retained litigation as a means of enforcing education entitlements and applying political pressure.[43]

The adoption of procedural safeguards. Due process protections for handicapped children had become a natural part of claims for a right to education. The use of quasi-judicial hearings in the *PARC* consent decree established due process as the presumptive means of protecting children's entitlements. Later court orders and the model statute used in several states' legislation routinely included similar requirements: notice of any changes in the child's program, access to all relevant records, representation by counsel, powers to introduce evidence and examine witnesses, access to a written record of the hearing, and the availability of an independent educational evaluation.[44]

The federal special education reform also naturally included procedural safeguards. However, the authors of the law relied on administrative mechanisms for enforcement. The initial version of the procedural safeguards only required prior notice to parents when the school proposed changes and an opportunity for an impartial hearing that included access to relevant records and an independent educational evaluation.[45] Several special education activists saw PL 94-142 as a new stage in cooperation with schools. They feared that reliance on hearings for enforcement would endanger that cooperation.

The Senate and the House passed legislation that included two different administrative enforcement plans. Only the Senate included the requirement of procedural safeguards.[46] Policymakers, particularly worried about noncompliance by schools, proposed that extensively specified procedural safeguards replace the administrative enforcement mechanisms in the two bills. Conferees adopted reliance on procedural safeguards, but school representatives and conservative congressmen balked at the five-page specification of procedures. Moderates worked furiously to effect a compromise between the two views by whittling down the detailed proposal. The schools' desperate need for federal assistance, the bargaining resolve of the hard-line advocate groups, and the already established constitutional basis for requiring hearings persuaded the school representatives and the conservatives to accept procedural safeguards much like the *PARC* provisions. The bargaining strength of the special education advocates derived from their willingness to return to a litigation strategy if lawmakers enacted diluted procedural safeguards.

The strategy of legalization. Child advocates supported the procedural safeguards for the same reasons that activists had adopted the litigation strategy. Representatives of the child had no power in the schools. School administrators and special education professionals had other concerns that often conflicted with the child's interest. Parents and child advocates did not have the institutional leverage needed. Impartial hearings grounded on the child's right to an appropriate education would secure meaningful representation for the child in school decisions. Parents would enter discussions to determine their child's program with the power to challenge unfavorable school decisions.

Due process hearings provide parents with a forum more accessible than litigation. Parents have to be informed of their rights to participate in their child's educational planning and to demand a hearing if they are not satisfied; parents are more likely to know of their child's entitlements. Also, the hearings do not pose intimidating obstacles to parents' claims. Parents are more comfortable at the neighborhood school than at the courthouse. Parents can pursue their own claims or use lay assistance; they do not need to deal with lawyers and the alien customs and language of the law. Also the due process hearings should be less expensive than litigation.

The procedural safeguards could also be a political tool. Hearings imposed costs on school districts just as litigation has. Schools must prepare for and hold the hearing. A hearing might result in orders for expensive services such as tuition for private education. In return for not demanding hearings, schools might give in on demands for special programs. This strategy seems particularly attractive to an advocate group seeking a policy change. Procedural safeguards of the requirements of PL 94-142 confer political leverage on representatives of the handicapped. As one advocate involved in the design of the safeguards said, "Even the presence of such a system would force the district to play more honestly."

Conclusion: The Prospects of Reform

Advocates for the handicapped adopted the legalization strategy in their reform efforts, first by pursuing right-to-education lawsuits, then by instituting procedural safeguards in schools. This strategy enabled the handicapped to overcome their longstanding political powerlessness. The extension of legal protections to disadvantaged groups, particularly the rights to equal education and due process, gave the handicapped a legal basis for demanding entry into the schools and provision of special programs. Because lawsuits to enforce these claims impose costs on the defendant schools, the handicapped were able to use threats of litigation as political resources, particularly in their successful campaign for federal reform legislation. In PL 94-142, special education activists reproduced their strategy of legalization within the schools. They institutionalized quasi-legal rights and a legal enforcement mechanism—a new legal order within the schools. Special education activists also continued using litigation to effectuate rights not made explicit in the legislation.[47]

Consequences of Reform

Special education has been transformed from small and often neglected "discretionary programs" excluding many handicapped children, to a national commitment to reach all handicapped children with appropriate education programs. The special education movement and the passage of PL 94-142 are the primary causes of this change. Several hundred thousand handicapped children have been brought into the public schools. Over 4 million children receive special education and related services. Ninety-four percent of school-age handicapped children receive special educational services in public schools. There has been an increase in placements of handicapped children in regular classrooms. More handicapped children are being given individualized education programs. Federal, state, and local expenditures for special education have rapidly increased.[48]

Role of Professionals.

The new position of special education professionals in the schools is a measure of the change effected by the strategy of legalization. In many ways, their role in school policymaking has been strengthened. PL 94-142 enacted many professional norms such as the access to education for all handicapped children and individualized education planning. Budgets for special education programs have substantially increased. As one school official commented, "Special education is a growth industry, about the only one in education." Finally, the adoption of procedural safeguards established a forum where professional opinions would receive great weight, particularly when the school refused to provide a special program. All of these changes have loosened constraints on special educators, expanding the scope of their involvement and capacity to act.

Even as the scope of the special educators' involvement has increased so has the outside control of their discretion. Parents have been given considerable say over the education their child receives. Some advocates supported the procedural safeguards because, "We felt we could not trust the professionals so we wanted a procedure whereby the parents could say, 'No, I don't want my child classified as retarded.'" Parents often disagree with professionals; their participation in the IEP meeting and access to procedural safeguards puts them in a position to make decisions that have, in the past, been left to special educators.[49]

The Effects of Legalization

PL 94-142 gives parents the capacity to challenge either denial of services or misclassification, by using the due process hearings as an enforcement or political strategy. The placement of procedural safeguards can effect school reforms through either strategy. Parents can use the hearings to enforce their child's entitlements, obtaining desired services from recalcitrant school officials. This scenario follows the traditional pattern of the legal enforcement of rights. If the hearings officer decides that the child is entitled to what the parent requests, the school must provide the service. Results of the hearings progressively elaborate the handicapped child's entitlements; cumulating decisions define the contours of "appropriate" education. School districts thus learn what services to provide under what circumstances, complying without the necessity of a hearing. Questions about the child's education are resolved in discussions between school officials and the parents "in the shadow" of the emerging standards.[50]

A second scenario shows parents using their new rights strategically in bargaining with school officials. Due process hearings can disrupt schools just as litigation did, though to a lesser degree. In contrast to the enforcement strategy, the political strategy capitalizes on uncertainty. Schools, like most organizations, are generally risk conscious; functioning smoothly requires routine. If educational entitlements are uncertain and the costs of determining them are high, schools will give up more. They will provide the disputed service to avoid a hearing.[51] The key to the political strategy is not what a child is entitled to, but what the school district will provide in order to avoid a hearing.

Recent implementation studies provide information for preliminary evaluation of the effects of legalization in terms of the two strategies.[52] An initially large number of hearings, many decisions for parents, and the emergence of coherent standards for determining entitlements would indicate an effective enforcement strategy. The services that parents claim and the amount of continued litigation are also important. The hearings' financial and psychological costs to school officials and the uncertainty of children's entitlements indicate the potential for parents using the political strategy. Finally, the evaluation of the effects of the procedural safeguards involves a third component: how the participation of parents and school officials in adversary hearings affects the continuing relationship between school officials and parent and child.

Enforcement strategy. The evaluations suggest that the enforcement strategy has played only a minor role. Due process hearings are so infrequent that their direct effect is negligible. In California, only .08 percent of handicapped children enrolled in public schools had a hearing during one year. Only 168 hearings were held in Pennsylvania during a four-year period. A national study found only seven of 22 districts had had more than one hearing.[53]

Of these hearings, parents are winning less than half in Pennsylvania and slightly more than half in California. Most of the hearings in California involve claims for private school tuition; since most of these children were, at the time, already in private schools, these hearings are of arguable value in effecting the goals of PL 94-142. Excluding the private school claims, parents are winning only about one-third of hearings.[54]

Hearings and appeals have not proved effective means of specifying the educational rights of the handicapped. Officials in Pennsylvania set up an appeals process to help define educational entitlements. The system has had only mixed success. The Pennsylvania report finds, "The apparent inconsistency of analysis and outcome in the appellate opinions calls into question the possibility of defining 'appropriateness' through lawlike mechanisms."[55] Once again the effect of the enforcement strategy appears minimal; there is no emergent certainty, only continued confusion. At least in Pennsylvania, the enforcement strategy holds little promise.

However, hearings may be having a significant direct effect in particular school districts. Some school districts have exceptionally large numbers of hearings. In California, two districts have had more than 40 hearings apiece; no other district has had more than 11. Several studies show that districts with large numbers of hearings also have long histories of disputes between parents and schools, so hearings may be important in enforcing children's entitlements in these districts.[56]

Political strategy. Though hearings are limited as a direct enforcement resource, they do provide significant resources to parents in dealing with school officials.[57] Parents, often with the assistance of advocates for special education groups, use demands for hearings as leverage in negotiations with school officials and school officials give parents what they request in order to avoid hearings. Although only the national study addresses this point, the evidence is clear:

> "In general, school districts try to find some way of accommodating parental demands without resorting to due process hearings . . . avoiding hearings is viewed as necessary for [several] reasons, [including]
> • The total cost in terms of time, fees, and inconvenience would be greater than the cost of providing the service in question
> • Adverse publicity would result for the district . . . .
> • Losing a hearing may set a dangerous precedent . . . .
> [S]everal parents were told 'off the record' that they would get the services they wanted if they would stop pressing for a hearing: 'If you don't do the due process and just be quiet, we'll give you what you want.'"

Schools compromise in the face of hearings except when the cost of compromise is too high—"In practice . . . the issues that tend to get resolved through formal hearings rather than through informal discussions and compromises are those on which administrators are strapped by resource limitations." Advocates also use the "hearings process more as a way of influencing the school system than as a way of filling the individual child's needs."[58] Comments by both school representatives and special education advocates and findings in other studies corroborate these points.

Adversary relationships. Due process hearings have also produced animosity between parents and school officials. They have not proved to be the effective forums for the amicable resolution of disagreements between parents and school officials that some congressional policymakers hoped they would. Instead, "Formality and an adversary atmosphere characterize most hearings. . . . They are often very nasty and [involve] legalistic maneuvering . . . lawyers lose sight of education issues and 'ride procedural issues.'" Parents and school officials have found hearings to be frustrating, painful, and destructive. As a parent said, "It's been hell. Absolute hell. I seldom speak about it, even to my husband."[59] The anger coming out of a hearing can seriously impair the continuing relationship between parent, child, and the school. This suggests that hearings have a negative effect, but the comment of one activ-

68

ist rings true—"The reality is that once you get to the hearing, you're already in an adversarial situation . . . it's a confrontation and you've got to get it over with."

The Future Challenge

The special education reform movement, using the political strategy of litigation, made great gains in the education of the handicapped. PL 94-142 institutionalized basic reforms and a strategy of legalization that appears effective in implementing these reforms. However, the greatest test of special education reforms, and the politics of legalization, lies ahead. Federal education support has been slashed; education budget cuts at the state and local level pose a serious threat to the presently favored status of special education. Special education advocates may be able to hold their ground. Continuing politics of legalization may protect the handicapped's share of government programs while other programs face the political reality of limits.

Notes

Acknowledgments: David Kirp has steadfastly provided the guidance and encouragement that has enabled me to complete this project. David Neal and Susan Sterett have also provided valuable research and writing assistance. I thank them all.

David Neal and I conducted interviews with several key participants; these provide the basis for this account of the special education movement and the passage of the Education for All Handicapped Children Act. The following people were quite generous with their time and thoughts. I wish to thank: Joe Ballard, Council for Exceptional Children; Jack Duncan, Staff of Representative John Brademas; Michael Francis, Staff of Senator Robert Stafford; James Galloway, National Association of State Directors of Special Education; Thomas Gilhool, Attorney for Pennsylvania Association of Retarded Citizens; Robert Herman, Bureau of Education for the Handicapped; Ron Howard, National Association of State Boards of Education; John Martin, Council of Chief State School Officers; Ray Millenson, Staff of Senator Jacob Javits; John Morris, Department of Education; Ann Rosewater, Staff of Representative George Miller; Marilyn Rauth, American Federation of Teachers; Gus Steinhilber, National School Boards Association; Lisa Walker, Staff of Senator Harrison Williams; Fred Weintraub, Council for Exceptional Children; Jim Wilson, Pennsylvania Association for Retarded Citizens; and Dan Yohalem, Children's Defense Fund. Because our sources granted interviews on the condition that we not attribute any specific comments, no references accompany quotes from the interviews.

Our sources were reporting events that had occurred up to eleven years previously, so we approached their accounts with a healthy skepticism. We sought to crosscheck these accounts with published material and with the comments of other sources. I have included documentary support where possible. I also submitted an earlier version of this paper to two of our principal sources to verify my recounting of the story. Finally, I presented this earlier version at the October 1980 meeting of the Special Education Collaborative Conference at Stanford University. The participants were extremely helpful in providing a broad perspective on the special education movement.

This is intended as a legislative history, so I have relied on the public record of PL 94-142 where possible. The primary source for this material has been the four sets of hearings that Congress held in 1973 and 1975. These are: U.S., Congress, Senate, Subcommittee on the Handicapped of the Committee on Labor and Public Welfare, *Education for the Handicapped*, 93rd Cong., 1st sess., 1973 (hereafter cited as *Senate Hearings 1973*); U.S., Congress, House, Subcommittee on Select Education of the Committee on Education and Labor, *Education of the Handicapped Act Amendments*, 93rd Cong., 1st sess., 1973 (hereafter cited as *House Hearings 1973*); U.S. Congress, Senate, Subcommittee on the Handicapped of Committee on Labor and Public Welfare, *Education for All Handicapped Children*, 94th Cong., 1st sess., 1975 (hereafter cited as *Senate Hearings 1975*); and U.S., Congress, House, Subcommittee on Select Education of the Committee on Education and Labor, *Extension of Education of the Handicapped Act*, 94th Cong., 1st sess., 1975 (hereafter cited as *House Hearings 1975*).

1. *Senate Hearings 1973*, p. 793.

2. *House Hearings 1973*, p. 88.

3. *Senate Hearings 1973*, p. 88. Testimony of Clarke Ross, United Cerebral Palsy Association.

4. Marcia Burgdorf and Robert Burgdorf, "History of Unequal Treatment: The Qualifications of Handicapped Persons as a 'Suspect Class' under the Equal Protection Clause," *Santa Clara Law Review* 855 (1975), p. 874.

5. Alan Abeson and Joseph Ballard, "State and Federal Policy for Exceptional Children," *Public Policy and the Education of Exceptional Children*, eds. Frederick Weintraub, Alan Abeson, and Joseph Ballard (Reston, Va.: Council for Exceptional Children, 1976) (hereafter cited as *Public Policy and Exceptional Children*); Frederick Weintraub, "Special Education and the Government—A History," *Encyclopedia of Education* (New York: Macmillan Co., 1971) 8; and Frederick Weintraub and Alan Abeson, "New Education Policies for the Handicapped: The Quiet Revolution," in Weintraub et al., eds., *Public Policy and Exceptional Children*.

6. Carl Milofsky, *Special Education: A Sociological Study of California Programs* (New York: Praeger, 1976).

7. 20 U.S. Code. 1401–1461.

8. Scheingold writes about how rights serve as political resources. Stuart Scheingold, *The Politics of Rights: Lawyers, Public Policy, and Political Change* (New Haven, Conn.: Yale University Press, 1974) See also Stewart Macaulay, *Law and the Balance of Power: The Automobile Manufacturers and Their Dealers* (New York: Russell Sage, 1966) and Leon Mayhew, *Law and Equal Opportunity: A Study of the Massachusetts Commission Against Discrimination* (Cambridge, Mass.: Harvard University Press, 1968).

9. 347 U.S. 483 (1954).

10. Weintraub and Abeson, "New Education Policies," in Weintraub et al., eds., *Public Policy and Exceptional Children*, pp. 8–13. See also Paul Dimond, "The Constitutional Right to Education: The Quiet Revolution," 24 *Hastings Law Journal* 1087 (1973).

11. Thomas Gilhool, "Education: An Inalienable Right," in Weintraub et al., eds., *Public Policy and Exceptional Children*.

12. James Wilson, "The Strategy of Protest: Problems of Negro Civic Action," V *Journal of Conflict Resolution* 261 (1961).

13. See, for example, Michael Parenti, "Power and Pluralism: A View from the Bottom," 32 *Journal of Politics* 501 (1970).

14. Mancur Olson, *The Logic of Collective Action* (Cambridge, Mass.: Harvard University Press, 1965), pp. 9–16, 43–52.

15. This analysis of the special education movement's use of litigation was stimulated by accounts of how disadvantaged groups have used protest to overcome their political powerlessness. Several works have been particularly helpful: William Gamson, *The Strategy of Social Protest* (Homewood, Ill.: Dorsey, 1975); E. J. Hobsbawm, "Should the Poor Organize?" *New York Review of Books* (March 23, 1978), p. 44; Michael Lipsky, "Protest as a Political Resource," 62 *American Political Science Review* 1144 (1968); Frances Piven and Richard Cloward, *Poor People's Movements: Why They Succeed, How They Fail* (New York: Pantheon, 1977); and Wilson, "The Strategy of Protest." Another work helped in my transferring the protest perspective to the use of litigation: Stephen Barkan, "Political Trials and Resource Mobilization: Towards a New Understanding of Social Movement Litigation," 58 *Social Forces* 944 (1980).

16. Alan Abeson, "Litigation," in Weintraub et al., eds., *Public Policy and Exceptional Children*; Thomas Gilhool, "Education: An Inalienable Right"; and Leopold Lippman and Ignacy Goldberg, *Right to Education* (New York: Teachers College Press, 1973), chap. 4.

17. See *Halderman* v. *Pennhurst State School and Hospital*, 446 F. Supp. 1295 at 1302–1312 (E.D. Pa. 1977).

18. See Dennis Haggerty and E. Sacks, "Education of the Handicapped: Towards a Definition of Appropriate Education," 50 *Temple Law Quarterly* 961 (1977).

19. 343 F. Supp. 279 (E.D. Pa. 1972).

20. 348 F. Supp. 866 (D.D.C. 1972).

21. Council for Exceptional Children, "A Continuing Summary of Pending and Completed Litigation Regarding the Education of the Handicapped," *House Hearings 1975*, p. 191.

22. *United States* v. *Carolene Products* 304 U.S. 144 at 152 n. 4 (1938) provides the theoretical basis for this expansion. For an excellent comment on the constitutional protection of disadvantaged groups, see Owen Fiss, "Foreword: The Forms of Justice," 93 *Harvard Law Review* 1 (1979).

23. *Brown* v. *Board of Education*, 347 U.S. 483 (1954); *Goldberg* v. *Kelly*, 397 U.S. 254 (1970). Tribe presents an excellent summary of the evolution of due process protections: Laurence Tribe, *American Constitutional Law* (Mineola, N.Y.: Foundation Press, 1978), pp. 506–532.

24. Council for Exceptional Children, "A Continuing Summary," p. 91.

25. Abeson, "Litigation," p. 241. See also Abram Chayes, "The Role of the Judge in Public Law Litigation," 89 *Harvard Law Review* 1281 (1976); Fiss, "Foreword"; Lon Fuller, "Forms and Limits of Adjudication," 92 *Harvard Law Review* 353 (1979); and Seymour Sarason, *The Culture of the School and the Problem of Change* (Boston: Allyn and Bacon, 1971).

26. Richard A. Rossmiller, "Financing Educational Programs for Handicapped Children," *Senate Hearings 1973*, p. 1900.

27. *Mills* v. *Board of Education of District of Columbia* 348 F. Supp. 866 at 876 (D.D.C. 1972).

28. A. B. Harmon, "The Kentucky Right to Education Litigation," in Weintraub et al., eds., *Public Policy and Exceptional Children*.

29. Leo Connor, "The Proposed CEC Policy Statement on Governmental Affairs," 36 *Exceptional Children* 539 (1970). See also Frederick Weintraub, Alan Abeson, and David Braddock, *State Law and Education of the Handicapped: Issues and Recommendations* (Reston, Va.: Council for Exceptional Children, 1971).

30. See generally, Frederick Weintraub and Alan Abeson, "Appropriate Education for All Handicapped Children: A Growing Issue," 23 *Syracuse Law Review* 1037 (1972) (reprinted in *Senate Hearings 1973*, p. 154); David Kirp, "Schools as Sorters: The Constitutional and Policy Implications of Student Classification," 121 *University of Pennsylvania Law Review* 705 (1973); and David Kirp, William Buss, and Peter Kuriloff, "Legal Reform of Special Education: Empirical Studies and Procedural Proposals," 62 *California Law Review* 40 (1974): pp. 40–155 (reprinted in *Senate Hearings 1973*, p. 1648).

31. See text accompanying n. 50.

32. Eugene Eidenberg and Roy Morey, *An Act of Congress: The Legislative Process and the Making of Educational Policy* (New York: Norton, 1969); Eric Redman, *The Dance of Legislation* (New York: Simon and Schuster, 1973).

33. *Senate Hearings 1975*, p. 160 (testimony of Terrel Bell, U.S. Commissioner or Education).

34. Eidenberg and Morey, *An Act of Congress.*

35. *Senate Hearings 1975*, p. 146 (testimony of Francis McIntyre, Assistant State Superintendent of Education, Maryland).

36. *House Hearings 1973*, pp. 26, 27 (testimony of Fred Weintraub, Council for Exceptional Children).

37. See e.g. *Senate Hearings 1973*, p. 430 (testimony of Jean Garvin, State Director of Special Education—Vermont).

38. Hargrove et al. described this idea in terms of "client politics" and "entrepreneurial politics" (from James Wilson, *The Politics of Regulation* [New York: Basic Books, 1980]). See Erwin Hargrove, Scarlett Graham, Leslie Ward, Virginia Abernethy, Joseph Cunningham, and William Vaughn, *Regulations and Schools: The Implementation of Equal Education for Handicapped Children* (Nashville: Institute for Public Policy Studies, 1981).

39. 20 U.S.Code 1401(18). Martin provides a straightforward discussion of the statutory provisions of PL 94-142 and their later interpretation. Reed Martin, *Educating Handicapped Children, The Legal Mandate* (Champaign, Ill.: Research Press, 1979), pp. 57–75.

40. 20 U.S.Code 1041(19); Martin, *Educating Handicapped Children*, pp. 77–84.

41. Galanter's analysis suggests that parents will be ill-equipped to overcome the advantages of the schools in the hearings. Marc Galanter, "Why the 'Haves' Come Out Ahead: Speculations on the Limits of Legal Change," 9 *Law and Society Review* 95 (1974).

42. 20 U.S.Code 1412(5)(B); Martin, *Educating Handicapped Children*, pp. 85–95.

43. 20 U.S.Code 1415(e).

44. See for example, *Mills* v. *Board of Education*, 348 F. Supp. 866 at 880-883 (D.D.C.) (court-ordered procedural safeguards); Alan Abeson, Nancy Bolick, and Jayne Hass, "Due Process of Law: Background and Intent," in Weintraub et al., eds., *Public Policy and Exceptional Children* (Tennessee and Massachusetts statutes).

45. The original procedural safeguards are set out in S. 6, §6(a)(1)(B), *Senate Hearings 1973*, p. 15.

46. Senate version: U.S., Congress, Senate, *Congressional Record* 121:19478–19482, June 18, 1975. House version: U.S. Congress, House, *Congressional Record* 121:25526–25531, July 29, 1975.

47. In fact the pace of litigation may have increased as courts wrestle with the provisions of PL 94-142, particularly the meaning of related services, the necessity of year round education, and the payment of tuition for private schools.

48. Department of Education, *The Interim Report, Secretarial Task Force on Equal*

Educational Opportunity for Handicapped Children (Washington, D.C.: Department of Education, 1980) pp. 7–14.

49. See Peter Kuriloff, David Kirp, and William Buss, "When Handicapped Children Go to Court: Assessing the Impact of the Legal Reform of Special Education in Pennsylvania" (Report prepared for the National Institute of Education, 1979), pp. 26–152, 215–248. See generally, Hargrove et al., *Regulations and Schools*; and Marian Stearns, David Greene, and Jane David, "Local Implementation of PL 94-142" (Discussion draft—SRI International, 1979, hereafter cited as *SRI*). See also Richard A. Weatherly and Michael Lipsky, "Street Level Bureaucrats and Institutional Innovation: Implementating Special Education Reform," 47 *Harvard Educational Review* 171 (1977). Kirp's discussion of the interplay of five policy frames—professionalization, politicization, legalization, bureaucratization, and market regulation—provides an interesting perspective here, particularly given his focus on professionalization and legalization. David Kirp, "Professionalization as a Policy Choice: British Special Education in Comparative Perspective," (this volume, p. 74–112).

50. Robert Mnookin and Lewis Kornhauser, "Bargaining in the Shadow of the Law: The Case of Divorce," *Yale Law Journal* (1979). See also Stewart Macaulay, "Non-Contractual Relations in Business," 28 *American Sociological Review* 55 (1963).

51. Thomas Schelling, *The Strategy of Conflict* (New York: Oxford University Press, 1960).

52. Several implementation studies of PL 94-142 and similar state legislation provide some data about the operation of the procedural safeguards. Milton Budoff and Alan Orenstein, "Special Education Appeals Hearings: Their Form and the Response of Participants," *Final Report on Due Process in Special Education: Legal and Human Perspectives* (Washington, D.C.: U.S. Department of Health, Education, and Welfare, 1979); Michael Kirst and Kay Bertken, "Due Process Hearings in Special Education: An Exploration of Who Benefits" (This volume, p. 136–168); Kuriloff et al., "When Handicapped Children," (Pennsylvania); Richard A. Weatherly, *Reforming Special Education: Policy Implementation from State Level to Street Level* (Cambridge, Mass.: MIT Press, 1979) (Massachusetts). These implementation studies are summarized in David Neal, "The Legalization of Special Education" (Paper prepared for the Institute for Research on Educational Finance and Governance, Stanford University, 1980).

53. Kirst and Bertken, "Due Process Hearings," p. 141; Kuriloff et al., "When Handicapped Children," pp. 159–169; *SRI*, p. 104.

54. Kirst and Bertken, "Due Process Hearings," p. 146–150; Kuriloff et al., "When Handicapped Children," pp. 168, 169.

55. Kuriloff et al., "When Handicapped Children," pp. 215–248.

56. Budoff and Orenstein, "Special Education Appeals Hearings," pp. 9–1, 13–15; Kirst and Bertken, "Due Process Hearings," pp. 141, 142, *SRI*, p. 101.

57. The SRI study also found that the IEP requirement has also provided bargaining leverage to parents. *SRI*, pp. 79–82.

58. *SRI*, pp. 101–104.

59. Budoff and Orenstein, "Special Education Appeals Hearings," pp. 9–11, 13–15, 17–27.

CHAPTER 4/

Professionalization as a Policy Choice: British Special Education in Comparative Perspective

DAVID L. KIRP

Policy Frameworks

The way a policy problem gets defined says a great deal about how it will be resolved. This link between definition and solution, question and answer, is most obvious with respect to the *scope* of an issue. Asking, for example, whether the welfare winter coat allowance should be increased generates a reply different in kind from a query about the rightness of any earmarked welfare allowance, or one comparing welfare and job training programs. The *framework* within which a policy issue is embedded involves a less familiar but equally significant policy choice; here again, conceptualization shapes response. This essay examines the consequences of choosing among policy frameworks, contrasting British and American approaches to the education of handicapped youngsters. The essay also speaks more generally to the impact of different social policy strategies.

Contemporary social policy is dominated by four distinct ways of characterizing an issue.[1] A given policy question may be regarded as best settled by recourse to professional expertise, and in that event, what experts say prevails. Alternatively, the question may be resolved by relying on political judgment, either through ideologically driven clashes or through the give and take of bargaining among the interested parties. Or it may be resolved by stressing legal norms, especially the norm of fair decision-making process. Or, finally, it may be resolved by depending on bureaucratic standards of consistency and internal accountability. Lurking in the background is a fifth possibility: the determination to let the market fix policy outcomes.

These alternative policy frameworks—professionalization, politicization, legalization, bureaucratization, and market regulation—coexist uneasily with one another. They are pursued by different policy actors for different reasons. They have distinctive potentialities and equally distinctive pathologies, and tend to fall in and out of favor with policymakers over time. Choosing among these policy frameworks affects the policy system and, vitally, the supposed beneficiaries.

We routinely link certain frameworks with particular policy domains. The treatment of criminals, for example, seems an essentially legal issue, while the care of thalidomide victims depends on medical and psychological expertise. Yet such categorizations offer only partial truths. Because crimes are defined by rules and because a rule-bound process determines guilt or innocence, law is a major—but not the only—framework applied in treating criminals. Talking about treatment as rehabilitation introduces professional concerns; the bureaucratic structure of the prison system may make alternative treatments unfeasible; and politics settles both what we mean by criminal behavior and whether resources are devoted to deterrence or rehabilitation. The thalidomide case is similar. While caring for thalidomide victims demands professional knowledge, the treatment itself depends on the legal rights enjoyed by the victim, the institutional structure within which help is provided, and the balancing of the claims of this group for political attention against those of another class of victims.[2]

As these illustrations suggest, few policy problems get defined exclusively in terms of one or another framework. They draw instead on elements of two or more frames. While the several frameworks can sometimes be brought into harmony—as students of policy implementation consistently remind us, for example, attention to how organizations work properly informs the analysis of any complex policy issue—conflict among frameworks, not harmony, is the norm.[3]

These frameworks are not merely descriptive devices. They also represent alternative values. Professionals regard expertise as a superior form of problem solving because it eschews petty partisanship, while the ideologue disparages claims of expertise as concealing political judgments. Bureaucratic norms are said to secure the fairness that results from checking discretion; on the other hand, legal standards supposedly provide a firmer protection against arbitrariness precisely because they permit careful inquiry into specific circumstances.[4] Such disagreements cannot be settled by recourse to an agreed-upon metric, for it is the metric itself that is the focus of contention. Choosing among these frameworks of analysis means selecting among ways of ordering the relevant policy universe.

Since each of the frameworks has its own built-in constituency with a special stake in the policy, this is no abstruse matter. Legalization is the lawyer's life blood. Organized interest groups see issues predominantly in political terms. Doctors and caseworkers routinely define questions as depending on expertise for their resolution. It is a trait of the vocation that being a lawyer or an administrator or a lobbyist means, among other things, that one regards problems in a distinctive light.

These distinctions among frameworks matter a great deal. They determine what will be provided, by whom, and on what terms. They fix the nature and extent of regulatory control. They shape how varied the good or service will be and identify who will benefit. Defining a policy problem primarily in terms of rights creates a different client class, with a different stake, than does treating the issue as one fit for professional discretion or suitably the ministerial responsibility of a bureau.[5] Because choices among frameworks embody choices about the allocation of power, how these choices are made becomes a central policy question.

Once a policy has been framed in a particular way, change usually comes slowly and at the margin. Here, as in so many aspects of the policy process, incrementalism embodies the norm: professional judgment may count for somewhat more or less over time, the significance of procedural protections varies, and so forth. More marked and ubiquitous changes can be detected in the longer run. Legalism has generally grown substantially more important in the United States during the past two decades, while bureaucratic standard setting—particularly important during the 1970s in the area of environmental protection, occupational safety, and consumer product regulation—has fallen from favor.[6] Comparable trends are evident in Britain, though they are both more recent and more tentative.

Why do these transformations occur? The explanations are sometimes issue-specific. New technologies, new ways of accomplishing a desired result, may prompt a realignment: the emergence of a promising professional cure for some social malady, for example, encourages increased dependency on expertise. Factors transcending any particular policy issue are also relevant: a shift in the political climate, for example, or newly felt constraints on the budget of the public household[7] may prompt what amounts to a paradigm shift. Each of these factors has been at work in the United States and Britain. Yet because policy issues are usually tacitly understood as inextricably linked to a given framework, it is often hard to reconceptualize the question in less incremental terms. Only by embracing a different kind of perspective, one that relies on historical or comparative insight, does it become apparent that a vital policy choice has indeed been made.

The evolution of educational policy for handicapped children in Britain, usually and euphemistically termed "special education," nicely illustrates these propositions.[8] In Britain, as in the United States, determination of handicap and prescription for handicapped youngsters were historically left to the medical profession. During the past 30 years, other professionals, notably psychologists and educationalists, have contended for dominance. The rightness of defining the issues almost exclusively in terms of professional expertise was not, however, called into question in Britain until very recently, and then only timidly. British policy statements have been largely dismissive of, or inattentive to, alternative frameworks that, by contrast, have enjoyed greater acceptance in the United States: restructuring the bureaucracy that delivers services, bringing the handicapped into the ordinary educational system as a part of an ideologically driven push for social integration, and enabling the handicapped significantly to shape their own treatment regime.

These alternatives surfaced in Britain between 1974 and 1978, during a period of intense policy review of the education of the handicapped undertaken by a government-appointed committee of enquiry. The concept of integration found its way into British law, but in toothless form, and the other alternative frameworks were effectively rejected. The committee of enquiry was familiar with these options. A committee delegation came to the United States to learn firsthand about the approach taken in the Education for All Handicapped Children Act, PL 94-142.[9] That legislation expands federal and state government control over local practice, elaborates substantive and procedural rights, and establishes a statutory preference for integration. The British committee chose instead to preserve a professionalized approach, and while its proposals have subsequently been modified by the government, nothing approaching the nature of the American undertaking has been suggested.

Why should such differences in approach arise? And to what effect? Succeeding sections recount this history, contrasting it both with British social policy in other spheres and with the American experience in special education. The concluding section considers impact of the choice of a policy framework on the lives of children.

The Evolution of British Special Education Policy

Recent policy reviews—including the report of the Committee of Enquiry into the Education of Handicapped Children and Young People (1978),[10] and the government's White Paper, *Special Needs in Education* (1980),[11] confirm the long-standing perception of British special education as almost exclusively the province of specialists, an institutionally marginal service isolated from ordinary schools and managed by a specialist group.

The Rise of a Professionalized Service

Special education was an afterthought in the history of publicly provided schooling in Britain.[12] While the first schools for the handicapped—asylums for idiots, academies for the deaf and dumb—were established a century before the 1870 Education Act, that act made no provision for handicapped youngsters. Over the next 50 years, the law was amended on a handicap-by-handicap basis, first to permit, and then to require, that local education authorities assume responsibility for providing basic schooling for these youngsters. Change in law proceeded slowly, and change in the schools was slower still. By 1909, for instance, only one-third of all authorities were providing schooling for the retarded. Twenty years later, the Mental Deficiency Committee established by the Ministry of Education reported that just one-sixth of all retardates had been ascertained and assigned to special schools—this at a time when almost all youngsters attended at least primary school.[13]

Gradual changes in the legislation did not affect the basic pattern of provision. Unlike ordinary education, primarily a state-provided enterprise, state-subsidized private schools were key providers of services for particular kinds of handicap. This remains true today, as four out of five blind children, approximately half of the deaf children, and one-third of those labeled as maladjusted are privately schooled. [14] Even when education for the handicapped was publicly supplied, it was a separate and distinct service, usually delivered in special schools the quality of which depended upon the resources a local authority chose to allocate. A series of reports issued by the Ministry of Education, beginning in the 1920s, recommended bringing special and ordinary students together in order to avoid the stigma of special treatment. [15] The reporters offered only advice and not mandates, advice that in this instance went ignored, since local authorities were more interested in providing some distinct type of schooling for handicapped youngsters.

The 1944 Education Act, which reshaped the system of British education generally, made the terms on which special education would be offered more coherent. That act treats "pupils who suffer from any disability of the mind or body" as a single group. Local authorities are obliged to ascertain who these children are, to determine their disability primarily through medical examination, and "to provide for the education of a pupil with a serious disability in an appropriate special school, or any other suitable school where this was impractical or the disability was not serious." [16]

During the parliamentary debate over the 1944 act, the government spokesman declared that "we desire to see as many children as possible retained in the normal stream of school life," [17] and a 1946 Ministry of Education report envisioned a special education system reaching as many as one-sixth of British youngsters. [18] Yet special education developed very differently, as a distinct service reaching a tiny fraction—fewer than 2 percent—of British schoolchildren.

The structure of the act helps in explaining this outcome. Because the handicapped child must be medically diagnosed, problems concerning a child's school experiences are less likely to be regarded as within the province of special education than are the more traditional maladies: it is rickets, not grading deficiencies or rebelliousness, that most readily commands attention. The act also makes special provision the norm, linkages to the ordinary system the exception; this structure also suggests a regime of narrowly defined concerns.

Institutional and professional preferences have reinforced these structural and legal tendencies, giving rise to a small and separate service. No one plumped for a vastly expanded conception of special children who would largely be integrated into the regular system. In a straitened postwar economy, priorities had to be determined. Children most evidently in need also seemed most deserving of help, and separate institutions appeared essential for this group. Those responsible for special education within the government set about persuading local authorities that there existed a specialty called special education and that programs should be established for each of the 10 diverse categories of handicap—ranging from educationally subnormal to blind, maladjusted to delicate—specified in department regulations.

The special education advocates created a job market for educational psychologists as professionals uniquely able to identify and sort certain kinds of special students, and fostered the development of distinct institutions walled off from ordinary schools. These schools had their own staffing patterns and resource requirements—both extremely generous in comparison with the ordinary system. The advocates' success is apparent in the increase of specialist professionals and special students. Guidelines for minimum numbers of specialist professionals,[19] issued by the Ministry of Education in 1959, were withdrawn in 1973, for by then every authority had exceeded the Ministry's recommendation.[20] The number of special students also grew. When compared with the ordinary population, they remained a minuscule and almost invisible group, a circumstance reinforced by their separation; but the increase in the numbers of students identified as special—from 38,499 in 1945 to 58,042 in 1955, and to 184,996 in 1979—is impressive evidence of system building.[21]

This newly strengthened special system identified its clientele in essentially medical terms. It attributed behaviors to individual organic deficiencies, whether the behavior in question was maladjustment or blindness. The increasing emergence of a psychological orientation among professionals dealing with certain kinds of handicap, notably maladjustment and so-called moderate educational subnormality, altered the specification of the illness but not the underlying perception that a personal disorder was at issue. Individual cure, or more likely, adjustment to a less-than-normal adult life, became the objective of the special system. An individual entering the system of special education was unlikely to return to ordinary school. Only after leaving school, if at all, might he disappear into the adult population.

The 1944 Education Act and subsequent professional efforts solidified a framework which defined as a professional concern the needs of a wide range of children who differed from the norm. Central government had a sizeable role in spurring these developments. While the government does not allocate resources for particular operational expenditures, it does approve school building requests. The Ministry explicitly favored special school construction during the 1950s, thus encouraging their construction. Between 1950 and 1977, the number of such schools increased from 685 to 1,882.[22]

A series of circulars and reports concerning aspects of special education, issued regularly since the 1950s, reinforced the professional character of the service. Some of the government reports—*Units for Partially Hearing Children*, for instance, or *Diagnostic and Assessment Units*[23]—set the standard for good practice in particular areas. Others, for example, the *Report of the Committee on Maladjusted Children*,[24] identified particular categories of handicap. That report defined maladjustment in the psychological language characteristic of the 1950s. Still others, such as the survey of special units for "behaviorally disturbed" students, undertaken in 1978, catalogued and implicitly legitimated new developments in special education.[25] Department of Education and Science (DES) reports also signaled the relevance of resource constraints as affecting local authorities' capacity to take up new ideas.[26]

These reports, although advisory, were not without effect. In British educational policy, orders are rare and "government by circular" the norm.[27] The system is perceived by its participants as depending on hint and signal, consultation and suggestion. Advice from central government commands, at the least, a respectful audience. A DES publication is followed by queries from Her Majesty's Inspectorate (HMI) during visits to local authorities, discussions with the national groups who regularly consult with DES, and the like. A DES publication will routinely stir discussion among the specialists, and may lead authorities to appoint working parties that make policy recommendations in light of the national advice. Policy change takes place gradually on an authority-by-authority basis. In the case of special education, policy reform was tied directly to expertise.

The clearest example of centrally promoted change is Circular 2/75, which addressed the assessment of handicapped children.[28] The 1944 act had required the certification of a doctor to identify a child as needing special education, and the circular could not, of course, countermand the law. Yet the assessment forms that the circular specified gave effective control to the psychologist, who would coordinate the appraisals of a number of professionals, including the doctor and classroom teacher, and also gather information from parents. The circular codified what was regarded as sensible practice, and, in a tone more directive than is customarily used, urged its application in all authorities. Circular 2/75 solidified the professional claim to competence, even as it altered the balance of authority among professionals within the special education system.

Debate over educational policy in Britain often assumes the form of discussions about sound educational practice, and in such an environment the role of HMI becomes crucial. HMI serves a dual purpose. Through its advising, HMI is supposed to improve local practice. The Inspectorate also brings information about existing practice to the attention of central government and recommends policy change. With respect to special education, HMI evaluations substantially affected the substance of departmental advice, and as consultant to local authorities, HMI took an unusually directive stance. While the Inspectorate, in effect, competes with a local authority's own advisers for attention with respect to other aspects of schooling, HMI has had an effective monopoly on special education expertise until the reorganization of local education agencies (LEAs) into larger units with their own special education specialists.

By 1971, when a committee of enquiry was established, by the secretary of state for Education and Science, to study children's special educational needs, those needs were defined almost exclusively in terms of specialist expertise. The field itself had been carved up, with experts for particular types of physical handicap, degrees of retardation, specimens of maladjustment. The determination that all children could benefit from professional intervention had led DES, in 1970, to assume responsibility for some 34 thousand severely handicapped children, previously the charge of the Department of Health and Social Services (DHSS).[29] As a result, professional staff interested in education supplanted the lay care that DHSS had historically provided, and local authorities' special education activities were extended to a new clientele.

Advice from advisory committees composed of fellow professionals led DES to recommend policy changes, but these involved tinkering with an enterprise that was considered essentially sound. From the viewpoint of DES, its specialist advisers, and practitioners in the field, progress in special education meant continuing the expansion of a distinct enterprise, particularly that of reaching handicapped children below formal schooling age or older than age 16.

The Rejected Alternatives

In molding special education policy in Britain, professionalism, intertwined with the bureaucratic structure, enjoyed near-absolute preeminence as a policy frame. Counterforces, alternative frameworks for thinking about policy, long went unheard in policy discussions. Neither politics nor law nor the market have effectively challenged professional hegemony.

Politics. Little political attention was paid to special education. There were no parliamentary calls for review of the legislative structure, even at a time when handicap groups, working with the parliamentary All Party Disablement Conference, were pushing for new legislation concerning accessibilty to public buildings and government job quotas for handicapped persons. At neither the national nor local levels of government did the treatment of handicapped pupils become an issue remotely comparable in importance to the treatment of a similarly small group, nonwhite students.[30] Policy was effectively fixed by administrators and professionals; and even where politicians got involved in particular communities, they had acted on behalf of professionally defined interests. "Those advising the politicians," a student of social service budget-setting observed, "are themselves professionals. There is a heavy professional social work involvement both on the demand and the supply side."[31]

Voluntary organizations concerned with particular handicap groups, such as the Royal National Institute for the Deaf, and the Spastics Society, do exist; but these are not interest groups. For one thing, they are typically charitable enterprises, not membership organizations designed to serve a particular group and not represent it. They are primarily engaged in improving the lot of handicapped individuals and their families, by offering support, not calling for government action; indeed, their legal status as charitable organizations formally precludes them from acting otherwise. For another thing, the special education lobbying efforts mounted from time to time have been hampered by the fragmentation of these groups. It is the needs of persons with a particular handicap, not the interests of all children who are, or should be, receiving special help in the schools, that define the main concern of each group. While there exists a Joint Council for the Educationally Handicapped, its activities embody what one senior DES official termed "the lowest common denominator of joint interest."

In a political system where interest group pressure is a way of life,[32] such efforts on behalf of the handicapped themselves are rare. The interest group activity which does occur has been orchestrated by the professionals. A small but energetic lobbying effort promoted by one of the senior professionals in the field led, first, to the 1970 legislation that extended DES authority over the profoundly retarded, and then to the formation of the committee of enquiry in 1974. Although these individuals lacked the power to change the law directly, their persistence— exemplified in letters to all MPs, a steady stream of correspondence with successive DES secretaries of state, endless speeches at professional meetings, and similar tactics—helped set in motion a train of events that has led over time to the desired changes.

Law. Legal norms have played an even more modest part than political action in fixing the course of British special education. Litigation concerning educational policy—like public law litigation in Britain generally—must identify a violation of a statutory duty; for, unlike in the United States, there are no sweeping constitutional principles on which to rest cases. The 1944 Education Act makes such claims enormously difficult to establish. While the courts have intervened with growing frequency in instances of apparently arbitrary administrative action, the scope of those interventions has been decidedly limited, at least by comparison with American court decisions.[33]

Where local authorities have failed to follow prescribed procedures, they have been overturned, but such decisions merely mandate that the authority take the proposed action in the legally correct way.[34] The leading decision on policymaking prerogative, the *Tameside* case, effectively insulates local authority action from both DES scrutiny and individual attack.[35] The court held in *Tameside* that the secretary of state could not reverse a local authority's policy determination unless the secretary concluded that the authority's action had no basis in reason. That decision twists a provision of the 1944 act, broadly empowering the secretary of state to act if "satisfied . . . that any local authority . . . have acted or are preparing to act unreasonably," into a defense of local variability; for under the *Tameside* standard it is hard to imagine what "unreasonable" action would entail. Although the act broadly authorizes initiatives by the secretary of state to "secure the effective execution of national policy," *Tameside* embraces a less centrist and more pluralist approach. After *Tameside*, DES can only act if it has a specific statutory mandate to do so. Because the 1944 act is drafted in broad terms, allowing much room for administrative discretion over policy matters, such specificity is the exception. The *Tameside* rationale also assures that parental complaints against an authority's action, based on the claim that the authority is acting unreasonably, will almost invariably be resolved in the authority's favor.

The *Tameside* decision strengthens the hand of local authorities, but even before that opinion, DES was reluctant to overturn local determinations. Under the 1944 act, parents can allege, in a complaint to the secretary of state, that an authority has acted unreasonably or has failed to perform some statutory duty. An estimated 100 such complaints concerning special education have been filed annually since 1970. As a matter of DES policy, these complaints are treated informally; there is not even a departmental record of their number. Only when a complaint uses the language of appeal does DES mobilize the administrative apparatus. Complaints are handled by a number of middle level DES administrators who apply no clear or fixed standard; consequently, the handling of a complaint substantially depends on who processes it. Parents' only hope of prevailing depends on the matter being treated informally, with DES urging a particular solution on the authority; for no formal request for DES intervention has succeeded during the period. These legal rights embodied in the 1944 act thus have no practical meaning.

This wholly discretionary system is peculiar to education. It is sharply distinguishable from the administrative appeals machinery which exists in other areas, most notably supplementary welfare benefits. It also represents a shift in departmental practice away from close administrative review of certain claims. Prior to the declaration, in the 1970 act, that all children were educable, parents could appeal to the secretary of state from local authority determinations that their child was "unsuitable" for education; the 1959 Mental Health Act tightened the standards for such determination. The history of DES reviews of these assessments reveals that a substantial number of complaints were lodged between 1951 and 1969:[36] between 369 (or 11.6 percent of all instances of locally determined ineducability) in 1951, and 139 (61.2 percent of all such instances) in 1969. In 1959, prior to the change of legal standard, the department was reluctant to reverse local decisions, doing so in just 1.6 percent of the cases in 1951 and 9.4 percent in 1960, the year before the Mental Health Act went into effect. The altered legal standard reduced the number of children identified as unsuitable for education and made the department much more willing to support parental appeals. In more than 20 percent of the cases filed each year between 1961 and 1969, appeals were upheld. This history confirms that in certain circumstances DES can manage an effective administrative appeals process. The present system—in which appeals are discouraged, seem always to fail, and are not recorded publicly—embodies a preference for professional discretion over formal, lawlike review.

Antagonism to the law remains the norm with respect to decision making in education. Those who manage and staff social programs distrust legalization because it interferes with the exercise of "enlightened and altruistic" administration, frustration what Richard Titmuss terms "a system of flexible, individualized justice based on considerations of dignity and self-respect."[37] Legalism is regarded as a pathological condition, undermining the realization of a purposive and benevolent administrative regime. Leftist critics are equally dismissive of legal intervention, but for another reason: they see law being used to thwart challenges to the prevailing political and economic order.[38] There are those who embrace a model of social service reform through legal change, but their successes have been few in number and modest in scope.[39]

The market. Although special education is offered both by private state-aided schools and local authority schools, the market does not discipline public sector behavior. There exists little real competition between the two sectors. Private schools provide specialized services that are either too costly for most local authorities to maintain (for instance, education for blind children) or that cater to the excess demand generated by the publicly run schools (for instance, schools for the maladjusted). The professionals who staff schools in the two sectors share similar values. In terms of how the educational system actually operates, it makes better sense to treat the public and private special education programs as components of a single system.

What Makes Special Education Special?

The preference for a professional solution to a social policy problem characterizes not just special education but also British educational policy and, indeed, British social policy generally.[40] The courts rarely act to fix policy; there is no British equivalent of the American welfare or desegregation cases. Central government has seldom exercised its broad powers under the 1944 act to shape the system. In education, the conversion of a three-tiered secondary school system into a comprehensive school regime and the restructuring of higher education stand as the two noticeable exceptions in nearly four decades.[41]

Special education is special only because it exaggerates these tendencies of British policy. What is supposed to distinguish special from ordinary education is the level of expertise involved. Everyone can claim to be an expert concerning ordinary schooling, if only because everyone has experienced it; by contrast, the demands of the retarded or blind child seem more exotic, the means of instructing such children outside the kit-bag of knowledge that leads many of us to imagine that we might competently manage the teaching of third grade mathematics or fifth grade English. Special educators are regarded, and regard themselves, as specialists, to a degree that the regular classroom teacher does not, and this bolsters their claims of expertise.

For their part, parents of handicapped youngsters are less willing, or able, to press a different understanding of the needs of their children. These parents bear a distinctive kind of burden.[42] Not infrequently, they perceive their children as a shame for which they themselves deserve some measure of blame, and assume responsibility for having produced a less-than-normal child. Their inclination is to protect that child—and themselves—by not asserting themselves; for assertion makes both parent and child visible in unwanted ways.[43] Such inclinations, while surely wrong, are nonetheless widely shared. Groups acting on behalf of particular handicaps seek to ease parents' isolation, but there is not much evidence that these parents regard themselves as a group, or that they have learned to make demands on behalf of, say, blind or spastic children; rather, they are grateful for what they get. There are, of course, the exceptional cases: a dispute over the appropriate education of an assertedly dyslexic child wound up in the courts, and the *Times* recounted the story of the protracted struggle of one parent, herself a well-known editor, to extract from the Inner London Education Authority a decent education for her child. But these are rare events, singular occurrences, that do not threaten the general dominance of the professionals.

With respect to two of the largest categories of handicap, learning difficulties and maladjustment, the fact that the handicap itself is so closely associated with a social misfortune—low income, family instability, and the like—means that the parents cannot defend the interests of their children by effectively confronting professionals and bureaucracies. It would be unrealistic to expect most parents of such youngsters, rightly attentive to the survival of their families, to be able to question professional judgment even if they were inclined to do so.

The apparently marginal policy importance of special education assures that issues of policy and practice rarely enter into general policy discussion. Such services as welfare, housing, health, and ordinary schooling affect sufficient numbers of people, and cost enough money, to merit routine scrutiny by local authorities, government departments, journalists, and students of politics and social administration. Special education, by contrast, occupies its own structurally differentiated niche within education. Because special education consumes only about 6 percent of the total education budget, it is largely insulated from detailed review. Social science and education faculties within the universities do not take much notice of special education; the favor is returned by academics in the special education field, who have not related the concerns of their domain to those of ordinary education or social services. Debates over special education policy are thus confined to a very small circle of people who have grown up in the field, and who share a commitment to basic assumptions, notably the primacy of expertise in policy shaping. The system whose workings the committee of enquiry undertook to examine was thus a largely self-contained and self-satisfied concern.

The Warnock Committee of Enquiry Report: Policy Review as a Laying On of Hands

Committees and the Conventional Wisdom

Committees of enquiry have been widely used in education to assess particular policy areas.[44] The appeal of this device is considerable. The appointment of a committee theoretically enables a knowledgeable group to take an unblinkered look at policy in a given domain. In practice, new ideas rarely emerge from these committees, although on occasion—as with the Plowden Committee's embracing of the open classroom concept—innovative practices are given legitimacy.[45] The committee tends instead to seize upon the prevailing conventional wisdom, and become a lobby for its own cause.

That committees of enquiry, set up with the apparent intention of seeing the world afresh, should instead see a more familiar world, is readily understandable. Committee nominees are reviewed by senior civil servants, and while there is of course some balancing to be done— maintaining parity among Welsh, Scottish, and English members, and making the requisite political appointments—most nominees have been proposed, if not actually approved, by DES. Members of the committee tend not to be sharp critics of present practice but to represent more mainstream views; the committee chairman, while deliberately chosen from outside the field being investigated, is reportedly selected from a list of candidates screened for reliability by the civil service. Any evident differences in viewpoint concerning the issue before the committee will be represented among its members, thus encouraging compromise.

The primary source of advice and support for the committee is DES itself, which assigns individuals both from the department and HMI to serve the committee. As representatives of DES, they are unlikely to hold heterodox positions. The committee staff brings a particular expertise to the enterprise. Because it drafts papers for the committee, the staff can shape the terms of discussion; its connections outside the committee determine the kinds of views that the committee hears; and it has that most precious resource, time, which enables the staff to undertake more than all but the most conscientious committee members.[46]

The tradition of moderation, characteristic of central policymaking generally, carries over to these committees. If the committee wishes to be taken seriously, it attunes itself to prevailing opinion. Consequently, what committees of enquiry repeatedly urge is a bigger and better-coordinated version of the present: provide more services or extend service provision to those previously unserved. This characterization aptly describes the Report of the Committee of Enquiry into the Education of Handicapped Children and Young People, commonly referred to as the Warnock Report.

The consequences of these twin sources of departmental power, a voice in committee appointments and a supportive relationship to the enterprise, are apparent in the composition and workings of the War-nock Committee. The committee was drawn almost entirely from the special education–related professionals. One-third of its members were associated with special schools. Committee members represented the medical, psychological, nursing, social work, and teaching professions. Its chairman, an Oxford philosophy don, was the one nonspecialist; its vice-chairman was a county education officer, long involved with special education. Only one of the committee's 26 members was the parent of a handicapped child. The special interest groups were unrepresented, for DES affirmed that it was not forming a constituent body. Despite the disproportionate number of nonwhite children who had been identified as educationally subnormal or maladjusted, no nonwhite served on the committee, nor was there a lawyer who might have spoken to the relevance of a legal-rights viewpoint. Nor was there a handicapped person.

The committee's staff developed material that reflected both the departmental position and viewpoints congenial with those of committee members. Although outside evidence was collected, both in hearings and written presentations, this material had scant influence on the committee. Concerning the critical matter of framing the policy question, there was little dissent among committee members and staff. As it saw its task, the committee had few fundamental choices to make.

What the Report Urges

The report reflects this general complacency. What commands central attention is not the system for special education, which is generally commended, but the ways in which special children are described in the law and regulations. Departmental regulations had created categories of handicap for which special services were to be provided. Those categories, the committee determined, were excessively rigid, and did not reveal the range of problems that might beset a child who was, say, physically handicapped and retarded. Categorization also imposed a label that could be applied in a stigmatizing fashion, rather than defining an educational deficiency. Moreover, the categories distinguished too sharply between the small fraction of the population with severe handicaps and the far larger proportion, estimated by the committee as nearly one in five, who would need special help at some point during their school careers.

The Warnock Report urged the abolition of these categories. Under its proposed scheme, records would be maintained and formal diagnoses carried out only for the most handicapped youngsters—the group roughly corresponding to those receiving full-time special education. These pupils would not be formally labeled as maladjusted or physically handicapped, but would instead be the recorded group, each individually described. The larger group with special needs would receive assistance without bearing any label at all, within the context of the school program. The labels would survive for purposes of description if not categorization, with one change: the educationally subnormal were henceforth to be referred to as children with learning difficulties.

The semantics of euphemism have had particular relevance to unfortunates, whether they be poor countries—underdeveloped, less developed, emerging nations—or handicapped pupils. While the regulations in force still refer to the educationally subnormal, this group was later called retarded and then slow learners. Now they are described as children with learning difficulties.[47] Less than a century ago, these youngsters were known as idiots and imbeciles. Such changes may signal a shift in attitude toward the population being described. Whether they imply new modes of assessment, and more critically whether assessment affects the education provided, are entirely different matters, about which the Warnock Report speaks with a less sure voice.

The proposed new assessment procedure relies heavily on Circular 2/75, which contemplates collecting a variety of professional views, coordinated by a psychologist, in ascertaining handicap. The Warnock Report expands this effort into a five-stage procedure, each stage calling on more and more refined expert judgment than the last. That model presumes what is highly problematic, that a handicap is comprised of a set of conditions diagnosable by professionals, and that within the professional ranks those with narrowly defined specialities are most adept at making assessments.

Psychologists often speak of assessment as if it were an end in itself, divorced from education, because they know so much more about the one than the other. Yet from the children's perspective, what matters most is the nature of the education received, who gets what kind of schooling in what setting. Here again, the Warnock Report's primary contribution is definitional and not substantive in nature. The report identifies four types of special education provision in ordinary schools—ranging from full-time instruction in an ordinary class with some supplemental support, to full-time education in a special class within the schools—without clarifying the circumstances that would make one or another the preferable alternative. Instruction in special schools is placed farther along the same continuum, with no adequate benchmarks. This section of the report is dotted with palliative phrases-—"children . . . who are more likely to thrive in the more intimate communal and educational setting of a special school"—which put the best, most expert-like face on what is in fact an absence of expertise.[48]

A full detailing of the educational offering would, to be sure, have lain outside the province of the committee. What is wanted is guidance, a hint as to what can be done. In place of such guidance, the Warnock Report says in effect: trust the professionals. The thinness of this undertaking becomes strikingly apparent in the discussion of curriculum. Here, even more plainly than in discussing the nature of the educational service, vacuous words such as "appropriate" and "needs" dominate, when in fact remarkably little is known about what approach should be adopted for which children.[49]

The Warnock Report describes the problem of special educational needs as one best resolved by the flexible application of expertise. The major fault that it finds with the present system, the rigidity of the categories of handicap fixed in the law, is really a plea for relying more on professional assessment. The *ad hoc* application of trained judgment to individual cases defines the course of reform. The report's other recommendations are consistent with the idea that special education's weaknesses are curable by professional determination. They call for expanding provision for handicapped children under age five and above age 16, and offering training to ordinary teachers, to enable them better to meet the demands of special children. Had the Warnock Report's recommendations been incorporated into the law, the scope of special education would have widened to serve the student population newly identified as special. Added money would have been spent on the service—how much is uncertain, since the report included no cost estimates—with new special services provided by specialists. In short, the Warnock Report spells more of the same.

What the Warnock Committee Didn't Consider

In the options that it dismisses as well as those it adopts, the Warnock Committee shapes the issue in terms of professionalism. Its resistance to the idea of integration because of the latter's ideological overtones, its discomfiture with full parental participation, its disregard of legal rights, and its inattention to questions of school organization are all compatible with a professional orientation.

Ideology and politics. During the period of the report's preparation, the Education Act of 1976 was amended to require that all children be educated in ordinary schools except where this was "impracticable or incompatible with the provision of efficient instruction in the schools; or would involve unreasonable public expenditure."[50] Section 10, inserted into the act by the House of Lords and unenthusiastically accepted by the government, embodies the weakest of preferences for the integration of handicapped and ordinary children. It does not speak of instruction in common classrooms but in "county or voluntary schools," and thus clearly contemplates the maintenance of units composed entirely of special children whose only contact with their schoolmates might come at meals or on the playground. The broad exceptions to the legislative requirement, which effectively enable an authority to base policy on its view of economic or educational concerns, make it hard to imagine any local judgment being overturned by a court or by DES.

Section 10 was nonetheless not without significance. As a political statement, it appeared to commit the government to the idea of integration, and it turned an educational question into a question of principle with deep symbolic importance. This very fact, coupled with the considerable opposition to Section 10 heard within the special education field, led the committee to choose a different course. It could not refute the section, which while not yet implemented—as written, it had to be effectuated by an order of the secretary of state—was nonetheless newly adopted law. Yet again the committee substituted definition for analysis. It identified three forms of integration—integration as a matter of physical location, social interaction, and educational interchange—and treated the choice among these as a matter of professional judgment.

More revealingly, the discussion of integration contrasts the educational needs of children with the social good of integration. Of particular concern in the report are the ordinary children, whose progress in schooling is regarded as jeopardized by excessive integration. In this calculus, the professional endeavor, education, is balanced against a social or political undertaking, integration, ignoring the likelihood that integration has educational as well as social consequences. Yet children learn at least as much from each other as they do from the particulars of curriculum or pedagogy. This latter proposition underlies the unhappiness with the three-tiered system of secondary schooling for ordinary children,[51] and seems to hold true for handicapped children as well. The efficacy of special programs for the mildly handicapped, particularly the maladjusted and retarded, has been seriously questioned.[52] These students—as well as other types of handicapped youngsters, including the deaf and blind—may well do better in ordinary classrooms with supplementary support, without hampering the progress of other children.[53] Though these data are hardly conclusive, they challenge the

Warnock Report's framework of analysis. Like so much that is of apparent relevance, they go undiscussed in the report.

Rights and law. The idea that handicapped children or their guardians might have legally cognizable rights scarcely figures in the Warnock Report. While one chapter describes "parents as partners," the terms of the partnership are fixed by the professionals. Parents are to be given information concerning available services as well as practical help, and are expected to contribute their knowledge of the child in the assessment procedure. Yet parents have only limited access to the material on which assessment decisions are based. While they are encouraged to discuss the educational program with school officials, there is no recourse in instances of disagreement. The report does not even mention the existing possibility of appealing to DES, let alone to the courts.

The issue of rights concerns not only individual families but also racial groups. Nonwhites, especially West Indians, are substantially overrepresented among those students labeled educationally subnormal,[54] and programs for maladjusted children, including the special units to deal with behavioral disturbance attached to a growing number of secondary schools, have been criticized on similar grounds. These revelations led West Indian community leaders to demand an investigation by the government's race relations agency. Despite this contretemps, race is nowhere mentioned in the Warnock Report. (The index to the report includes West Germany but not West Indians.) Racial overrepresentation is an unknown concept. The discussion of testing students whose native language is not English refers only to Welsh and Gaelic, despite the fact that many nonwhite immigrant youngsters lack fluency in English. Because the question of nonwhites and special education raises not one but two red flags—it poses the specter of legal rights and it is politically volatile—the committee opted to ignore the issue entirely.

The very idea of rights was unsettling. Those committee members who visited the United States came away horrified by the reliance there on administrative hearings and litigation over matters that seemed either petty or unsuitable for such review; it was as if Richard Titmuss's warnings about hearings over the cost of a new toothbrush had been realized in American special education. Hearings were thought to breed controversy when consensus was the objective. In the framework of the Warnock Report, rights would war with the idea of efficient service provided by professionals acting to the best of their abilities, and hence were pernicious. As committee chairman Mary Warnock declared: "There is something deeply unattractive about the spectacle of someone demanding his own rights." [55]

Organization. The Warnock Report focuses on the needs of individuals, not on the structure that will meet those needs. Three paragraphs are devoted to "organization's ability to adapt to new demands." The level of discussion is unspecific, even in comparison with the rest of the document. "The demands may be relatively simple or more complex and varied according to circumstance." [56] the report announces. The only concrete organizational recommendation envisions establishing a special education unit, with its own head, within the ordinary school, a notion inconsistent with the reconceptualization of special education set out elsewhere in the report. The Warnock Report does offer one other suggestion with organizational implications. It proposes that a named person, the head teacher in the school, help parents in bringing together the several special education services. Insofar as the named person is to act as the intermediary between these services and the child's advocate, the head teacher seems a strange choice, if only because the parent may be unhappy with the school itself. The committee's failure to recognize this potential for conflict reveals either naiveté concerning how schools work—unlikely, since a number of committee members were themselves school officials—or a preference for letting professionals determine organizational configurations for themselves.

Organizational concerns are the predicate for the effective delivery of any service, since support for a redefined special education has little meaning if the structure is unfit for the task. A school system which rigidly observes the demarcation between ordinary and special education will make one thing of the notion of an expanded special program, while a system working to connect up ordinary and special instruction assumes a rather different set of tasks. To link the futures of handicapped children to the ordinary schools demands attention to, among other things, teaching skills required in heterogeneous classrooms, the quality of interchange among students with diverse backgrounds and abilities, the relationshp between the ordinary program and supplementary support, and the fears concerning the impact of the venture on the quality of education. Ignoring these matters puts the pedagogical and psychological cart before the organizational horse. The Secondary Heads Association made this point rather more poetically: "The Warnock owl has told the grasshopper to change into a mouse but if asked how this can be done suggests that owls only deal with policy." [57]

The consequences of disregarding the organizational aspect of the issue are most apparent in the Warnock Report's treatment of maladjustment as an individual problem, to be remedied by professional attention. The reported incidence of maladjustment has increased far more rapidly than any other handicap. While only 3,544 children in Britain were identified as maladjusted in 1950, the number steadily climbed, to 6,033 in 1961, 14,534 in 1971, and 22,402 in 1979, a rate of increase surpassing that of any other category of handicap. [58] These figures significantly understate the size of the maladjusted population, because they do not include children assigned, without benefit of any formal ascertainment, to special units within the ordinary school. A DES survey, published in 1978, revealed 3,932 places in such units, while a 1980 questionnaire returned by only half the authorities in the United Kingdom reported 5,837 places. [59]

Why such rapid growth in the maladjustment category? For one thing, the expanded presence of psychologists trained to identify maladjustment almost guarantees that more maladjusted individuals will, in fact, be identified, since professionals create their own clientele. For another thing, changes in educational policy of wider scope have doubtless had an impact. Extending the school leaving age to 16 has forced ordinary schools to figure out how to deal with students who would otherwise have left school for work at the onset of adolescence. The merging of secondary modern and grammar schools into comprehensive schools, during the late 1960s and 1970s, also compelled authorities to educate a more diverse student population under one roof. One way of coping with a larger population of badly educated, resentful secondary school youngsters, who can no longer be kept out of the patch of the academically ambitious by assignment to a secondary modern school, is to create a special program for them.

That strategy responds, in part, to real and individual problems. As educationalist Peter Newell notes, "Some students exhibit irrational or disturbing behavior, and behavior which would damage others in schools, because of provocations in their lives which in a sense having nothing to do with the schools." But Newell adds that "while schools retain structures and practices which are entirely undemocratic, and which only allow as alternatives apathetic or active conformity or disruption and rejection, it is the schools we must label as disruptive and not the students."[60] Although the criticism is overstated, establishing new programs for the maladjusted does place the burden of adaptation on the student, not the school. As sociologists Ian Lewis and Graham Vulliamy have written: "Problems endemic to schools become easily translated to become problems of particular children, and practice suggests that categorization is followed by isolation, rather than eradication of the causes of the problem."[61] Such considerations go unnoticed if one sees the phenomenon solely through the eyes of the experts.

The Government's Response: Warnock without Tears?

The government's response to the Warnock Report, a White Paper entitled *Special Needs in Education* (1980), adopts the report's reconceptualization of special educational needs, without providing any of the additional resources for the under-fives, over-sixteens, teacher retraining, and the like, that the Warnock Committee had recommended. The government has tried to reconcile the framework of expertise with the bare government cupboard of the 1980s by transforming the problems besetting special education into a matter of semantics.

The Warnock Report invites such a response. With 224 policy recommendations, mostly unranked, and not a cost calculation in the lot, the document seems to have been drafted for earlier, more affluent times. "A mass of uncosted idealism," one DES official termed it. The report's ambiguous treatment of so many issues permitted enthusiasts to embrace it for wholly inconsistent reasons. The author of Section 10 of the 1976 Education Act, which proposes integration of handicapped children, lauded the effort as a "magnificent and important"[62] endorsement of integration, even as the general secretary of the National Union of Teachers observed that, "We are glad that the Warnock Report does not advocate speedy integration."[63] Such ambiguity, coupled with the report's emphasis on good practice as opposed to policy, left the government free to argue that there was little that the central government ought to do.

The government has proposed abandoning the categories in force since 1945, substituting the distinction between recorded and unrecorded children with special needs set out in the Warnock Report. That reformation of the issue, the White Paper argues, will permit "the gradual redeployment of resources." The source of funds for such new ventures as the proposed preschool program is unspecified. The government speaks of "coordination," "good practice," and "good will," language vainly searching for some meaning.

The White Paper differs from the Warnock Report in one significant respect. In lieu of implementing Section 10, it permits parents of handicapped children to appeal the local authority's evaluation of the child or the proposed placement to an LEA appeals committee, thus giving some recognition to the idea of legal rights. This change in the law is, however, a modest one and should be appreciated in the context of broader educational reforms. Under the 1980 Education Act, parents of ordinary children make their preferences known to the educational authority and, if dissatisfied with the authority's decision, can bring their dispute to a local appeals committee. The 1980 Education Act explicitly denied parents of handicapped children the right to lodge an appeal, and that slight produced the first glimmerings of political mobilization on behalf of handicapped school children. The All Party Disablement Conference, previously little concerned with education issues, questioned this distinction and persuaded the government to change its mind.[64] Yet disputes concerning handicapped children are still treated differently from those involving ordinary youngsters. For the former group, the appeals committee can only recommend a course of action to the authority, while for the latter, the appeals committee may actually reverse the authority. The difference is defended by recourse to what is almost a tautology: "the circumstances may be very special" for handicapped children.

The introduction of the concept of rights, even if in weakened form, potentially alters the way special education is conceptualized. The framework for policy remains overwhelmingly rooted in professional judgment, but a contending notion has been given some legitimacy. In its attentiveness to fiscal constraints and its willingness to speak in terms of rights, the government policy toward handicapped children may signal a possible sea change in thinking about British social policy.[65]

Professionalization Versus Rights

The American Experience

What are the consequences of professionalization? The question is best approached by comparing the quite different British and American experiences. The course of special education policy in the United States followed a pattern roughly akin to Britain's until the late 1960s.[66] Service was provided in separate units within the public school system to those children capable of benefiting from an education.[67] The more seriously handicapped youngsters were treated as ineducable and denied a publicly supported education; some received instruction in private schools, paid for by their parents and not by the government. The terms of service were set by the professionals who offered it. During the 1950s and 1960s, pressure for a new special education teaching credential and the development of more sophisticated assessment techniques revealed a strengthening of the professional status of the field.

As in Britain, special education was a policy backwater, whose critics tended to come from inside the profession. That pattern changed for several reasons. Programs for the mildly handicapped, particularly the so-called educable retardates, drew political fire as inefficacious and, more potently, as dumping grounds for minority youngsters.[68] The IQ tests, which brought the bad news of weak academic performance and which were the primary basis for assignment to these classes, sparked particular criticism for their supposed racial bias. The denial of any education for the most profoundly handicapped was attacked as inhumane, and as resting on erroneous judgments about personal potential.

These points were aggressively pressed by a lobbying group that borrowed many of its tactics from the civil rights movement, and that consequently undertook to convert the issues surrounding the education of the handicapped into questions of civil rights.[69] Isolating the mildly retarded from normal school life and depriving the seriously handicapped of any schooling were both depicted as inequitable, and like so many other inequities were brought to the courts. Arguments over policy were turned into constitutionally rooted claims of unequal educational opportunity.

The several strands of litigation were pursued with varying degrees of success. It was hard to craft a legal argument for providing a better education, since that sounded too much like pure policy. But for those who had been excluded from school, the courts could and did insist that "appropriate" or "suitable" instruction be offered, and, without much analysis, this right was extended to encompass all handicapped children.[70] Nonwhites could not convince the courts to shut down classes for the mildly retarded, for that too seemed a matter of policy. Yet they were able to force school systems to stop relying primarily on IQ tests to determine who was retarded; more generally, the hostility toward labeling children as retarded led school districts to rely less on this classification.[71]

Federal courts had laid down broad maxims concerning equality of opportunity for handicapped youngsters by the mid-1970s. All children were deemed entitled to some form of education (here the courts achieved, through reliance on constitutional principle, what had been earlier recognized by legislation in Britain). The specifics of that education should fit the child's own needs. Where the suitability of the educational program was a matter of dispute, parents were entitled to a full-dress review of the dispute, in a due process hearing presided over by a neutral official. Parents could be represented at the hearing, introduce evidence, and scrutinize the evidence presented by the school authorities. The outcomes of these hearings were appealable to the state commissioner of education and, ultimately, to the courts. Children should be schooled in a setting as close as possible to the ordinary classroom consistent with their special needs. Other things being equal, regular class placement, supplemented by itinerant special help, was legally preferable to full-day special classes, and special classes were preferable to special schools.

The 1975 Education for All Handicapped Children Act[72] embraces and expands upon this concept of equal opportunity. The act entitles all children to a suitable education, incorporates the presumption that all children be treated as normal whenever possible, includes detailed due process protections, and cautions against discriminatory assessment measures. It also requires an individual education plan for every handicapped schoolchild, diagnosing the child's condition and specifying a prescriptive regime to be prepared and approved by the child's parents. Although the legislation has been funded at relatively modest levels—$874 million in 1981, as compared with an authorization of $2.32 billion—this has not prevented Washington from closely monitoring state and local activities, insisting that states live up to their obligations under the act or risk fund cutoffs.

That the claims of the handicapped were not to be treated as subject to the whim of federal largesse, but embodied personal rights, was underscored by the interpretation of companion legislation, the Rehabilitation Act,[73] passed the previous year. This bill, which demanded "nondiscrimination" in education on grounds of handicap, was modeled after earlier civil rights legislation. The obligation to secure nondiscrimination, the Department of Health, Education, and Welfare held, imposed on states essentially the same requirements concerning suitable education for the handicapped as did the Education for All Handicapped Children Act. Even those states that chose not to accept federal money for handicapped students were nonetheless obliged to take the same actions on their behalf as those that did; this was a matter of the civil rights of the handicapped, not mere governmental largesse.

The formal differences between the British and American approaches are obvious. While in Britain special education remains essentially a bureaucratized, professionally run undertaking, the American reforms introduce several new elements into the policy equation. The education of handicapped youngsters remains rooted in professional judgment—in a period characterized by professional expansion into so many spheres of personal and family life, it is hard to imagine a policy toward the handicapped that did not pay considerable deference to the professionals.[74] But the new American approach to special education policy also draws on each of the other policy frames as competing approaches. It sets up a tension between bureaucratic concerns for control and accountability on the one side, and professional interests in autonomy on the other. It places the issue of special education within a larger political framework: the preference for what is termed "mainstreaming," while defensible in terms of educational efficacy, essentially constitutes a political judgment. Special education—"appropriate" special education—has also become a legally recognized right, not an artifact of governmental generosity or professional judgment. The due process hearing system stands as a procedural safeguard for substantive claims to a suitable and individually determined education.

The Impact of Rights

It is the idea of legally enforceable rights that is critical here.[75] Thinking about special education in terms of political and legal rights forces a consequential recharacterization of special education. The distribution of resources, relationships among the affected parties, and levels of disputatiousness are all affected by the introduction of the rights perspective, as is the very conception of handicap.

Resources. Consider first the issue of resource allocation. In a sector where the demand for a service is powerfully determined by supply, there are never enough resources. This has been true both in Britain and

America, where waiting lists for special programs have been the measure of insufficiency. Expenditure for special education in both countries has grown during the past two decades at a rate exceeding that for social services generally. What distinguishes America from Britain is the *attitude* toward resources, and the influence of the rights orientation on that attitude.

What handicapped children receive in Britain depends on what the government determines that it can afford, and that holds true whether one is focusing on a local authority or on DES. DES circulars in the early 1970s made explicit reference to resource constraints as justifying local authority failure to implement concededly beneficial reforms. Section 10 of the 1976 Education Act, which called for integrating handicapped children into ordinary schools, was not implemented partly because the resources were unavailable; DES would neither require authorities to find the funds themselves nor promise the seemingly unattainable. The 1980 White Paper permits local authorities to reject the recommendation of a local appeals committee concerning special education programs if the decision has "substantial resource implications." The failure to fund the new special programs urged by the Warnock Report is premised on a lack of resources, not a rejection of the proposal's merits.

The American structure of rights, by contrast, does not formally treat resource limits as constraining what can be provided. Court decisions rejected school district arguments that certain needs of handicapped children were unaffordable.[76] The Constitution, said the courts, does not carry a price tag, the implication being that these needs were not demands to redistribute resources that might be compared with other demands, but were absolute entitlements. The Education for All Handicapped Children Act has received less federal financial support than was authorized, a tacit concession that the hoped-for funds were not available. But the claim of a child to an appropriate education remains a claim of right that the states must somehow support. The due process hearings held pursuant to the act illustrate the implications of this standard. Most of the hearings have involved claims that a costly nonpublic institution could do a better job than the public school in meeting a particular child's needs, and that the school district was therefore obliged to pay the child's tuition.[77]

Limited resources remain a reality in American special education. Yet obligatory official disavowal of resource constraints forces cost calculations below the surface of policy, and this gives advocates for the handicapped an edge in competition with other groups not similarly regarded as enjoying rights. The rights orientation also helps to explain both the rapid expansion of special education provision in American schools—8 percent of American students as compared with fewer than 2 percent in Britain have been assessed for special needs[78]—and the more rapid rate of growth of special education expenditure in the United States than in Britain over the past decade, when the rights orientation took firm hold.

Relationships. Interchanges between individuals are harder to appraise than expenditure patterns, but here too the differing orientation to rights has apparent implications. Discussion of the needs of the handicapped in Britain is routinely coupled with concern for ordinary children. Nowhere is this made plainer than in the Warnock Report, which balances the social gains to handicapped children stemming from integration with the costs that integration may impose on the rest of the school. The American rights orientation renders such balancing odious; a quota on handicapped students in any ordinary school, proposed by the Warnock Report, sounds something like the discredited "benign quotas" for black students in desegregating schools. Although the dilemmas of association across the boundary of handicap raised by the Warnock Report are familiar in both countries, the British approach weights interests, while the rights orientation places the burden of adjustment on the ordinary school. In the American context, it becomes hard to ask "How will the *other* children fare?," and consequently integration has been promoted far more energetically than in Britain.

Conflict. The orientation to rights also encourages more apparent conflict than a professionally dominated environment, a decidedly mixed blessing. In the United States, conflicts find formal manifestation in due process hearings and appeals,[79] as well as in the continuing press for judicial solutions to policy conflicts.[80] Since 1978, for instance, lower courts have ordered a halt to IQ testing in one state, forced the shutdown of another state's institution for mentally retarded students (intimating that institutionalization itself might be impermissible), and looked closely into New York City's program for emotionally disturbed students.[81] Litigation and administrative appeals have been rare and unsuccessful in Britain, and even were such a challenge to succeed, the outcome would directly affect only the litigants, while in the United States these cases, if ultimately upheld, mold policy for school districts or even entire states, thus making the conflict more consequential. The differing norms of the two policy systems encourage these variations in behavior. The receptivity of American courts to policy issues promotes disputatiousness, even as the diminution of disagreement in Britain— exemplified by repeated references to "good will" in the White Paper and the belief, expressed in the Warnock Report, that "partnership," not conflict, is the desired end—muffles disputes.

This disputatiousness affects the educational system in a variety of ways. The American habit of publicly challenging the enterprise furthers change and reform under the banner of rights. It may lead school authorities to offer students an education that is measurably better than would otherwise have been provided, and, in general, it fosters a dynamic, rather than a static, policy. Yet conflict carries a heavy price. It threatens the element of trust in relationships among the parties to the process, essential if a helping relationship is to be maintained.[82] Conflict also promotes discomfort, and for that reason not even those who instigate disagreements thrive in this climate of disputatiousness. It is, however, clear that parents feel driven to exercise their right to protest by the severest of provocations, and that failing to assert their child's rights will lead to a most malign neglect.[83] The problem is one of striking a balance. Describing parents as partner, as the Warnock Report does, is Pollyanna-ish; but "see you in court" is not the happiest rejoinder.

The degree of conflict is influenced by differences in how the relationship between central and local government is structured in the two countries. In Britain, the central government's primary source of contact with local authorities, HMI, offers professional guidance. Pressure, in the unsubtle sense of threatening to withhold government aid, is unknown. The British aspire to lift the weakest authorities to the level of the best over time. By contrast, local authorities in the United States are legally required to meet a minimum level of performance. This produces a tension between levels of government, akin in some ways to tensions within American schools, that does not find its counterpart in Britain.

The meaning of handicap. The most profound of the ideas of rights may be that of how handicap is understood in the two nations. Through political astuteness and judicial successes, handicap groups in the United

States have forced their way onto the center stage of policy.[84] Their concerns are related to those of other groups who see themselves as victims of discrimination; their policy proposals are presented as part of a larger struggle for equity. The Education for All Handicapped Children Act signals a considerable success in this effort, for it sets a higher authorization level than any other federal education legislation. The integration of handicapped children into the educational mainstream, although not so highly charged as the integration of blacks and whites, is similarly premised on a claim of rights. Both groups, historically invisible, have made themselves profoundly present. In this respect the enactment of rights affords a predicate for the assertion of self.[85]

The handicapped in Britain remain for the most part beneficiaries of what Charles Dickens tellingly termed "telescopic philanthropy," a form of benevolence in which "the further away the object of our compassion lies the more intense will be the feelings of concern and obligation which it evokes."[86] This compassion, while real enough, conflicts with the idea that the handicapped are persons in the full sense, capable of participating in the definition of their own interest. They have remained substantially a dependent class, the wards of caring professionals. What the handicapped receive is still treated as a matter of grace, a contribution made by the larger society to help a small and distinct group. The lack of a counterforce may mean that they have embraced this socially held view as their own.

Choosing Between Policy Frameworks

The British and American approaches, the one professional-centered and the other more rights-centered, embrace different conceptions of good social policy. The rights orientation of American special education policy is consistent with a view of social welfare espoused during the Great Society, which generally stressed individual entitlement to governmentally subsidized benefits.[87] That approach creates an inherently uneasy relationship between the client and the government agency. The client's worth is understood to be predicated on his being something more than a supplicant, and the experience of being a client is supposed somehow to be empowering. The ideal is a social welfare system true both to its own mission and to the expressed wishes of its clients, one that combines fairness and efficiency—avoiding racism, sexism, ageism, and the other isms—with attention to individual clients' needs and preferences. This ambitious aspiration is doomed to failure, for the internal contradictions among the demands are too profound and the counterforces are too powerful.[88] Yet special education policy, as it works in practice, suggests a more feasible goal.

The American approach, though rights-centered, creates a *dynamic tension among the competing frameworks, a tension in which varying conceptions of the good social welfare system are pressed by all who have been invited into the house of policy.*[89] Professionalism, legalism, bureaucratization, and politicization pull and tug against one another. Given such a conception, problems arise when one or another framework becomes too powerful; when, for instance, legalism engulfs in procedural snarls questions which may either be unresolvable or better resolved less formally; when professionals deprive parents of an effective voice in decisions concerning their children; or when bureaucratic rules undermine the exercise of wise professional discretion. Policy remedies take the form of redressing the balance among these frameworks.

The British aspiration has been wholly different: *enabling professionals, through the exercise of benign discretion, to offer the highest level of service on the least stigmatizing terms possible, given available social resources.*[90] This model of social welfare does not recognize conflict; it is silent concerning politics, and actively antagonistic toward law. It contemplates professionals and administrators working on behalf of an ever-expanding clientele toward an agreed-upon common good.

Such an approach is well suited to a period of social prosperity, when a nation can afford to provide more services for more people. It fares less well when economic growth slows, or when the social services are being trimmed. That situation fosters a reexamination of how available resources are distributed, and this may reduce professional discretion. The new British emphasis on parental choice in education illustrates this reexamination at the micro-level. Each family becomes, in effect, a semi-sovereign, able, under certain circumstances, to override professional judgments: since the beneficiaries cannot have more, as in the past, the temptation is to give them a greater say concerning what they do receive. At the macro-level, the government has sought to rationalize the distribution of funds by replacing the growth-oriented rate support grant—which, in effect, permitted local authorities to determine expenditures—with a more uniform national standard. This too constricts the authority of professionals and local program administrators.[91]

Both increased parent choice and the promise of more rationalist central government control identify the ambiguity of power relationships within the British policymaking system, and suggest the circumstances under which the unquestioned dominance of professional values in social welfare policy may come to an end. Neither the imminence nor the importance of these changes should be exaggerated. Parent choice and greater centralization remain merely proposals of uncertain impact, and because special education is so small in scope and structurally so isolated, these proposals may well have little obvious or direct impact, even if implemented. Yet to the extent that change is marked, it will curb the authority of the professional providers, and so move British special education policy somewhat closer to the American model.

Notes

Acknowledgments: This paper was prepared for the Program in Law, Institute for Research on Educational Finance and Governance, Stanford University. The advice and comments of colleagues on both sides of the Atlantic—Michael Adler, Eugene Bardach, David Cohen, Maurice Kogan, Henry Levin, Stuart Maclure, Paul Peterson, and Martin Trow—are gratefully acknowledged.

1. The discussion of frameworks borrows at least in spirit from other and very diverse attempts to examine the implications of choosing among ways of ordering the world, including: Brian Barry, *Sociologists, Economists, and Democracy* (London: Collier Macmillan, 1970); Michael Sherwin, *Logic of Explanation in Psychoanalysis* (New York: Academic Press, 1969); Charles Lindblom, *Politics and Markets* (New York: Basic Books, 1977); Judith Shklar, *Legalism* (Cambridge, Mass.: Harvard University Press, 1964); E. P. Thompson, *Whigs and Hunters: The Origin of the Black Act* (New York: Pantheon Books, 1975); Michel Foucault, *Madness and Civilization* (New York: Vintage Books, 1973); Paul Diesling, *Five Types of Decision and Their Social Conditions* (Urbana: University of Illinois Press, 1962); Murray Edelman, *Political Language: Words That Succeed and Policies That Fail* (New York: Academic Press, 1977); Morris Kline, *Mathematics: The Loss of Certainty* (New York: Oxford University Press, 1980); Michael Polanyi, *Personal Knowledge* (Chicago: University of Chicago Press, 1958); Charles Lindblom and David Cohen, *Usable Knowledge: Social Science and Social Problem Solving* (New Haven, Conn.: Yale University Press, 1979).

2. The particular case of thalidomide victims is analyzed in depth in Jonathan Bradshaw, *The Family Fund: An Initiative in Social Policy* (London: Routledge and Kegan Paul, 1980).

3. See for example, Eugene Bardach, *The Implementation Game* (Cambridge, Mass.: MIT Press, 1977); Erwin Hargrove, *The Missing Link: The Study of Implementation in Social Policy* (Washington, D.C.: Urban Institute, 1975); Michael Lipsky, *Street Level Bureaucracy* (New York: Russell Sage, 1980).

4. For thoughtful treatments of this tension between legalism and bureaucratic norms, see Robert Kagan, *Regulatory Justice* (New York: Russell Sage, 1969) and Philippe Nonet, *Administrative Justice* (New York: Russell Sage, 1967).

5. See generally, John Chubb, *The Politics of Energy: Interest Groups and the Bureaucracy* (Stanford, Ca.: Stanford University Press, 1981).

6. On the spread of legal norms, see Philip Selznick, *Law, Society, and Industrial Justice* (New York: Russell Sage, 1969). On deregulation see Eugene Bardach and Robert Kagan, *Going by the Book: Enforcement of Protective Regulation* (report prepared for Twentieth Century fund, 1980; published as *Going by the Book: The Problem of Reg latory Unreasonableness* [Philadelphia: Temple University Press, 1982]); Charles Schul12e, *Public Use of Private Interest* (Washington, D.C.: Brookings Institution, 1977); James Q. Wilson, ed., *The Politics of Regulation* (New York: Basic Books, 1980).

7. The term is drawn from Daniel Bell, *The Cultural Contradiction of Capitalism* (New York: Basic Books, 1976).

8. The discussion of British special education policy rests heavily on interviews with key figures in the field. These interviews assume special importance because of the paucity of relevant writing. In most instances interviewees were unwilling to be quoted for the record, and for that reason specific interviews are not cited in the notes. Those interviewed include: Naomi Angell, Children's Legal Centre; John Bagley, Principal, Department of Education and Science (DES); John Banks, Assistant Secretary, DES; Professor Tessa Blackstone, Institute of Education, University of London: W. K. Brennan, former Assistant Education Officer for Special Education, Inner London Education Authority (ILEA); Kenneth Burgin, Principal, Economic Analysis, DES; Geoffrey Cockerill, former Undersecretary, DES; George Cooke, Vice-Chairman of Warnock Committee, Secretary General of Society of Education Officers, former Chief Education Officer, Lincolnshire; Dr. D. M. C. Dale, Institute of Education, University of London; John Fish, Staff Inspector for Special Education, Her Majesty's Inspectorate (HMI); Doreen Flint, National Society for Mentally Handicapped Children and Adults; Richard Gray, The Spastics Society; John Hedger, Assistant Secretary, DES, and Secretary to the Warnock Committee; Dr. Seamus Hegarty, National Foundation for Educational Research, Slough; Professor Jeffrey Jowell, Faculty of Law, University College, University of London; Dr. Harry Judge, Department of Education, Oxford University; Professor Maurice Kogan, Department of Government, Brunel University; Peter Litton, Undersecretary, DES; Eric Lord, HMI; Stuart Maclure, Editor, *Times Educational Supplement*; Bert Massey, Royal Association for Disablement and Rehabilitation (RADAR); Peter Mitchell, RADAR; Dr. Peter Mortimore, Head of Educational Research, ILEA; Peter Newell, Advisory Centre for Education; Patricia Pearce, parent governor, Alexander Priory, London; Morag Plank, Campaign for the Mentally Handicapped (CMH); Philipa Russell, Voluntary Council for Handicapped Children; Stanley Segal, Ravenswood Village Community, Berkshire; Tony Smythe, National Association for Mental Health; Barry Taylor, Chief Educational Officer, Somerset; Felicity Taylor, education writer, London; Winifred Tumin, parent member of Warnock Committee; Lord Vaizey, Professor, Brunel University; Mary Warnock, Chairman of Warnock Committee, and Senior Research Fellow at St. Hughes College, Oxford; Professor Klaus Wedell, Institute of Education, University of London; Shirley Williams, former Secretary of State, DES; Allison Wortheimer, Campaign for the Mentally Handicapped; Lady Janet Young, Minister of State, DES.

9. Public Law 94-142, 89 Stat. 773 (1975), codified at 20 U.S. Code 1401-1461.

10. *Special Educational Needs: Report of the Committee of Enquiry into the Education of Handicapped Children and Young People* (London: HMSO, 1978) (hereafter referred to as *Warnock Report*).

11. *Special Needs in Education* (London: HMSO, 1980) (hereafter referred to as *White Paper*).

12. The historical material is derived primarily from *Warnock Report*, pp. 8-36; and D. G. Pritchard, *Education and the Handicapped: 1760-1960* (London: Routledge and Kegan Paul, 1963).

13. *Report of the Joint Departmental Commission on Mental Deficiency (London: HMSO, 1929).*

14. *Patricia Rowan, What Sort of Life?* (Slough, England: National Foundation for Educational Research, 1980).

15. *Report of the Committee of Enquiry into Problems Relating to Partially Sighted Children* (London: HMSO, 1934); *Report of the Committee of Enquiry into Problems Relating to Children with Defective Hearing* (London: HMSO, 1968); *Report of the Joint Departmental Commission on Mental Deficiency* (London: HMSO, 1919).

16. *Education Act* (1944) 7 and 8 George VI, C. 31 (London: HMSO).

17. Hansard vol. 398, col. 703 (21 March 1944).

18. *Special Education Treatment* (London: HMSO, 1946).

19. *The Handicapped Pupils and Special Schools Regulations* (London: HMSO, 1959).

20. *Staffing of Special Schools and Classes*, Circular 4/73 (London: HMSO, 1973).

21. *Warnock Report*, p. 22; *White Paper*, p. 8.

22. *Warnock Report*, p. 121.

23. *Units for Partially Hearing Children* (London: HMSO, 1966); *Diagnostic and Assessment Units* (London: HMSO, 1968).

24. *Report of the Committee on Maladjusted Children* (London: HMSO, 1955).

25. *Behavioural Units* (London: HMSO, 1978), vol. 42.

26. *Staffing of Special Schools and Classes*

27. See generally, Bryan Keith-Lucas and Peter G. Richards, *A History of Local Government in the Twentieth Century* (London: Allen and Unwin, 1978); Robert E. Jennings, *Education and Politics* (London: Batsford, 1977).

28. *The Discovery of Children Requiring Special Education and the Assessment of Their Needs*, Circular 2/75 (London: HMSO, 1975).

29. Education (Handicapped Children) Act 1970, Elizabeth II, C. 52 (London: HMSO); *The Last to Come In* (London: HMSO, 1971).

30. See David Kirp, *Doing Good by Doing Little: Race and Schooling in Britain* (Berkeley: University of California Press, 1979).

31. Howard Glennerster, "The Determinants of Social Expenditure," *Planning for Welfare: Social Policy and the Expenditure Process* ed. Timothy Booth 3, 12 (Oxford: Basil Blackstone and Martin Robertson, 1979).

32. On interest group activity generally, see S. E. Finer, *Anonymous Empire* (London: Pall Mall, 1958); Graham Wooton, *Interest Groups* (Englewood Cliffs, N.J.: Prentice-Hall, 1970).

33. For a general treatment of these questions, see Stanley A. de Smith, ed., *Judicial Review of Administrative Action* (London: Stevens, 1973); Harold Wade, ed., *Administrative Law* (Oxford: Oxford University Press, 1977). The British and American approaches to "making" law are contrasted in H. L. A. Hart, "American Jurisprudence through English Eyes: The Nightmare and the Noble Dream," *Georgia Law Review* XI (September 1977): 969–991.

34. See for example, *Bradbury* v. *Enfield London Borough Council* 1 WLR 131 (1967).

35. *Secretary of State for Education and Science* v. *Tameside Metropolitan Borough Council* 3 WLR 64 (1976).

36. *Annual Report of School Medical Service: Numbers of Cases, 1944–1970* (London: HMSO, 1970).

37. Richard Titmuss, "Welfare Rights, Law, and Discretion," *Political Quarterly* 42 (April/June 1971): 113–132.

38. See generally, John Griffiths, *The Politics of the Judiciary* (London: Fontana,

1977). Compare E. P. Thompson, *Whigs and Hunters: The Origin of the Black Act* (New York: Pantheon, 1975), pp. 258–269.

39. See for example, Tony Prosser, "Politics and Judicial Review: The Atkinson Case and Its Aftermath," *Public Law* Vol. 1979 (Spring 1979), pp. 59–83.

40. On the professionalization of social services, see Eliot Friedson, *Professional Dominance: The Social Structure of Medical Care* (New York: Atherton, 1970); Robert Vinter, "Analysis of Treatment Organizations," ed. Yehaskel Hasenfeld and Richard English *Human Service Organizations* 33 (Ann Arbor: University of Michigan Press, 1974); Jeffrey Berlant, *Professions and Monopoly: A Study of Medicine in the United States and Great Britain* (Berkeley: University of California Press, 1975); Everett Hughes, *Men and Their Work* (Glencoe, Ill.: Free Press, 1958); Magali Larson, *The Rise of Professionalism* (Berkeley: University of California Press, 1977); Harold Wilensky, "The Professionalization of Everyone?" *American Journal of Sociology* 70 (September 1964): 133–158. With respect to child policy and professionals, see Alfred J. Kahn and Sheila B. Kammerman, *Child Care Programs in Nine Counties: A Report* (Washington, D.C.: U.S. Department of Health, Education, and Welfare, 1976).

41. See generally, Maurice Kogan, *Educational Policy Making* (London: Allen and Unwin, (1975); Michael Locke, *Power and Politics in the School System* (London: Routledge and Kegan Paul, 1974).

42. See Jules Henry, *Pathways to Madness* (New York: Random House, 1971); Robert Edgerton, *Cloak of Competence: Stigma in the Lives of the Mentally Retarded* (Berkeley: University of California Press, 1967).

43. See Bradshaw, *The Family Fund.*

44. See for example, *Half Our Futures* (London: HMSO, 1963) (Newsom Report); *Report of the Committee on Higher Education* (London: HMSO, 1961–63) (Robbins Report); *A New Partnership for Our Schools* (London: HMSO, 1977) (Taylor Report).

45. *Children and Their Primary Schools* (London: HMSO, 1967).

46. On the power of the British civil service generally, see Geoffrey Smith and Nelson Polsby, *British Government and Its Discontents* (New York: Basic Books, 1981), pp. 144–168.

47. *Warnock Report.*

48. *Warnock Report*, p. 123.

49. In citing the report of the Schools' Council Project, "The Curriculum for Slow Learners," the Warnock Committee recognizes this weakness in the curriculum, yet it makes nothing of it (*Warnock Report*, p. 219).

50. Education Act (1976), Elizabeth II, C. 81 (London: HMSO, 1976).

51. See generally Jean Floud and A. H. Halsey, *Social Class and Educational Opportunity* (London: Heineman, 1956).

52. David Galloway and Carole Goodwin, *Educating Slow-Learning and Maladjusted Children: Integration or Segregation?* (London: Longman, 1979).

53. D. M. C. "Educating Deaf and Partially Hearing Children Individually in Ordinary Schools," *The Lancet* 884 (October 21, 1978); Martin Milligan, "Accepting Blind Children in Ordinary Schools—Everyone Benefits," *Where* 142 (October 1978): 275.

54. See Bernard Coard, *How the West Indian Child is Made Educationally Subnormal in the British School System* (London: New Beacon, 1971).

55. Quoted in *Times Educational Supplement*, 25 February 1977.

56. *Warnock Report*, p. 109.

57. Quoted in *Times Educational Supplement*, 2 June 1978. See generally Seymour Sarason, *The Culture of the School and the Problem of Change* (Boston: Allyn and Bacon, 1970).

58. Data concerning the number of children ascertained as maladjusted come from De-

partment of Education and Science, "Educational Provision for Handicapped Pupils," *DES Statistics of Education*, for the relevant years; the source of the 1979 figure is *White Paper*.

59. *Behavioral Units* (London: HMSO, 1978), vol. 49; "ACE Survey: Disruptive Units," *Where* 159 (June 1980): 10.

60. Peter Newell, "Sin Bins: The Integration Argument," *Where* 160 (July/August 1980): 8.

61. Ian Lewis and Graham Vulliamy, "Warnock or Warlock? The Sorcery of Definitions: The Limitations of the Report on Special Education," *Educational Review* 32 (February 1980): 3–10.

62. Quoted in *Times Educational Supplement*, 23 June 1978.

63. Quoted in *Times Educational Supplement*, 26 May 1978.

64. Hansard, April 7, 1980. For a discussion of the political history of this legislation, see David Bull, "School Admissions: A New Appeals Procedure," *Journal of Social Welfare* 7 (September 1980): 209.

65. On the possibility of capitalizing on the contraction of the educational system to accomplish good educational ends, see Harry Judge, "After the Comprehensive Revolution: What Sort of Secondary Schools?" *Oxford Review of Education* 5 (June 1979): 137–146.

66. This history is recounted in Seymour Sarason and John Doris, *Educational Handicap, Public Policy, and Social History: A Broadened Perspective on Mental Retardation* (New York: The Free Press, 1979); David Rothman, *The Discovery of the Asylum: Social Order and Disorder in the New Republic* (Boston: Little, Brown & Co., 1971); Jane Mercer and John Richardson, "Mental Retardation as a Social Problem," in Nicholas Hobbs, ed., 2 *Issues in the Classification of Children* 131 (San Francisco: Jossey-Bass, 1975); Willard Gaylin, Ira Glasser, Steven Marcus, and David Rothman, eds., *Doing Good: The Limits of Benevolence* (New York: Pantheon, 1978); Marvin Lazerson, "The Origins of Special Education," (this volume, p. 00).

67. Carl Milofsky, *Special Education: A Sociological Study of California Programs* (New York: Praeger, 1976).

68. The references are collected in David Kirp, "Schools as Sorters: The Constitutional and Policy Implications of Student Classification," *University of Pennsylvania Law Review* 121 (April 1973): 705–797.

69. See Alan Abeson and Jeffrey Zettel, "The End of the Quiet Revolution: The Education for All Handicapped Children Act of 1975," 44 *Exceptional Children* 115 (1977); David Kirp, William Buss, and Peter Kuriloff, "Legal Reform of Special Education: Empirical Studies and Procedural Proposals," *California Law Review* 62 no. 40 (1974): 40–155; David Neal, "The Legalization of Special Education" (Paper prepared for the Institute for Research on Educational Finance and Governance, Stanford University, 1980); Jack Tweedie, "Federal Reform of Special Education: An Exploration into Policymaking Style" (Paper prepared for the Institute for Research on Educational Finance and Governance, Stanford University, 1980).

70. *Pennsylvania Association of Retarded Citizens* v. *Commonwealth of Pennsylvania*, 342 F. Supp. 279, 295 (E.D. Pa. 1972); *Mills* v. *Board of Education of District of Columbia*, 348 F. Supp. 866 (D.D.C. 1972).

71. *Larry P.* v. *Riles*, 343 F. Supp. 1306 (N.D. Cal. 1973) *aff'd*, 502 F. 2d. (63 [9th Cir.] 1974).

72. See n. 9.

73. 29 U.S.C. [?]794 (1976).

74. For an empirical confirmation of this proposition, see Richard A. Weatherly, *Reforming Special Education: Policy Implementation from State Level to Street Level* (Cam-

bridge, Mass.: MIT Press, 1979). See also Christopher Lasch, *Haven in a Heartless World* (New York: Basic Books, 1979).

75. See John Gliedman and William Roth, *The Unexpected Minority: Handicapped Children in America* (New York: Harcourt Brace Jovanovich, 1980); Kirp, "Schools as Sorters."

76. See for example, *Mills* v. *Board of Education.*

77. See Michael Kirst and Kay Bertken, "Due Process Hearings in Special Education: An Exploration of Who Benefits" (Paper prepared for the Institute for Research on Educational Finance and Governance, Stanford University, 1980).

78. Count of children taken by the states, December 1, 1979. This annual count serves as the basis for allocation of funds appropriated under PL 94-192. Department of Education, *The Interim Report, Secretarial Task Force on Equal Educational Opportunity for Handicapped Children* (Washington, D.C.: U.S. Department of Health, Education, and Welfare, 1980).

79. See for example, Kirst and Bertken, "Due Process Hearings"; Peter Kuriloff, David Kirp, and William Buss, "When Handicapped Children Go to Court: Assessing the Impact of the Legal Reform of Special Education in Pennsylvania" (Report prepared for the National Institute of Education, 1979).

80. See generally, David Kirp and Mark Yudof, *Educational Policy and the Law* (Berkeley: McCutchan, 1981).

81. See *Larry P.* v. *Riles; Halderman* v. *Pennhurst State School and Hospital*, 446 F. Supp. 1295 (E.D. Pa. 1977), *aff'd* in part and *rev'd* and *remanded* in part, 612 F. 2d 84 (3rd Cir. 1980), *rev'd* 49 U.S.L.W. 4363 (1981); *Lora* v. *Board of Education*, 456 F. Supp. 1211, 1268 (E.D. N.Y. 1978), *rev'd* 623 F. 2d. 248 (2d. Cir. 1980).

82. On the importance of trust relationships in the management of schools, see David Kirp, "Proceduralism and Bureaucracy: Due Process in the School Setting," *Stanford Law Review* 28 (May 1976): 841–876. Compare Mary Metz, *Classrooms and Corridors: The Crisis of Authority in Desegregated Secondary Schools* (Berkeley: University of California Press, 1978).

83. Milton Budoff and Alan Orenstein, "Special Education Appeals Hearings: Their Form and the Response of the Participants," *Final Report on Due Process in Special Education: Legal and Human Perspectives* (Washington, D.C.: U.S. Department of Health, Education, and Welfare, 1979).

84. See for example, Wolf Wolfensberger, *Citizen Advocacy for the Handicapped, Impaired, and Disadvantaged: An Overview* (Washington, D.C.: U.S. Department of Health, Education, and Welfare, 1972).

85. See Robert B. Edgerton, *Cloak of Competence.* .

86. The Dickens observation, made in *Bleak House*, is quoted and elaborated upon in Robert Pinker, *The Idea of Welfare* (London: Heineman, 1979), p. 3.

87. See for example, Charles Reich, "The New Property," *Yale Law Journal* 73 (April 196?): 733–787; Frances Piven and Richard Cloward, *Regulating the Poor: The Functions of Public Welfare* (New York: Free Press, 1971).

88. See for example, Daniel P. Moynihan, *Maximum Feasible Misunderstanding: Community Action in the War on Poverty* (New York: Free Press, 1969).

89. Compare Michael Walzer, *Radical Principles* (New York: Basic Books, 1980), pp. 23–53.

90. See for example, Richard Titmuss, *Commitment to Welfare* (London: Allen and Unwin, 1968); Robert Pinker, *Social Theory and Social Policy* (London: Heineman, 1971).

91. See Tyrell Burgess and Tony Travers, *Ten Billion Pounds: Whitehall's Takeover of the Town Halls* (London: Grant McIntyre, 1980); Richard McAllister and David Hunter, *Local Government: Death in Our Time* (London: Outer Circle Policy Unit, 1980).

PART III/

Implementation of
Special Education

CHAPTER 5

Organizational Barriers to Full Implementation of PL 94-142

JANE L. DAVID and

DAVID GREENE

Introduction

The recent history of federal policies designed to change school-level behaviors is characterized by stories of failures to change behavior in expected ways. Research on program implementation illustrates the importance of the local context in shaping programs and suggests that externally generated demands which ignore this context will be thwarted. Hence federal policies intended to change schools will succeed only to the extent that they reflect an understanding of the conditions under which the policies are to be implemented.

PL 94-142, the Education for All Handicapped Children Act, is one example of federal legislation in education designed to change local behavior and, as such, serves to illustrate the broader issue of the gap between the assumptions of "top-down" reform and the realities of local school systems. PL 94-142 exemplifies the problems that can arise when a federal policy meets the organizational reality of school systems head on. This chapter illustrates some of the ways in which full implementation of PL 94-142 is constrained by certain organizational characteristics of school systems that were not taken into account in formulating the legislation.

The conceptualization of the law and its implementation context, as well as the specific findings reported here, are drawn from a study designed to assess progress in implementing PL 94-142 at the local level over a four-year period beginning in 1978, the first year in which a noticeable infusion of federal funds reached local school systems.[1] The findings reported in this chapter are drawn from the first two years of data collection;[2] some of the material from the original study has been reorganized and supplemented.

The analysis of the law and the "bottom-up" perspective that guided the study, are described first, followed by an overview of the design of the research. The highlights of the findings are then presented together with an analysis of the obstacles to implementation, the analysis emphasizing orgnizational barriers.

The Provisions of PL 94-142

In November of 1975, Congress passed the Education for All Handicapped Children Act (PL 94-142). Modeled on progressive state legislation and based on modern theories of instruction and learning, the act represents a statement of national goals, and is sometimes referred to as a civil rights act because it incorporates judicial decisions ensuring due process and equal access to education for handicapped children. It also affirms a respect for individual differences. Inherent in this act is the belief that handicapped children, although exceptional along certain dimensions, share with other citizens the right to an appropriate, publicly funded education. The law emphasizes the role of the parent, guardian, or parent surrogate in serving as advocate for the child and as the agent to whom the educational system must be accountable.

The philosophy reflected in the major provisions of PL 94-142 includes the following concepts:

- Schools are responsible for reaching out and ensuring that no child is excluded from an appropriate education at public expense.
- Handicapped children should be identified, evaluated, and prescribed appropriate educational services without being mislabeled, stigmatized, or discriminated against.
- Each child must have an individualized education program (IEP) that includes present level of performance, annual goals, specific objectives, special education and related services to be provided, and time schedules, and the IEP should be reviewed and reconsidered at least annually.
- Handicapped children should be educated in the least restrictive environment (LRE) possible.

- The process by which the child's program is decided should involve the child's parents and the child (where appropriate), as well as the child's teacher and a representative of the responsible agency of the public school system and other qualified professionals.
- Parents must be notified about a child's identification, evaluation, and placement; parents should participate in decisions and must give informed consent to program changes; due process rights to a fair hearing are to be provided when parents and the school cannot agree on a child's evaluation or program.
- Local education agencies (LEAs) should participate in state personnel development systems to ensure that staff involved in the education of handicapped children are qualified for their jobs.

PL 94-142 can be viewed from many perspectives: civil rights, educational, local, state, or federal. This chapter specifically views the act from the perspective of educators at the local level. This viewpoint is reflected in the following characterization of the law's requirements and the context in which it is being implemented.

Goals for Implementation

PL 94-142 includes two overriding goals that pertain to LEAs: the provision of a free appropriate public education (FAPE) to all handicapped children and the protection of the rights of handicapped children and their parents. FAPE is a broad, overarching concept that subsumes the "procedural safeguards" concerned with placement in the least restrictive environment and with nondiscriminatory evaluation. In this view, due process procedures (e.g., for parental notification and informed consent, and for hearings to resolve disputes between parents and the schools) serve the specific function of protecting the right of all handicapped children to FAPE.[3]

The study presumed that few, if any, LEAs were operating so as to achieve the goal of providing FAPE to all handicapped children. Implementing the law, therefore, would require LEAs to bring about changes in prevailing practices. By comparing the traditional practices of most local special education systems with the ideal system implicitly described in the law, two fundamental action implications, or implementation goals, that LEAs should strive for were derived: (1) increasing the scope and comprehensiveness of special education services, and (2) changing current procedures so they result in individually appropriate services for children.

117

The first of these implementation goals requires LEAs to reach out and serve all children in need of special education services (i.e., to eliminate inappropriate exclusion from the system). It also encompasses an increase in the range and flexibility of services available to eligible children. This has merit in its own right and is based on the presumption that a wide, flexible range of services facilitates movement toward less restrictive placements. In short, LEAs must identify and serve all eligible children.

The second implementation goal requires changing traditional practices in specific and fundamental ways; this amounts to a paradigm shift in how schools decide what services each child receives. Traditionally, special education practices have rested on classification: a child is classified as having one or more handicapping conditions that then determine what services are to be delivered, by whom, and where. The intent of PL 94-142 is to alter this system fundamentally by shifting the focus of special education from categories of disabilities to individual children's needs. The law now requires that a child's unique needs be identified and that services appropriate to these needs be provided. Instead of fitting children to available programs, schools are now required to design an individually appropriate program for each child. The procedures specified to accomplish this goal necessitate basic, structural changes in how educational programming decisions are made. These basic, structural changes must be one of the fundamental implementation goals for LEAs.

The FAPE Schema

Figure 5-1 is a schematic representation of what the law says about how an ideal special education system should operate under full implementation of PL 94-142.[4] The FAPE schema explicitly represents the relationships among the mechanisms, values, and goals in PL 94-142 that characterize an ideal local special education system. By this is meant a school system that is set up to achieve the goal of providing FAPE to all handicapped children in its jurisdiction, and in which due process procedures are functioning effectively. Thus, the FAPE schema serve as a working definition of the intent of the law.

The ultimate goal of the system depicted in Figure 5-1 is to provide a free appropriate public education for all handicapped children. This requires that two complementary questions be decided about each handicapped child: (1) what educational goals and services are individually

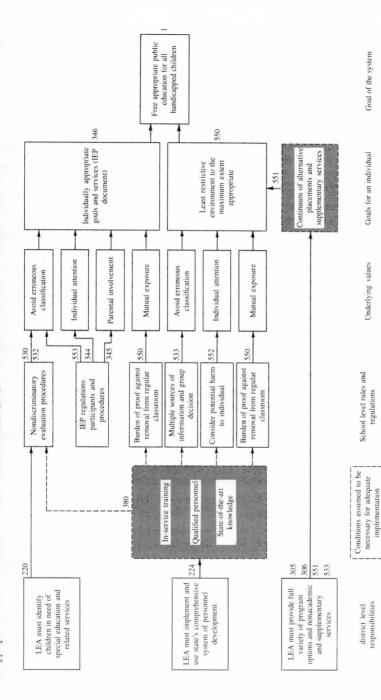

Note: Numbers near boxes refer to Regulations 121a.1 through 121a.754

appropriate for the particular child?, and (2) what is the least restrictive environment in which the child can be provided with the services appropriate to his/her needs?

Central to these decisions, and hence shown directly to their left in this schema, is a set of four basic values that can be inferred from a close reading of the legislative history of PL 94-142. Most crucial is the need for individual attention. Complementing this is the imperative of avoiding erroneous classification. Together, these two values constitute a fundamental shift in emphasis away from a system in which the assignment of a child to a category was the most significant event in the child's special education career. The third basic value is that of parental involvement. The final value derives from an awareness that both handicapped and nonhandicapped children benefit from the mutual exposure that "mainstreaming" provides.

Decisions about what is "appropriate" should result from treating the child individually, involving the child's parents, avoiding erroneous classification, and considering the benefits of mutual exposure. Decisions about what environment is least restrictive should result from a balancing act in which the "mainstreaming" goal of the law is reconciled with the child's best interest.

The law also includes specific requirements that should encourage the consideration of these basic values in the decision-making process. These requirements appear in the federal rules and regulations that are shown to the left of the boxes labeled "Underlying Values." In determining which services are most appropriate for the child, the key regulations concern IEP procedures, testing and evaluation procedures, and the need to justify removing a child from the regular classroom. To determine the least restrictive setting appropriate for the child, the salient regulations are those concerning multiple sources of information and multiple participants in decision making, consideration of potential harm to the child and, again, the justification for removing a child from the regular class setting.

These requirements, and the values they promote, are considerations primarily dealt with by people at the school level (teachers, evaluators, principals) who work directly with the handicapped child. The role of the LEA administration in the law's implementation hierarchy is to provide the conditions necessary for school level personnel to carry out their functions as intended. These conditions are presented in the shaded boxes.

To choose a placement that is the least restrictive environment appropriate for the child, decision makers must have some range of placements available from which to select. Similarly, to enhance the appropriateness of identification, evaluation, placement, and services, and to permit the decision making and service delivery mechanisms to operate as intended, the LEA must provide qualified personnel, in-service training, and the dissemination of "state-of-the-art" knowledge. Thus, the LEA is required to identify all children in need of special education and related services so that their individual needs can be determined. The LEA is also required to implement and use the state's comprehensive system of personnel development. Finally, the LEA must provide a full variety of program options and nonacademic and supplemental services in order to ensure that there is a continuum of alternative placements and supplementary services.

The main advantage of the FAPE schema is that it shows the relationships among the literal and implied requirements of the law and its regulations. It is not intended to describe what actually happens in a school or district; instead, it describes the considerations that ought to influence the way school systems refer, evaluate, place, and provide services for handicapped children. If current practices in LEAs do not reflect these considerations, then the law intends that such practices change.

Context for Implementation: The Bottom-Up Perspective

The preceding analysis of the law's requirements and their interrelationships presents an idealized version of its intent. The law, however, is not being implemented in a vacuum but rather in ongoing systems of regular and special education—systems with particular organizational characteristics, traditions, and roles.

On the basis of the experience with this study, the Rand study of educational change by Berman and McLaughlin (1978), and the hindsight afforded by Weatherly's (1979) detailed study of the implementation of Chapter 766 (the special education law) in Massachusetts, it is clear that local contextual factors play a major role in shaping the specific nature of the inevitable tradeoffs and coping strategies of both individuals and organizations.[5] Along with the Weatherly and Lipsky (1977) "street level bureaucrat" model,[6] we take the perspective that the individuals most closely in contact with the client are making policy by their day-to-day interaction with the client. From this point of view, the higher federal and state administrative levels function as constraints on the range of options available to these local "policymakers." What this means is that individuals in public service bureaucracies are always being "squeezed" between constraints from above and demands from below.

This study of local implementation focuses on two levels of local special education systems: the administrative (district) level and the service delivery (school) level. These two levels, with their respective contexts, are depicted in Figure 5.2. The top half of the figure represents the administrative level. Assuming the administrative unit is a district office, the State Education Agency (SEA) at the top sends down regulations and money, monitors the district office, and provides technical assistance. Immediately below are the schools, needing and demanding as much help from the district office as they can get. As an organization, the district office has certain attributes ("within-office factors") that may facilitate or inhibit its capacity to get things done.

The office is conceived of as figuratively "bursting its seams" because of pressures from top and bottom, with the specific, concrete, day-to-day details of the local context determining where the figurative "bulges" occur. Thus, for example, a district with little or no organized parent pressure will find it relatively easy to place a low priority on the parental involvement requirements of the law. On the other hand, a district with organized and vocal parent pressure cannot long avoid responding to the parent involvement requirements, despite the heavy commitment in time and personnel that this entails.

The bottom half of Figure 5-2 depicts the service delivery (school) level. At the top is the district office, representing both the helpful and restrictive constraints that act on the local school. Below are the children to be served. The quality of school personnel and leadership (and other "within-school factors") varies as it does at the district level. Given the view that schools operate at or near their capacity, when they are caught up in the demands-resources squeeze, their priorities depend a great deal on the specific, concrete, day-to-day details of the immediate context.

In summary, this model of the implementation context adopts a "bottom-up" perspective on implementation. This approach tries to share the point of view of the individuals who deal most directly with handicapped children and their parents. These "street level bureau-

Figure 5-2. Model of Implementation Context

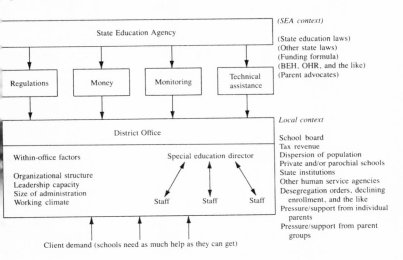

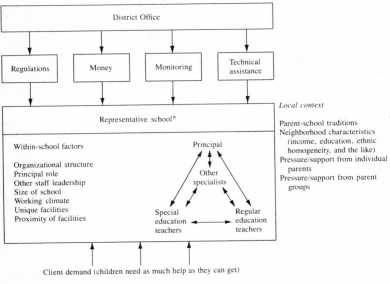

*Districts vary in heterogeneity among schools.

crats," be they teachers or school level administrators, are the individuals whose responses to the requirements of PL 94-142 determine whether or not the intent of the law is met. Their responses, in turn, reflect the circumstances of their daily lives, of which the federal law is only one factor. Thus, to understand local implementation, how the requirements of the law do or do not mesh with preexisting local practice must be understood.

The Study Design

The findings that are described below are from the first year of a longitudinal study based on a multiple case study design. The design was chosen to balance the need for conducting personal interviews to understand complex organizations with the need for generalizing beyond the sample so as to be useful for federal policymakers. The sample consisted of 22 local education agencies (LEAs) chosen to reflect wide variation in the factors expected to strongly influence the implementation of PL 94-142. The LEAs were selected in two stages. First, nine states were chosen to provide variation on three factors: the similarity between current state special education law and PL 94-142, state funding formulas for special education, and the organization of the state system of special education. Within each state, two or three LEAs were selected to vary on resource availability (amount of funding, staff, etc.) and resource accessibility (size and population dispersion). The variation and importance of these factors were verified during the first year's site visits.

In 1978/79, a team composed of two researchers visited each site for two to four days, once in the fall and again in the spring. The site visits consisted primarily of interviews with LEA and school staff, parents, and representatives of community groups and agencies. The interviews were structured by a common set of topics in the form of an interview guide. Specific questions were tailored to individual respondents and their situation.

The topics in the interview guide provided the framework for writing a case study for each district as the first stage of analysis. The common format for collecting and presenting the data was designed to facilitate the second stage of analysis, across sites. Cross-site analyses were designed to generate inferences about LEAs in general—to test the extent to which statements of findings could be supported across all the sites or could be associated with differences among the sites.

These analyses began with statements of findings, generated by the site visitors and from reading the case studies; the statements were then organized and refined by topic. These statements were then reviewed by each researcher for the sites he/she had visited. The result was a set of statements that had been "fine-tuned" to describe carefully findings that applied either to some or to all of the LEAs. In each case, a finding was stated as a generalization but its domain of applicability was carefully limited to what the data actually supported.

The following section summarizes many of the general findings and conclusions from the first year of data collection (i.e., the 1978/79 school year). At the level they are described here, none of these findings was altered by the findings based on the second year of data collection (1979/80). After presenting these highlights, the characteristics of local educational agencies shared by all districts and their effects on the process of implementing PL 94-142 are discussed.

Selected Findings

In terms of meeting the federal mandate to seek out and provide for all children within their jurisdiction who are handicapped and in need of special education, staff in all the LEAs in this study are heavily influenced by what kinds of programs the LEA provides directly, what the LEA obtains routinely from others, and how many "slots" remain open in these programs to serve additional children. Thus, whether a handicapped child will even be identified as a potential beneficiary is determined to a large extent by the availability of appropriate programs in his/her school or district and the discretion exercised by staff in making eligibility decisions during the referral-to-placement process. Moreover, all the districts in the study face some program limitations relative to the need or demand for services in their sites, and all have backlogs of children waiting for evaluation, for placement, or for both. For this reason, efforts to seek out unserved handicapped children are rarely launched except when a new program option is made available and "caseloads" or classes need to be filled as a result.

Schools are by and large meeting the letter of the IEP provisions. Although parts of the document are often drafted prior to the IEP meeting, the meetings are usually held with the required participants and the written document usually includes the required components. At the present time, however, for the vast majority of students found eligible for special education, the decisions about what services and placements they will receive are essentially determined by what is known to be available. If a service is not already available, there is no assurance that additional funds will be forthcoming to pay for the new service. Since school districts become legally liable for providing a service that is recommended on the IEP, the conservative approach is usually taken—recommend on the IEP only those services that can be delivered with certainty, that is, what is already available. The most common area in which this problem occurs is that of related services, e.g., physical therapy, occupational therapy, transportation (except that directly to and from regular instruction). Moreover, since services are tightly linked to the settings in which they are delivered (except for learning disability programs), the placement decision is made automatically once services have been determined, or vice versa. Currently, because a range of placement options for a given service rarely exists, the placement decision seldom entails a separate consideration of the setting's restrictiveness.

Schools are also meeting their legal obligations to involve parents in decisions concerning their children. The local school systems that were visited have forms and procedures in place for informing parents of their legal rights, notifying parents about actions to be taken regarding their children, and obtaining their signed consent to these actions. LEAs have also established procedures for inviting parents to participate in various phases of the IEP development process and many parents take advantage of these opportunities. Although some sites had various parent consent procedures and individual education planning practices before PL 94-142, the universal conformance to procedural requirements by LEAs in the sample and the increased contact reported by school staff and parents of handicapped children attests to the impact of the federal law.

The fact that procedures are in place does *not* mean, however, that parental consent is necessarily "informed," nor that parents are making substantive contributions to school decision making. Although the law is unclear as to what is the appropriate role of parents in making decisions jointly with school staff, it is clear that presenting parents with an already complete IEP document or involving them on a pro forma basis—as frequently happens—is not what the law intended.

In-service training of one form or another is occurring in all the districts. However, the training is primarily concerned with the procedural requirements of the law, not with substantive (i.e., "how to") questions. Service delivery personnel who take advantage of the usual in-service training opportunities find them generally informative but not relevant to the practical problems and issues they face.

Finally, due process mechanisms, from notification and consent through complaint and fair hearings procedures, are in place. Issues of appropriateness are resolved through hearings procedures, rather than through informal negotiations, primarily when the LEA cannot afford to acquiesce to parental requests. Thus, most hearings have been concerned with parental requests for the LEA to pay for private school placements or for related services that are provided by some other agency. Argument in hearings revolve around the meaning of "appropriateness," but the issue of whether the LEA is required to pay for services, rather than the issue of what is most appropriate for the child, underlies most hearings.

In general, the findings as a whole can be characterized as procedural compliance: the letter of the law is being met, by and large. Yet this falls far short of meeting the spirit or intent of the law. In the following section, the major obstacles to achieving full implementation of PL 94-142 that were found by the study are reviewed.

Obstacles to Implementation

Standing in the way of full implementation are three broad classes of obstacles: limited resources, the state of the art, and organizational characteristics of LEAs. Less time will be spent in discussing on the obstacles posed by limited resources and the state of the art because it is more useful to draw implications for policy that are not dependent upon the unrealistic assumption that large amounts of new money and new knowledge are imminent.

Resources

The most obvious obstacle—both to serving all handicapped children and to enabling services to be determined on the basis of individual needs—is the inadequacy of resources for special education and related services. This leads directly to a shortage of program openings and, thus, to a lack of alternative service and placement options that can be considered in determining what is appropriate for individual children. It also produces a backlog of handicapped children waiting to be served.

To meet the full intent of the law, LEAs must also see that their special education staff are qualified, that regular teachers, principals, and other staff are prepared to play the roles implied in the law, and that their programs are coordinated with private schools and with other agencies to ensure that full services are delivered at no cost to parents. These changes cost money as well as time and effort. In spite of the fact that expenditures for special education have increased relative to other education outlays, limitations on funds currently available force LEA administrators to make choices between expanding direct services to children and changing the delivery system (e.g., in-service training, working with parents, and coordinating services). They must also choose among groups of children eligible to receive services.

State of the Art

A different set of problems results from the fact that the law requires educators to make judgments about appropriateness and need that would defy the proverbial wisdom of Solomon. Currently, there are no generally accepted guidelines regarding which related services for which needs are "necessary for a child to benefit from the educational program." Still unaddressed are questions about how to determine the *amount* of a particular related service necessary to meet a child's educational needs. Although the law lists counseling as a (potential) related service, every school district "holds the line" at a different point. For example, in one site a learning disabled child with emotional problems will get individual psychotherapy from a private practitioner at the expense of the public schools; in many other sites, it would be *suggested*, but not *recommended*, that the parents consider taking the child to the community mental health agency for some counseling (a recommendation would require that staff write the service on the IEP, thus making it the LEA's responsibility to pay for the service). The latter districts have, in effect, defined counseling as not necessary for the child to benefit from his/her educational services.

There are two other related areas in which state-of-the-art problems abound. One is identifying learning disabled children. Particularly difficult is the judgment as to whether a given child's "deficits" are attributable to "processing" disorders *rather* than "environmental, cultural, or economic disadvantage." Yet for many practitioners the final eligibility decision often rests on this very judgment. The other problem area is the provision of an appropriate program for serving seriously emotionally disturbed children in a public school setting. For most LEAs, this is an area of almost total ignorance.

Finally, LEAs face a problem in the state of the art of staff development, and particularly in-service training. Neither general orientation to the 1975 act, information on new procedural requirements disseminated through administrative channels, nor in-service training courses offered by institutions of higher education are perceived by professionals as meeting their needs. In making sure that staff are qualified to fill their roles as intended in the act, LEAs face difficulties in relying on staff development programs in their current form.

Organizational Characteristics of LEAs

Public service bureaucracies. Local education agencies share several features with other public service bureaucracies in which change has been studied. Police departments, welfare agencies, and school systems, among others, share certain characteristics that affect their capacity to change. One such feature is their public service orientation. Unlike organizations motivated primarily to maximize profits, public service bureaucracies are oriented toward satisfying their clients' needs for services; and client demand always expands to absorb all the services the system can deliver. A corollary is that problems literally never go away. Thus, a teacher can never meet all the individual needs of all her or his students, and at the same time meet the expectations of colleagues and superiors. Similarly, a district office can never meet all the legitimate needs of all the schools it serves and the agencies to which it is responsible. It follows that public service bureaucracies are chronically short of resources and are forced to compete for a limited share of them. Their most basic need, adequate and reliable financial support, is dependent on politics and usually beyond their control.

The combination of unlimited demand and limited resources means that individuals in public service bureaucracies inevitably develop coping strategies. These strategies implicitly place different priorities on different demands and result in tradeoffs; for example, deciding which clients to serve first and establishing routine procedures for meeting their demand so this can be done without thinking is a common strategy. Given that people already had too much to do prior to the passage of PL 94-142, it is not surprising to see a pattern of procedural requirements being met superficially with little basic change in attitudes and intent. With priorities already in place, there is little incentive for substantial change in an already overloaded system. This is particularly true when such changes are imposed from the outside and hence carry with them a threat of removing personal discretion—the very discretion that allows personnel to function effectively. Thus, the most likely response to any new demand is to develop a set of routinized behaviors that minimize the demand's interference with traditional practices.

Finally, although mission-oriented, public service bureaucracies, as complex organizations, are also structured to maintain stability. Consisting of individuals whose role relationships are well defined, they do not change readily or by fiat. Hence, attempts to introduce fundamental change into a system like the public schools are bound to encounter some resistance and predictable problems.

Traditional boundaries. Traditional boundaries between parents and schools and between schools and other agencies serving handicapped children pose significant obstacles to implementing the intent of PL 94-142. Meeting the intent of PL 94-142 to have parents actively participate with school staff in making decisions about their children will require changes in traditional parent-school roles. Although parent notification and consent procedures are in place and parents have much more contact with appropriate school staff, parents do not know what is expected of them, or they are intimidated by the number of professional staff involved in the process. School staff are limited in the amount of time they can devote to counseling parents and are faced with a conflict if parents ask for services the school district does not provide. Because most parents seem to be satisfied with the extent of their participation and trust school staff to make decisions for their children, the incentive is lacking for school staff to make efforts to change their roles.

The traditional roles and boundaries between education agencies and other agencies providing services to handicapped individuals also affect the LEAs' ability to implement PL 94-142 as intended. Under PL 94-142, LEAs, as responsible local agencies of the state, are faced with renegotiating their boundaries with other agencies, because the education agency alone must ensure that all related services necessary for children to benefit from their education are delivered, that education and related services are provided appropriately whatever agency delivers them, and that such services are provided at no cost to parents. However, other agencies do not necessarily put a priority on providing services to children referred to them by the school system, nor do their regulations necessarily permit them to provide services free. In fact, some agencies have withdrawn services previously provided to handicapped children, assuming that the school would increase its services accordingly. Nonpublic schools and other institutions are not used to following specifications from the public education agency regarding what constiutes an appropriate individual education program. The fact that LEAs do not have the clout to require other agencies to honor education agency priorities, submit to LEA supervision, or provide free services to education agency clients, usually reflects a similar circumstance at the SEA level. LEAs in this situation cannot look to their SEAs for support or clarification of their legal and financial responsibilities.

Special education systems. Although the structure of special education systems does differ from place to place, particularly as a function of the size of the administrative unit, three characteristics are remarkably uniform: specialization of functions, division along the lines of different disabilities, and separation between the special and regular education systems.

Every special education system performs the same basic functions in the same basic sequence: students are identified and referred, evaluated, placed, and provided with services. In all but the smallest districts, different personnel are involved at different stages in this series of functions. Thus, to implement change (e.g., to break down the historic tendency to provide services solely on the basis of a child's classification), the effort must be coordinated so that each person in the process is working toward that goal. In a small district, this effort may amount to little more than the psychologist who is "in charge" of special education informally communicating a new concept to the appropriate people. In larger LEAs, however, assessment functions and service delivery functions are often performed by personnel reporting to entirely separate organizational entities, neither of which has a direct line relationship to other school level personnel. Specialization of function is at its greatest here; before a new concept can have significant impact at the school level, coordination must begin at the highest level of the administrative ladder and be passed down step by step.

The traditional division along the lines of different disabilities is an even more fundamental obstacle for PL 94-142 implementation. For historical reasons, the typical special education system of today is literally designed to channel handicapped children into one of a fixed number of programs; the larger the system, the larger the organizational structure of each separate program. In its most extreme form, each organizational unit charged with the delivery of services for a particular disability may even have its own referral form and its own IEP format. Within such a system, the best efforts of an EMR (educable mentally retarded) coordinator to teach regular teachers to use a referral form may actually work at cross-purposes to the efforts of an LD (learning disabilities) coordinator doing the same job. Clearly, it is difficult to implement goals that emphasize the individual, in a system so firmly rooted in classification by type of disability.

Finally, there is an organizational boundary between regular and special education that also has deep historical roots. Although districts vary among themselves, special education has always been "different," either subordinate to the regular education system, or autonomous but with a much more limited budget or line authority. This separation typically exacerbates the stigma often associated with handicapped children and limits the ability of special education administrators to effect changes in policy. Moreover, this organizational distance hampers communication between regular and special education teachers, resulting in a lack of understanding of each others' situations as well as a lack of coordination of efforts. Hence, responsibility for a handicapped child is likely to be fragmented. This poses particularly difficult challenges for implementing the IEP and LRE requirements of the law—requirements that often demand cooperation and coordination across the boundary between regular and special education.

Implications for Policy

The preceding emphasis on barriers to implementation, from money to organizational boundaries, communicates at best a pessimistic outlook for the major systemic changes (paradigm shift) intended by PL 94-142. Nevertheless, in spite of such extensive obstacles to full implementation, we have seen some LEAs with schools that reflect the progressive spirit of the law. Some of this progressiveness would not be possible without unusual affluence. But some progressive practices do not depend on a surfeit of resources. What the latter have in common are strategies designed to overcome organizational barriers.

One such strategy reflects an attempt to span the boundary between regular and special education. This strategy rests on the designation of a role for the express purposes of facilitating communication and coordinating activities between special education and regular education teachers. This role is referred to as "boundary crosser," and has been reported in a variety of guises.[7] A boundary crosser may, for example, provide direct assistance to a regular teacher with mainstreamed students; manage the IEP process, soliciting input from regular and special education teachers; or develop mechanisms for coordinating special and regular educational services for children who receive services in more than one setting.

A second, related, strategy is the provision of one-to-one training, particularly for regular teachers. It is related to the boundary crosser strategy inasmuch as the role of a boundary crosser often includes the provision of one-to-one training. The essence of the strategy is having someone available to respond to the very specific, day-to-day problems faced by teachers. This is particularly salient for regular teachers facing pressure to increase the accuracy of their referrals and to provide services to mainstreamed students. This type of training not only meets the immediate practical problems of "What do I do now?" but also reduces the fears and anxieties associated with new and challenging demands (role changes).

These strategies are more successful than most practices in meeting the intent of the law because they tackle organizational barriers *and* they embody two important principles of change: local adaptation and use of persons rather than materials. Boundary crossers and one-to-one trainers both respond to the needs of particular teachers in particular settings and involve personal relationships developed on an individual basis.

What do the characteristics of these strategies—together with the implementation study's general finding of procedural compliance—suggest for policy? First, they suggest that local solutions should be encouraged; this translates into a need to emphasize assistance rather than monitoring. If procedural compliance can be substantially achieved without realizing the intent of the law, heavy-handed monitoring will not significantly improve practices regarding handicapped students. Second, the design of technical assistance strategies must acknowledge the constraints within which local districts operate. These strategies must take into account the limits on resources and the types of organizational barriers that hinder implementation.

Finally, assistance should emphasize those domains that allow the use of people rather than materials, and that focus on facilitating change in existing roles. This suggests disseminating strategies like boundary crossers and one-to-one training in areas such as in-service, support to regular teachers in referral, IEP participation, and mainstreamed students.

These implications for policy extend beyond the specific provisions of PL 94-142. They represent one approach to easing the tension between top-down, externally imposed change efforts and bottom-up, locally designed efforts. As federal policymakers seek ways of reducing regulations associated with categorical programs, approaches designed to take local needs and conditions into account will have the greatest likelihood of changing local practices.

Notes

1. The descriptions of findings and the interpretations presented in this paper are ours and should not be taken as representing the views of SRI International nor the Office of Special Education, U.S. Department of Education.

2. Data collection consisted of visits twice a year to approximately 20 districts chosen to reflect variation on characteristics deemed relevant to implementation such as district size, previous state requirements, and wealth of district. For a detailed description of the design of the study the reader should refer to M. Stearns, D. Greene, and J. L. David, "Local Implementation of PL 94-142: First Year Report of a Longitudinal Study," (Menlo Park, Ca.: SRI International, April 1980).

3. Requirements for placement in the least restrictive environment and for non-discriminatory evaluation are classified differently in the regulations than in the law itself. In the regulations, the procedures concerned with placement in the least restrictive environment and with nondiscriminatory evaluation are classified, along with due process procedures, under the rubric "Procedural Safeguards" (subpart E). In the law itself, however, the section titled "Procedural Safeguards" (Section 615) covers due process procedures exclusively. In light of this classification difference between the law and the regulations, we reasoned that the key distinction is between that which is being protected (i.e., the FAPE rights that are being guaranteed by the law) and that which is doing the protecting (i.e., the due process procedures designed to back up the guarantee). Thus, although evaluation procedures and placement procedures logically may be construed as belonging in either category, we have included them as integral components of the FAPE goal.

4. The schema omits the due process procedures, not because they are any less important than the FAPE provisions, but simply because, conceptually and graphically, it is unwieldy to depict both on the same diagram. Parents who have a complaint may invoke due process procedures with respect to virtually any matter shown in the FAPE schema. Thus the protection afforded by the due process requirements is intended to permeate the entire system rather than be localized anywhere that might be usefully depicted in the schema.

5. P. Berman and M. W. McLaughlin, "Implementing and Sustaining Innovations," *Federal Programs Supporting Educational Change*, vol. 7, R-1589/8-HEW (Santa Monica, Ca.: Rand Corporation, 1978); Richard A. Weatherly, *Reforming Special Educa-*

tion: Policy Implementation for State Level to Street Level (Cambridge, Mass.: MIT Press, 1979).

6. Richard A. Weatherly and Michael Lipsky, "Street Level Bureaucrats and Institutional Innovation: Implementing Special Education Reform," *Harvard Educational Review* 47, no. 171 (1977): 171–197.

7. See David Greene, "Local Implementation of PL 94-142: The Crucial Role of 'Boundary Crossers'" (Menlo Park, Ca.: SRI International, 1980).

CHAPTER 6/

Due Process Hearings in
Special Education:
Some Early Findings from California

MICHAEL W. KIRST and

KAY A. BERTKEN

From the outset of policy debates over the education of handicapped students, concerns about fairness and equity have been central.[1] Landmark court cases found that special education programs discriminated against not only handicapped pupils generally, but also minority students, who were disproportionately assigned to special education classes on the basis of biased testing or procedures.[2] PL 94-142 sought to remedy these inequities by distinguishing the handicapped population with the right to "a free and appropriate education . . . designed to meet their unique needs." Procedural due process, including the right to an impartial hearing in cases of dispute, was afforded to protect this entitlement. It is ironic that now the hearings themselves might be a source of inequity in the provision of educational services.

Two equity questions motivated this research of due process hearings. First, what is distributed in these hearings? Scattered reports of the special education hearings that have been held around the country suggest that extravagant and expensive service demands are being made by parents and granted through this hearing mechanism.[3] These reports have provoked both worry and cynicism on the part of educators in the field. While some handicapped children may still lack a basic program, other individuals can demand and get expensive private school tuition payments or individual counseling by a private therapist. In a context of limited resources, case-by-case allocations can yield distortions in the distribution of public funds.[4]

The second question is related to the first. Who benefits from these hearings? Are relatively affluent and resourceful parents further advantaged through this hearing mechanism? If hearings are a source of educational resources, then equal access to that source is essential to a fair distribution. Studies of administrative hearings in other settings and some early reports of special education hearings suggest that hearing processes favor relatively advantaged people. This bias results in part from the fact that poor and less informed sectors of the population are less likely to know about, or choose to engage in, legalistic modes of action. In addition, the poor, less powerful, and less educated are unlikely to achieve favorable outcomes in adversary proceedings wherein decisions may depend upon the skillful presentation of persuasive evidence.[5]

In order to inform these policy discussions, a study was undertaken to determine the outcomes and beneficiaries of due process hearings in California. The study found the following:

1) There were relatively few hearings in California during the first year of the new procedure, but individual hearings were relatively expensive and time-consuming.

2) The single most important issue raised in the hearings was private school placement and tuition.

3) Hearing decisions resulted in allocations of expensive services and overturned district service determinations in a majority of cases. However, decisions were strongly conservative, supporting current service arrangements more often than allowing change.

4) Minorities and low-income parents used the hearing process less often than their numbers in the eligible population would have suggested. Relatively high income–ranked parents used the hearing procedure slightly more often than their number in the population would have suggested.

5) Once parents participated in the hearings, positive—i.e., favorable to parent—hearing resolutions were inversely related to income status.

6) Private service providers participated in many of the hearings and in some cases provided legal representation for the parents. Nearly all low-income parents had such help.

Each of these points will be discussed in order, after a review of the hearing process and description of the study.

Hearings in California

California regulations governing the hearing process, and supplanting older provisions concerning hearings for private placements, became effective statewide on July 1, 1978.[6] These regulations established a single hearing mechanism, conforming to the federal guidelines, for the resolution of all disputes arising from the diagnosis, classification, or placement of handicapped children by the public schools. Under the new provisions, either school personnel or parents can request a fair hearing whenever these disputes are not resolved in the course of regular contact between the parties. Prior to the formal hearing, the district must arrange an informal meeting between the parent and the superintendent's representative. If they cannot reach a resolution, then the district must arrange for a formal hearing.

Fair hearings in California conform to the general mandate of federal law. Both sides have the right to call and present evidence and have the facts weighed by an impartial decision maker. Either party may be represented by an attorney or an advocate. Both parties have the right to appeal a decision to a designee of the state superintendent of public instruction. If dissatisfied with the state appeal resolution, either party may appeal to a court of competent jurisdiction.

The significant elaboration of the federal guidelines in the California provisions involves the use of a hearing panel of three persons to hear the local cases. One member of the panel is chosen by the parent, one by the district, and the third by mutual agreement of the first two. All panel members must be knowledgeable in special education and the handicapping condition of the child at issue. None may be an employee of the local school district or of a private school where a child's placement may be considered.

In practice most of these panelists have been employees of neighboring school districts or county offices, university departments of special education, private schools, or agencies serving the handicapped. A few have been attorneys and judges. Because of the provision for local panel selection, there has been no specially trained cadre of hearing panelists in the state. For some panel members, knowledge of hearings is limited to the single case before them. Some others have been selected for many panels and have developed considerable experience. Although copies of decisions are sent to the Office of Special Education, of the California State Department of Education, there has been no formal provision for communicating decisions or developing precedent in local cases. Each is a relatively independent and isolated event.

Since September 1979, with the passage of SB 1149, the state law allows the party requesting the hearing to by-pass the local panel hearing and have a case heard initially by a staff hearing officer. None of the cases reviewed in this research used that option; all were heard first by a local panel.

The setting of hearings in a context of state special education reform is important. Under the California Master Plan for Special Education (AB 4040, 1974; and AB 1250, 1977) the state has assumed major new responsibility for the funding of special education. In a phase-in program that began in 1975 and will include all of the school districts by 1981/82, California has supported comprehensive planning and special education services. Over just a three-year period, 1978–1981, the real and anticipated increase in general fund contributions to special education will be more than $70 million.

The Research Project

Data for this research were collected in two phases. First, in order to determine the frequency and distribution of hearings in the state, a phone survey was conducted. Nearly 500 out of the 1,043 school districts and all of the county offices were called to get an accurate tally of the hearings that had been held by each responsible local agency between July 1, 1978 and July 1, 1979.

In that survey, only nine districts reported having had more than five hearings. Visits were made to each of the nine. The decisions and school records related to all of the hearings held in each of those districts from July 1, 1978 to the date of the visits in November and December, 1979, were reviewed, and interviews were conducted with school personnel. For purposes of this research, unusual access to hearing and student records was provided through the cooperation and support of the California State Department of Education.[7]

Several qualifications should be made concerning these data. First, the selection of the nine participating districts was made on the basis of the number of hearings they reported in the phone survey. These nine were the districts in the state reporting the highest number of hearings, five or more apiece. Together they represented nearly half of the total number of hearings reported in the entire state. However, when records were reviewed in these districts, it was found that several of the districts had overreported the number of hearings that had been held during the first year. Instead of the nine districts with the greatest hearing experience therefore, the districts represented a range of experience. The four districts with the most hearings were still included, but five districts were included that had hearing frequencies similar to many others in the state. The nine still contained about half the number of cases in the state.

The nine districts were not representative of the state as a whole. They were not a random sample. Two of the districts included in the study accunt for the large majority of cases reviewed, 104 out of 145. Each had held 52 hearings by the time of data collection. The general results reported in this paper were highly dependent upon the occurrences in those two sites. Where appropriate, findings that were peculiarly influenced by one or another of those districts are distinguished and explained.

While all of these conclusions were drawn from a limited number of school district sites and were especially influenced by two, a review of the formal decisions from an additional 46 local hearings held during the same time period in other districts around the state did not suggest any important contradictions.[8] Results of this research are largely congruent with the major findings of the longitudinal evaluation of PL 94-142, which gathered information from districts in a number of states, and with other extant reports of due process hearings in special education.[9]

Number of Hearings

At the time of this research a minority of the school districts and a very small proportion of the state's students participated in hearings. Only 278 local special education hearings were held in California in the first year of uniform state regulations.[10] One-third of those hearings were held in two school districts. The others were scattered among 100 of the remaining 1,041 school districts and 58 county offices of education that make up the nation's largest school system. The modal number of hearings held in California districts was zero. Only six districts held five or more hearings in that first year.

Most hearings were concentrated in the more densely populated urban counties of the state and in the large urban and suburban school districts within those counties. However, size of district was not perfectly correlated with the frequency of hearings. Some of California's largest districts had no hearings, or a very small number, while a few very small districts, with less than 500 students in their total enrollments, reported hearings.

The special education enrollment in California for 1978/79 was nearly 350 thousand. A large number of diagnostic and service decisions were required for each of those students, any one of which could have been disputed and brought to a hearing. The 278 hearings represented .08 percent of the state's special education enrollment, assuming only one hearing per student.

This finding of relatively few hearings is consistent with reports of special education hearings elsewhere in the country. Only seven of the 22 sites included in the national evaluation of PL 94-142 had more than one hearing. In Massachusetts, reports indicate that hearings were concentrated in relatively affluent suburban communities. Reports of experience from Washington, D.C. indicate some increases in the numbers of hearings after the initial months.[11]

In the nine districts where individual cases were reviewed for this research, there were 129 hearings during that first year. All of these districts were large urban or suburban districts. Their combined enrollment represented 20 percent of the state total; their special education enrollments constituted about 18 percent of the state's.

By the time data were gathered in these districts in November and December 1979, 16 more hearings had been held, for a total of 145 over an 18-month period. The distribution of these hearings across the nine districts is shown in Table 6.1. The rate of hearings for the first six months of the second year was well below what it had been the first year in all of the districts. Even within these districts, which had relatively high concentrations of hearings, the proportions of the special education enrollments participating in hearings was still quite small, ranging from .12 percent to 1.5 percent. In only two districts did the proportion of participating special education students reach 1 percent.

While special education hearings were not a widespread phenomenon in California, and did not directly affect a large number of students, individual hearings did prove to be time-consuming and relatively expensive mechanisms. Four of the nine districts included in the study estimated their average hearing costs. The estimates varied widely, depending on the length of hearings, the stipend payments to panel mem-

Table 6-1. Distribution of Local Hearings in Nine Districts

District	No. of hearings, 7/78–7/79	No. of hearings, 7/79–12/79	Total	Percentage of special education enrollment involved
1	8	1	9	.48%
2	51	1	52	1.5%
3	4	0	4	.5%
4	6	0	6	.17%
5	41	11	52	.12%
6	2	0	2	.13%
7	3	2	5	1.2%
8	3	0	3	.6%
9	11	1	12	.14%

bers, and the number of district personnel involved in the cases: $384, $900, $1,400, and $1,800. The estimates variously included professional and clerical time, panelists' fees, and any district legal fees; they did not include parent costs.

The modal local hearing review lasted nearly three hours and involved three district professionals. Individual hearings ranged from 15 minutes to 36 hours in length and involved as many as 11 and as few as one district employee. The mean number of school personnel hours absorbed in the actual conduct of a local hearing was 11.5. Preparation time was likely to double that figure.

Hearing Issues

The most frequent question debated in these hearings was whether or not children ought to be served in private schools at public expense. *Private day school placements and tuition payments were the primary issues in 110 out of the 145 hearings and in eight out of the nine districts. Including suits for residential school placement, 119 or 82 percent of the hearings centered on the issue of private placement.*[12]

The second most frequent set of issues concerned related services—individual tutoring, testing, counseling, various therapies or transportation services. In 32 different hearings, parents sought these services. *More than half of these issues were parent requests that the school districts pay for specific services provided by particular private practitioners.* Several parents wanted an extended school year for their children beyond the regular school year and summer session that were provided by the district.

Six hearings debated whether or not a child was eligible for special education. All of these issues were coupled with parental desires for particular services; none of these parents wanted their children excluded from special education programs. Three additional hearings involved parents who wanted changes in their children's handicap diagnoses related to desired changes of placements.

In the 145 local hearings reviewed, 180 different formal issues were debated.[13] Most of the hearings were held to resolve a single issue; 26 involved from two to four issues each. Table 6.2 indicates the issues and their frequency in this collection of local hearings.

An important distinction among these cases was the current placement and service status of the child whose program was in dispute. Many parents requested hearings in order to defend a current, district-financed service. In these cases it was the school district that wanted to change the child's program and the parents who contested that proposed change. These hearings were often precipitated when districts, able to serve children in their own new programs, recommended that a private school placement was no longer necessary for a child. Indeed, many

Table 6-2. Frequency of Issues Debated in Local Hearings

Issue	No. of times issue was addressed*	No. of hearings considering issue[†]
Private day school placement or payment	111	110
Residential school placement or payment	9	9
Related services		
Private	24	19
Public or unspecified	9	6
Transportation	6	4
Extended school year	3	3
Eligibility for special education	6	6
Classification	3	3
Public placement	4	4
IEP language	2	2
Others[‡]	3	3

*Out of 180 total issues.

†Out of 145 total hearings.

‡These miscellaneous "others" included a request to have a record removed from a child's folder; the one hearing initiated by a district, a request by the district that a child return from an out-of-district transfer in a neighboring district to a program in the child's home district; and a request by parents to meet with and approve their child's proposed teacher prior to consenting to placement.

Table 6-3. Change Orientations of the Issues in Local Special Education Hearings

Issue	No. of parents wanting to preserve status quo	No. of parents wanting district to fund a current service	No. of parents wanting a new service
Eligibility	2	0	4
Private day school	69	36	6
Residential school	2	3	4
Public placement	2	0	2
Related services			
Private	0	22	2
Public	0	0	9
Transportation	1	4	0
Extended year	0	1	2
Other	1	0	0
Total (n=172)*	77 (44.8%)	66 (38.4%)	29 (16.9%)

*Eight issues were not compatible with this classification scheme. Most were debates between alternative proposals for new services unrelated to current services.

California districts have changed their programs substantially since initial placements were made.

A second set of cases involved parents who wanted school district funding for ongoing services. In these instances the children were already in private schools or receiving particular services, but at their parents' or someone else's expense.[14] A common variation in these cases involved parents seeking reimbursement for money they had already spent.

Requests for completely new services were relatively uncommon in the hearings. Only 16.9 percent of the issues involved parents pursuing new services for their children. Many more issues involved disputes over who would fund a current or prior service (38.4 percent). The largest proportion of issues (44.8 percent) involved parents who were defending against a change proposed by a district. Table 6-3 indicates parent positions relative to each of the issues of concern in the local hearings.

Hearing Decisions

In only 43 out of the 145 local hearings did decisions support the school districts' positions and deny parents their claims. In 49 hearings parents were granted everything they asked for. In the remaining hearings decisions were split, granting some things and denying others, or granting part of a single request—three days a week of speech therapy instead of five, for example. Seven cases were conceded prior to the panel determination, six by districts and one by a parent. Six cases were left unresolved pending more information.

Of the parent requests that specifically required allocations of resources by the districts, private school tuitions were granted most often. Residential school placements were granted about half the time, while related services and public placements were denied more often than they were allowed. The panels did not decide any of the classification disputes and left one-third of the eligibility questions unresolved. In all of these cases the panels suggested further testing, or meetings that might be held, but deferred to the district to make the diagnostic determinations on the basis of new information.

Table 6-4 displays the fair hearing panel resolutions of each of the issues presented in these 145 hearings.

Of the original 145 hearings, 48 were appealed: 33 by parents, nine by districs, and six more by both parties.[15] For the most part, parents appealed local decisions that denied them their claims, and districts appealed decisions that granted parent claims. All six joint appeals were of compromise decisions. Parents appealed about 60 percent of the individual issues that were resolved in favor of the district. Districts, in contrast, appealed only 11 percent that favored parents.

Nearly half of the reviewed issues were overturned on appeal, generally in favor of the parents. Only five state appeal hearings resulted in decisions that changed panel decisions to the benefit of districts; 16 resulted in new full grants and two in new partial grants to parents. All of the appeal resolutions are shown in Table 6-5. Four new issues introduced at the appeal hearings are shown in parentheses.

In general parents fared well in these hearings, achieving at least partial grants of their claims in 49 percent of the local decisions and the same proportion in the state appeals.[16] They did even better in obtaining private school tuitions, improving their proportion of favorable outcomes to 73 percent, including the concessions and reversals on appeal. Eighty-one of 111 requests for private day school placement, and six out of 10 appeals for residential placement, were ultimately granted through the hearing and appeal process.

Valuable resources that had previously been denied to them by their school districts were distributed to parents in these hearings.[17] Many of these impressive grants, however, represented extensions of previously

Table 6-4. Local Hearing Resolutions by Issue

Issue	No. granted	No. denied	No. of compromises*	No. unresolved or dropped†
Private day school	39	36	22	14
	(35.1%)	(32.4%)	(19.8%)	(12.6%)
Residential	4	4	1	0
	(44.4%)	(44.4%)	(11.1%)	0
Related services				
Private	4	13	6	1
	(16.7%)	(54.2%)	(25%)	(4.2%)
Public	2	4	1	2
	(22.2%)	(44.4%)	(11.1%)	(22.2%)
Transportation	2	2	0	2
	(33.3%)	(33.3%)	0	(33.3%)
Extended year	1	2	0	0
	(33.3%)	(66.7%)	0	0
Eligibility	2	2	0	2
	(33.3%)	(33.3%)	0	(33.3%)
Classification	0	0	0	3
	0	0	0	(100%)
Public placement	0	2	1	1
		(50%)	(25%)	(25%)
IEP language	1	0	1	0
	(50%)	0	(50%)	0
Other	2	1	0	0
	(66.7%)	(33.3%)	0	0
Total (n=180)	57	66	32	25
	(31.7%)	(36.7%)	(17.8%)	(13.9%)

*Compromise decisions as used in this report refer to partial grants of the parent's original request. In several cases panels granted private school placement pending the completion of a new IEP or an assessment. This was recorded as a compromise decision although in some cases it translated in practice to a full grant. Thirteen out of 22 compromise decisions eventually resulted in full grants of private day school tuition without recourse to an appeal.

†These issues were not specifically decided by the hearing panels. Included are seven hearings over private placement that were conceded, one by the parent and one by the district, prior to the panel determination. Also listed here are issues that the panel left unresolved pending the collection of further information. These decisions supported the status quo and gave the school districts the responsibility to decide the case at a later date. A few of these unresolved issues were simply not mentioned in the decision.

funded services. *The proportion of favorable local decisions was significantly higher for parents defending against change.* More than twice as many decisions favored parents as favored districts when parents were supporting the status quo. In contrast, for parents who wanted a

Table 6-5. State Appeal Resolutions by Issue

	Appeal Resolutions						
	No. granted		No. of compromises		No. denied		No. unresolved
Issue	Sustain	Overturn	Sustain	Overturn	Sustain	Overturn	
Private school placement (n=27)	1	9	2	2	10	1	2 (conceded by district)
Residential placement (n=7)	2	2	0	0	2	1	0
Related services							
Private (n=13)	0	3	2	0	6	2	0
Public (n=3)	0	0	0	0	3	0	0
Transportation (n=5)	1	1	0 (1)*	1	1	0	0
Extended year (n=3)	0 (1)*	0	0	0	2	0	0
IEP language (n=1)	0	1	0	0	0	0	0
Continued public placement (n=1)	0	0	0	0	1	0	0
Other (n=3)	1 (1)*	0	0	0	0	0	0 (1)*
Subtotal (n=63)	5 (2)*	16	4 (1)*	3	25	4	2 (1)*
Total	23 (36.5%)		8 (12.7%)		29 (46.0%)		3 (4.8%)

*New issues introduced at the appeal hearings.

Table 6-6. Local Hearing Resolutions by the Change Orientation of the Parent Claims

Parent claims	No. granted	No. denied	No. of compromises	No. unresolved or dropped
Continue status quo (n=77)	30	21	15	11
	(39%)	(27.3%)	(19.5%)	(14.3%)
Change funding (n=66)	15	34	13	4
	(22.7%)	(51.5%)	(19.5%)	(6.1%)
Provide new service (n=29)	9	11	3	6
	(31.0%)	(37.9%)	(10.3%)	(20.7%)

*Comparing proparent vs. prodistrict decisions (where there were proparent grants and compromises) for three categories of cases and omitting decisions not specifically made by the panels (chi square = 6.94 [significant at .05]).
†Comparing proparent vs. prodistrict decisions for three categories of cases, chi square = 3.31 (not significant at .05). Frequencies are small in some cells, however.

148

change, decisions supporting the districts were more frequent than decisions granting parent claims. At the local level, parents who wanted a completely new service did proportionately better than parents who wanted districts to assume funding responsibility for a current service or to reimburse them for previous expenditures.

Table 6-6 shows all of the local hearing resolutions for parents who wanted to preserve the status quo, to obtain new funding for a current placement, or to obtain a new services.

As displayed in Table 6-7, parents defending current services and funding arrangements did better in the appeal hearings also than parents seeking any change. The differences, however, were not statistically significant. Parents who wanted the district to assume the cost of a service they were paying for did better than they had in local hearings, especially in cases of private placement; but those who wanted a completely new service lost services that they had previously won.

A brief history of one of the district's hearings illustrates a source of this conservative effect. In district no. 2, 34 out of 52 hearings involved parents who were defending arrangements whereby their children had been served in private schools in the communtiy. Many of these children had been attending these schools for several years at public expense because the district did not have the programs or space in its existing classes to serve them. The district initiated a number of new services as a result of new state funding and sought to return students from the private schools to these programs.

Parents, with help from the private schools, resisted the proposed moves; and all of them won continued private placement. They did not win their cases because the district did not offer appropriate programs. They won because the districts had not met certain procedural requirements of the law—assessments were not current or complete, required timelines were not met, or IEPs were not specific in their placement recommendations. In some cases, they won because the panel or appeal officer determined that a change in placement might be harmful to the child at that time.[18] Procedural requirements and the weight of historical evidence supporting a current placement (compared to speculation about how a child might do in a new program) made it difficult for that district to withdraw funding of a child's current program. Representatives of the private schools who were strongly motivated to maintain current service arrangements, were instrumental in the participation and case presentations of many parents.

149

Table 6-7. Appeal Decisions by the Change Orientation of the Parent Claims

Parent Claims	No. granted		No. denied		No. of compromises		No. unresolved
	Sustain	Overturn	Sustain	Overturn	Sustain	Overturn	
Continue status quo (n=11)	1 (54.5%)	5	3 (27.2%)	0	0	0	2 (conceded by district) (18.2%)
Change funding (n=36 + 1)	1 (29.7%)	10	15 (48.6%)	3	4 (1)+ (21.6%)	3	0
Provide new service (n=10 + 1)	2 (1)+ (27.3%)	0	6 (72.7%)	2	0	0	0

n = 59*

* Four of the 63 issues heard on appeal cannot be classified by this scheme.
+ New issues introduced at the appeal hearings.

150

These same four factors—evidence of procedural noncompliance by the districts, attention to the effects of a change in placement on the child, evidence of current success or satisfaction, and assistance by private schools—also contributed to decisions that required districts to assume the funding of placements parents had inititated.

Participation and SES

Specific data on the education, income, and occupation of the families of school district pupils are not generally available. A detailed analysis comparing hearing participants to the eligible population was not possible from school district reports.[19] However, available information could support a few important observations.

First, while there were black and Hispanic participants in the hearings, their proportion was significantly lower than their proportion in these nine districts.[20] Twenty-five of the 145 hearings (17.2 percent) involved black or Hispanic families.

Table 6-8 distinguishes the nine districts and indicates the expected number of minority participants, given the composition of each district, compared to the observed number.[21]

In five of the nine districts there were no minority participants. The relatively low number of hearings in each of these districts, however, made the observations unconvincing evidence of within district underrepresentation. Likewise, the one minority case out of three in district no. 8 was not statistically significant. With the exception of that one case, all of the minority cases occurred in the three districts where dis-

Table 6-8. Number of Minority Hearing Cases in Nine Districts Compared with Expectation Generated from District Enrollments

District	Number of cases	Expected number of minority cases	Expected % minority in district	Observed number of minority cases	% Minority of all district cases
1	9	1.0	11.9	0	0
2	52	19.0	35.8	11	21.2
3	4	0.5	12.4	0	0
4	6	1.0	15.9	0	0
5	52	31.0	59.5	12	23.1
6	2	0.1	4.6	0	0
7	5	0.2	4.6	0	0
8	3	0.1	3.1	1	33.3
9	12	3.6	29.6	1	8.3

Table 6-9. Number of Minority Hearing Cases in Three Districts Compared with Expectations Generated from Special Education Enrollments

District	Expected no. of minority participants	% Minority in special education	Observed no. of minority cases
2	30.2	(58.1%)	11*
5	30.7	(59%)	12†
9	4.2	(35%)	1‡

*Chi square = 27.62 (significant at .05).
†Chi square = 26.34 (significant at .05).
‡Chi square = 1.75 (not significant).

trict proportions would have suggested more than one. While all of these three did have minority participants, none of them had as many as would be expected in an exact replication of the school district enrollments.

The underrepresentation noted in this comparison may understate the real discrepancy between the actual and expected participation of minority families. The proportion of minority students in the school district pupil counts is undoubtedly lower than the proportion in the special education programs. Information on the ethnic distribution of handicapping conditions is complicated by inequities in special education enrollments, in part because of the criteria used for diagnosing and classifying students. On the other hand, studies of poverty in the United States frequently find associations between poverty, minority status, and a whole range of physical, mental, and emotional conditions recognized by the schools in special education programs.[22]

Special education enrollments by ethnicity, available only for districts no. 2, no. 5, and no. 9, show a greater proportion of minority students in the special education programs in two out of the three districts than in the total district student populations. Table 6-9 displays the expected number of minority participants, given California State Department of Education figures on each of these three districts' special education programs, compared to the observed number.

Twelve of the 145 hearings involved families known to rely on public assistance as their primary means of support.[23] Seven more probably qualified for and received AFDC support, for a total of 13.1 percent of the hearing participants.[24] This number is significantly lower than the proportion of AFDC recipients in these districts taken as a whole (23.2

percent), and even lower than estimates of the proportion of children from poverty level families likely to constitute the handicapped population and the special education programs of these districts.[25]

As shown in Table 6-10, nearly all of the low-income participants came from district no. 2. Only one other district, district no. 5, had any low-income participants, and participation there was significantly less than expectations derived from that district's population characteristics.

While the above analysis suggests that very low-income parents were underrepresented except in one district, evidence from this study does not support a view of the hearings as dominated by affluent parents. The nine districts varied in their demographic characteristics and in the characteristics of the parents who appeared in hearings. However, the known occupations of participating employed parents in the nine districts taken together did not differ significantly from the occupational distribution of family heads generally in California or in the five metropolitan areas encompassing these school districts.[26]

Sixty-six percent of the hearing participants were white-collar workers; 10.5 percent of those, female clerical workers. Twenty-three percent were blue-collar craftsmen, operatives, or transport workers. One percent were farm workers, and 8 percent held service occupations. White-collar workers were slightly overrepresented because of a larger

Table 6-10. Number of Low-Income Hearing Cases Compared with Proportions in School District Enrollments and Expected Number Generated from Estimates of Proportions in Special Education Programs

District	No. of hearings	% AFDC in district	% AFDC in special education	Expected no. of low-income cases	Observed no. of low-income cases
1	9	3.7	4.3	.4	0
2	52	21.2	23.7	12.3	16 (30.7%)*
3	4	3.3	3.7	.1	0
4	6	7.3	8.6	.5	0
5	52	27.3	30.6	15.9	3 (5.7%)†
6	2	5.8	6.3	.1	0
7	5	3.3	4.2	.2	0
8	3	.3	0.4	.01	0
9	12	15.9	18.8	2.3	0‡

*Chi square = 1.09 (not significant at .05).
†Chi square = 13.93 (significant at .05).
‡Chi square = 1.74 (not significant).

than expected number of self-employed professionals (doctors, dentists, attorneys): eight, instead of the anticipated one or two. Blue-collar workers were slightly underrepresented, 23 participants compared to an anticipated 35.

Other evidence contributing to an impression of a range of socio-economic participation in these hearings included the fact that 45 out of the 145 original hearings involved single female heads of families, most of them receiving public assistance or employed in clerical or service jobs with relatively low associated mean incomes.[27]

Hearing Outcomes by SES

Given the high proportion of outcomes favorable to parents in these hearings, the key to receiving benefits, especially for low-income parents, was the willingness or capacity to contest school district decisions. Once parents participated in the hearings, positive hearing resolutions were inversely related to income status.[28] Table 6-11 indicates the resolutions of local issues by the economic status ranking of the parents. Resolutions are divided between private school and all other issues. Residential school placement cases are distinguished in parentheses.

For private school and other issues, low income-ranked parents fared the best, winning at least partially favorable resolutions of 75.1 percent of the private school issues and 83.3 percent of all other issues. High income-ranked parents fared the worst. Only in cases involving this latter group did school districts have their positions supported more than half the time.[29]

It is important to note, however, that low-income parents pursued a much narrower range of claims than middle and high-income parents. None in the low-income category claimed residential placements or changes in public placement, transportation services, or an extended school year. One eligibility question, two requests for private related services, two for publicly provided related services, and one request for a record to be removed from a folder constituted the six issues, other than private placement, raised by low-income parents.

Low income-ranked parents were also less likely to pursue change through the hearings. In most cases they were defending against any changes in the current services provided for their children, and this accounted for some of their relative advantage in obtaining favorable hearing decisions. However, for every kind of issue—defense of the status quo, pleas for the district to accept funding responsibility for a current

Table 6-11. Local Resolutions of Private School and Other Issues for Parents in Three Income Rankings

Income ranking	No. granted	No. denied	No. of compromises	No. unresolved or dropped
Low				
Private school (n=16)	7	2	5	2
	(43.8%)	(12.5%)	(31.3%)	(12.5%)
Other (n=6)	5	0	0	1
	(83.3%)			(16.7%)
Middle				
Private school (n=88)	28 (4)*	25 (4)*	16	11
	(36.4%)	(33%)	(18.2%)	(12.5%)
Other (n=36)	7	16	5	8
	(19.4%)	(44.4%)	(13.9%)	(22.2%)
High				
Private school (n=16)	4	9	1 (1)*	1
	(25%)	(56.3%)	(12.5%)	(6.3%)
Other (n=18)	2	11	4	1
	(11.1%)	(61.1%)	(22.2%)	(5.6%)

*Residential school placement cases.

†Omitting decisions not specifically made by hearing panels and comparing proparent vs. prodistrict decisions for three income-ranked groups, chi square = 13.32 (significant at .05):

Income ranking	Proparent	Prodistrict
Low	17	2
Middle	60	45
High	12	20

service, or requests for completely new services—decisions favorable to parents decreased with increased income ranking.[30] Table 6-12 displays the relationship between hearing decisions and parent income-ranking according to the change orientations of the issues.

The same general pattern obtained in the appeal decisions. Although they participated in only four appeals (three appealed by parents and one by a district), low income-ranked parents won completely favorable decisions in all of them.[31] Two of the appeals overturned local denials and one case was conceded by the district prior to the appeal hearing, changing a local denial to a full grant of the parent's request. The remaining appeal sustained a local decision favorable to the parents.

Middle and high income-ranked parents appealed a broader range of issues than low income-ranked parents, whose cases involved only one

Table 6-12. Local Hearing Issue Decisions by Parent Income Ranking for Various Change Orientations of the Issues

Income ranking (by decision)	No. granted	No. denied	No. of compromises	No. unresolved or dropped
Continue status quo				
Low (n=14)	7	1	4	2
	(50%)	(7.1%)	(28.6%)	(14.3%)
Middle (n=55)	20	16	10	9
	(36.4%)	(29.1%)	(18.2%)	(16.4%)
High (n=8)	3	4	1	0
	(37.5%)	(50%)	(12.5%)	
Change funding				
Low (n=4)	2	1	1	0
	(50%)	(25%)	(25%)	
Middle (n=47)	11	22	11	3
	(23.4%)	(46.8%)	(23.4%)	(6.4%)
High (n=15)	2	11	1	1
	(13.3%)	(73.3%)	(6.7%)	(6.7%)
Provide new service				
Low (n=3)	2	0	0	1
	(66.7%)			(33.3%)
Middle (n=16)	5	7	0	4
	(31.3%)	(43.8%)		(25%)
High (n=9)	1	4	3	1
	(11.1%)	(44.4%)	(33.3%)	(11.1%)
n=171*				

*Omitted from this table are the nine issues that do not correspond to this scheme.

issue other than private day school placement and tuition. Both high and middle ranked groups improved on their local results through the appeals and had local hearing decisions overturned in their favor. However, middle income-ranked parents received grant or compromise decisions on 60 percent of the issues they argued in the appeals, while high income-ranked parents received favorable grant or compromise resolutions to only 25 percent of their appealed claims.

A favorable bias toward parents defending the status quo existed in appeal decisions as it had in local decisions. *However, for every category of claim—defense of the status quo, requests for funding of a current service, or requests for a new service—the smallest proportion of favorable decisions accrued to the higher income-ranked parents.*

Representation by attorneys, often presumed to be a source of advantage for high-income participants in legal proceedings, did not prove to be a particular asset in this collection of local hearings.[32] Parents who were represented by attorneys received the same proportion of favorable outcomes as parents who were not. At the appeal level, however, parents with attorneys did somewhat better than those without.[33]

Surprisingly, attorney representation was inversely related to income status at both levels. At the local level 63 percent of low-income parents, 46 percent of middle income, and 29.2 percent of high-income parents were represented by attorneys. At the appeal level too, low income – ranked parents were represented proportionately more often than other parents. They were accompanied by attorneys in all of their three appeals that went to hearings. Middle and high income – ranked parents were represented in 15 out of 32 and seven out of 14 appeals respectively. Low-income parents received legal assistance from a variety of sources including Legal Aid, the Western Center for Law and the Handicapped, the California Association for Private Special Education Schools, and County Vocational Rehabilitation Offices. None employed private attorneys.

Private Interests in Special Education Hearings

As has been noted, a large proportion of the hearings reviewed dealt with private school placement and tuition payments (82.1 percent). Most of these were cases involving children enrolled in private schools at the time of the hearings (59 percent were in private schools at district expense; another 32.3 percent at parents' or another agency's expense). Representatives of the private schools that these children attended participated in their hearings in a variety of ways—providing evidence of the current services and progress of the children and, in some cases, providing legal representation for the parents.

Private school representatives, usually principals or directors, accompanied parents at local hearings in at least 78 out of 110 day school cases.[34] Residential school personnel attended only one out of nine cases. Private school personnel attended most often when hearings concerned children who were already enrolled in their schools. They attended only two out of six hearings debating the transfer of children currently in public schools. *Parents who wanted to maintain current public funding of private schools did significantly better when they were accompanied by private school personnel. For other kinds of cases private school representation was not associated with improved outcomes.*[35]

Attendance at hearings by private school representatives was generally higher for low-income and minority parents, perhaps contributing to the willingness of those parents to participate. All low-income parents requesting private school tuition payments were asking for continued payments, and all of them were accompanied by private personnel at their hearings. In contrast, private school personnel accompanied middle and high income—ranked parents in 67.9 percent and 46 percent respectively of the hearings in which the children involved were currently in private placements. Minority parents were accompanied in 17 out of 20 of their private school cases (85 percent) compared with 67 percent for nonminority parents.

The cases in district no. 2, which had 52 hearings, represented more active private school involvement than cases in any of the other districts. It was also district no. 2 that accounted for the large majority of low-income participants. As was discussed before, a majority of cases in that district grew from the district's attempt to return pupils from private schools to new district programs. In that district the directors of involved private schools attended in 47 of the 48 cases that concerned students already in their schools. In addition, the law-student director of a private school association represented parents in 35 out of those 48 cases.[36]

Two examples of entrepreneurial participation in hearings in district no. 5 (also with 52 hearings) are illustrative of other sorts of private involvement. In four different local hearings and three subsequent appeal hearings, the same debate was raised—the billing of speech therapy, as a supplementary service rather than as part of the severe oral language-aphasia program provided in that school for some of the district's pupils. The district declined to pay for the supplementary service, contending that the regular program tuition should cover it. The director of that private school attended all of the hearings and appeals. The hearings only nominally involved the parents and children, who were caught up in a contractual disagreement between that private provider and the district.

In that same district in a set of five separate local hearings and two appeals, parents and a representative of a private service claimed the district ought to pay for privately provided itinerant services at a private school site where a number of district children were enrolled (not at district expense). The district won all of the cases and prepared itself to provide the itinerant service at the private school. None of the parents, however, accepted the district services; all continued to employ the private provider.

These hearings were typical of others in which the hearing debates did not specifically address a child's unmet service needs, but rather, the division of clients and responsibilities between the private and public sector. In a statewide context of expanding public services and commitment to comprehensive public programs, the use of individualized hearings to sustain or initiate private services was noteworthy.[37]

Conclusions and Recommendations

The impact of hearings in settling disputes and protecting the educational entitlement of handicapped children deserves longitudinal research.[38] Given the concerns that have risen in response to hearings in other public administrative settings—their infrequency of use, their individual expense, the lack of participation by the neediest groups— careful attention to the effects of the process in education is important.[39] The present study of some early experiences with the hearings in California revealed some support for these concerns and others, as well as some surprises.

First, the hearings were not widely nor frequently employed except in two large districts where managing hearings became a full-time job for at least one district employee. While each local case was time-consuming and often resulted in a second appeal hearing, few of the students in the state were directly affected.

The issues in these hearings were narrow, restricted to highly individualized claims to services usually outside of the public sector. Decisions resulted in few, if any, changes in general district programs. The major impact of these hearings was fiscal—the expense of holding the hearings and providing for the individual awards. District administrators did report, however, that as a result of hearings, their districts have become more careful in complying with the procedural mandates of the federal and state laws. Signatures, deadlines, adequate documentation, thorough and timely assessments have all assumed new importance. In addition, defensive behaviors have developed in some of the districts, including the taping of meetings with parents and more frequent district use of attorneys.[40]

The educational programs of children from a wide variety of backgrounds were the subjects of hearings, but low-income and minority children were underrepresented relative to their populations except in one district where parents received notable assistance from interested private schools. Low-income and minority parents rarely participated without the help of a private service provider, another community agency, or legal services. There were no observable differences between minority and nonminority parents in the claims they brought to hearings or in the decisions they received. When they participated, low-income parents pursued a narrower range of claims than high and middle income–ranked parents. Contrary to expectations, however, low-income participants won favorable decisions significantly more .often than middle and high income–ranked participants. Minority parents did as well as nonminority parents.

These hearings offered an effective appeal from the regular administrative decisions of the school districts. Parents often won their claims to services that the districts had denied them. Relatively few new services were allowed by the hearing decisions, however. Decisions favored defensive claims. Procedural omissions and violations by districts frequently supported claims to sustained services. Evidence of noncompliance was not particularly influential in justifying grants of new services, however. The status quo seemed to operate as the default value, frustrating both those parents and school districts desiring change and perhaps delaying the implementation of comprehensive public services under the California Master Plan.

If the conservative trend is not simply a peculiarity of hearings in these nine districts, hearings are likely to prolong current service arrangements and re-create any inequities contained in those arrangements. Children getting private school support may get more, children already getting special education attention may get more, but obtaining new services through hearings is less likely. The relative infrequency of low-income parents even requesting new service adds to this concern.

The structure of the hearing process in the state is still evolving. State Senate Bill 1870, passed in the summer of 1980, provides for mediation prior to a hearing before a state-appointed hearing officer. It eliminates the provision for the local panels, which proved difficult to assemble, and whose decisions were sometimes difficult to implement and often appealed. The effects of the new process—who participates and who benefits—should be monitored and compared with the evidence from these local panels where a kind of reverse discrimination seemed to operate.

Given the infrequency of hearings and evidence of biased participation rates, it is not reasonable to assume that hearings will provide an adequate check on school district decisions related to the programs of special education students. To ensure that decisions for all students are made fairly and with appropriate care, hearings in cases of dispute need to be supplemented with strong quality assurance programs within districts. Periodic administrative evaluations of a random sample of IEPs could be made, for example. Standards specifying the minimal content of the IEPs and prerequisites for any proposed changes in a child's program should be developed, shared, and used to guide the administrative evaluations. If this kind of self-monitoring were initiated in all special education programs, some hearings might be avoided while the rights of all special education clients would be protected.

At the same time, steps might be taken to equalize access to the hearing process in cases of disputes. In the hearings reviewed here, the participation of a large proportion of low-income and minority parents seemed to depend on the vested interest and involvement of private service providers. Without that interest, it is likely that low-income and minority participation would have been even more infrequent. Positive advantage might be taken of the knowledge that there are poverty law centers that assisted some parents in their pursuit of benefits through these hearings. Providing such centers with detailed explanations of hearing procedures and parent rights and encouraging their assistance in specific cases, as well as in the general development of any future rules governing the conduct of the hearings, would promote more equitable and informed use of the process in cases where it is necessary. Almost as important, it would give the public schools the initiative in developing positive cooperative relationships, instead of adversarial ones, with other agencies interested in the welfare of school clients.

Over time it is likely that the relationship between the public and private sector will stabilize, and the preponderance of cases dealing with such issues will diminish. The relationship is uneasy now, however. *From this collection of hearings it looks as though it will be difficult for public schools to reclaim students from private schools where they are satisfied. Some districts have already stopped trying.* Public funding for such placements may be necessary for awhile even as appropriate public placements become available. Funding formulas which reward districts that initiate disputes by trying to remove students from present settings ought to be reconsidered.

There is a demand for private school services among parents of handicapped children. An assumption that parents want a mainstream educational setting for their children is false. A large number of parents requesting renewed or new private school funding expressed strong preferences for the protected environment of relatively homogeneous private schools and considerable fear of integrated public schools. Many of these parents had suffered with their children through difficult experiences in previous public placements. They were reluctant to go back. Efforts to inform and involve such parents in new public programs should replace summary notification that the public schools no longer find it appropriate to fund their private placements. This kind of attention to the feelings of these families might have prevented some of the hearings reviewed here.

If the public schools continue to fund students in private facilities, and it looks as if this will be the case, some monitoring of the tuitions in those schools is imperative. Since the public schools have assumed 100 percent of the cost of private tuition for students who are recommended for private placement, those tuitions have risen substantially. In one district included in this study, they rose an average of 33 percent in one year. In another district there was evidence that charges to the district exceeded charges to individual parents for the same service.

Private day school tuitions granted in these hearings averaged more than $5 thousand per year per child, with some tuitions exceeding $9 thousand. Residential placements were, of course, much higher, more than $15 thousand per year in several cases. In comparison with the state allocations for students in public programs, many of these tuitions were quite high. The proposed increases in state allocations for public programs for 1980/81 provide $3,100 per child in special classes and centers and $1,200 per child in resource specialist programs, plus slightly more than $800 per child in support and management services. While these figures do not include all the costs of the regular school programs and facilities also provided for some of these children,[41] they are substantially lower than the outlays required by the average private placement.[42]

Given evidence from this research that public funding of private placements was difficult to withdraw, these services, once granted, can be assumed to obligate the district for a number of years. Some contractual agreement between the state and private special education school associations, or with the individual schools themselves, to limit tuition increases for publicly funded students is in order.

A final comment is more general. The vague legal entitlement to an "appropriate" education needs careful evaluation, especially as it guides these hearings. There is precedent for the use of hearings to settle disputes over claims to public benefits, but special education hearings are distinguished from other claim settling hearings by the lack of specificity in the controlling statutes. In the case of claims to AFDC or Veterans' Benefits, for example, there are relatively well-specified benefit schedules that define the public obligation to various defined classes of recipients. The role of the hearing officer is most often to decide, on the basis of evidence, whether the claimant has been misclassified or remuneration has been inaccurately figured. While there are some areas of discretion, the substantive consequences of the classifications are given.[43]

In these special education cases, however, consequences were not given. Hearing panels each defined the substance of an appropriate education and the corresponding public obligation to provide it.[44] A notable example was provided in two cases in which parents requested funding for the full calendar year at a residential school where both their children were placed at public expense. The district denied that it was obligated to pay for a school year longer than the one it provided in its own program. One hearing panel (made up of three judges) allowed the funding. Subsequently the district settled the other case, which had been taken by the parents to court rather than to a hearing, and provided the funds. The district had accepted the new responsibility. Meanwhile, in a neighboring district no such responsibility existed. Standard district policy there limited funding to children in residential schools to the length of the school year it provided for students in its own programs.

In a context of limited resources, case-by-case allocations, unconstrained by explicit and shared decision criteria, can yield distortions in the distriction of public funds. Some very generous grants were provided in these hearings. Taxi transportation to and from school at a cost to the district of $20 per day, and private counseling at a cost of $40 per hour once a week were two examples. While each may have been individually fair, the effect of these highly particularized provisions, superimposed on a general distribution of district resources, was alleged to be unfair. Several district administrators complained that while individual decisions may have been warranted, they all knew other children who deserved at least as much tutorial help or speech therapy or even residential care away from a difficult family situation.

Specific definitions of the services appropriate to classes of special education children is neither desirable nor appropriate to the spirit of PL 94-142, which recognizes the highly individualized needs of special education students. But some limitations on the extent of the public obligation ought to be considered, especially in the following areas:

- Some definition of the length of the school year.
- Some prerequisites for educationally warranted residential care.
- Restrictions on hearings relevant to the *amount* of a service to be provided. While parental claims that a service ought to be provided are appropriate to a hearing, the frequency of a service ought to be based on district standards allowing for the needs of all of the district students. Hearings are probably a poor forum for deciding whether a child ought to have completely individualized or small group speech therapy, for example.
- Consideration of a rule regarding the initiation of private school placements when public funding is sought. A small number of parents have taken advantage of the law's provision for the continuation of present program placement pending dispute resolution and have placed their children in private schools prior to initiating a hearing; then they have claimed a move would harm the child.

For the most part, the records of hearings held in these nine districts showed them to be highly personalized forums that attended to the issues and the facts and feelings of the parties before them. The hearings provided effective recourse from administrative decision, encouraged procedural compliance on the part of districts, and devoted considerable resources to the resolution of disputes arising out of the new legal entitlement. They were not powerful tools for change. On the contrary, they impeded change efforts by districts and infrequently allowed new services to parents. Nor were they a particularly equitable means for redistributing district resources. While they allocated valuable services and evidenced a decision bias toward low-income parents, the restricted and unequal use of the process portends a somewhat regressive impact.

To promote the goal of equity in education, refinements in the current hearing system are called for by these findings. Research into the costs of the process and possible alternatives to individualized hearings for ensuring fairness in the administration of special education services warrants continued attention.

Notes

1. For a review of the history of PL 94-142, see Frederick Weintraub, Alan Abeson, Joseph Ballard, and Martin Lavor, eds., *Public Policy and the Education of Exceptional Children* (Reston, Va.: Council for Exceptional Children, 1976).

2. *Mills* v. *Board of Education of District of Columbia,* 348 F. Supp. 866 (D.D.C. 1971); *Pennsylvania Association of Retarded Citizens* v. *Commonwealth of Pennsylvania,* 334 F. Supp. 1257 (E.D. Pa. 1971) and 343 F. Supp. 279 (E.D. Pa. 1972); *Larry P.* v. *Riles,* 343 F. Suppl. 1306 (N.D. Ca. 1972).

3. For example, Carrie Peyton, "Fair Hearings: School Administrators Want a Better Way," *Palo Alto Times,* 11 January, 1979.

4. For a general discussion of equity and legal processes, see John Arthur and William Shaw, *Justice and Economic Distribution* (Englewood Cliffs, N.J.: Prentice-Hall, 1978). For an empirical example, see Robert Rabin's study of the effects of CO status appeals in draft board hearings, "Do You Believe in a Supreme Being—The Administration of the Conscientious Objector Exemption," *Wisconsin Law Review* (1967): 642.

5. See Jeffrey Jowell, *Law and Bureaucracy: Administrative Discretion and the Limits of Legal Action* (Port Washington, N.Y.: Dunellen Publishing Co., 1975); Jerry Mashaw, "The Management Side of Due Process: Some Theoretical and Litigation Notes on the Assurance of Accuracy, Fairness and Timeliness in the Adjudication of Social Welfare Claims," 59 *Cornell Law Review* 772 (1974); For comment on the Massachusetts experience, see Richard A. Weatherly, *Reforming Special Education: Policy Implementation from State Level to Street Level* (Cambridge, Mass.: MIT Press, 1979). On hearings pursuant to the *P.A.R.C.* decision in Pennsylvania, see David Kirp, William Buss, and Peter Kuriloff, "Legal Reform of Special Education: Empirical Studies and Procedural Proposals," 62 *California Law Review* 40 (1974).

6. The old Sedgewick Act and regulations pursuant to it provided for administrative hearings, generally conducted by the county offices of education, if a parent wanted funding at a private school. The new sections of the Education Code, 56030–56038, integrate the issue of private school placement into the development of a comprehensive educational plan wherein placement determinations proceed from an evaluation of the child's needs. Any provision of that plan, including but not limited to private placement, may now be the subject of a hearing. Private placements are no longer singled out as distinct from the total process.

7. Special acknowledgment and appreciation go to former Director of the State Office of Special Education Gordon Duck; and to Gail Imoberstag of the Legal Services Office, as well as to the special education personnel in the nine participating districts.

8. One distinction that emerged was that in the 46 hearings, districts won a slightly greater proportion of decisions supporting their denial of private school placement and funding, nearly one-half compared to one-third in the nine districts of this study.

9. Marian Stearns, David Greene, and Jane David, "Local Implementation of PL 94-142" (Discussion draft), SRI International, Menlo Park, Ca., 1979). The only major area of difference with their report involved their statement that "many decisions have upheld the LEA's case." In the current study, more decisions supported parents' claims than districts'. See Sibyl Mitchell, "Parental Perceptions of Their Experiences with a Due Process [sic] in Special Education: A Preliminary Report" (Cambridge, Mass.: Research Institute for Educational Policy) (Paper presented at the 1976 meetings of the American

Educational Research Association, San Francisco, April 8, 1976); James Johnson, Robert McCary, and Richard Stiavelli, "Fair Hearings Have Big Impact on Local Agencies," *Thrust* (November 1979) 9:17. See also, Weatherly, *Reforming Special Education*.

10. The total from the phone survey was 290. Visits to the nine districts that reported having held 141 out of the 290 hearings revealed overreporting by 12 hearings, some of which had been held prior to July 1, 1978, and others of which represented reporting errors. It is possible that the number 278 exaggerates the total number of local hearings in the state.

11. For Massachusetts, see Weatherly, *Reforming Special Education*; for Washington, D.C., see Kirp, Buss, and Kuriloff, "Legal Reform of Special Education."

12. The California history of hearings dealing with private school placement may have contributed, although the private school issue also predominated in the national review of hearings for the evaluation of PL 94-142 and in reports from Massachusetts; see Stearns et al., "Local Implementation of PL 94-142," See also Mitchell, "Parental Perceptions," and Weatherly, *Reforming Special Education*.

13. An issue here refers to a debate over the substantive provisions of a child's program of diagnosis and placement. While claims of procedural irregularity did arise in these hearings and were important to the resolutions, they were not the focus of the disputes. Procedural matters were introduced to support claims to particular services.

14. In six cases the services had been funded by another public agency or by insurance.

15. Thirteen of the original 145 local hearings were held jointly by state hearing officers and local panels. All panel decisions were sustained and signed by the state representative and the state superintendent of public instruction. This procedure represented a transition to the new local panel hearings and occurred early in the first year of hearings in three of the districts. None of these are counted as state appeals. The proportion of appeals was, then, 48 out of 132 or 36.4 percent.

16. One case was appealed to the courts, an appeal for a new residential placement. It was denied by the court as it had been in the local and state hearings.

17. Private day school tuitions averaged $5,670 per child per year. Residential schools averaged $17,674. Related service grants averaged several hundred dollars each, although a few, including one grant for private counseling services, cost more than $1 thousand per child.

18. This information was taken from the decision rationales included in the written decisions of panels and appeal officers.

19. The population eligible to participate in hearings is undefined. It includes all students enrolled in special education programs plus others. It is an explicit function of hearings to decide cases of children excluded from special education services who seek such services. Six out of the 145 hearings reviewed here involved children not in special education. An appropriate comparison population for hearing participants is something between the populations of school district enrollees and special education enrollees, although even the former will exclude some.

20. For all of the districts compared to their minority-nonminority compositions weighted by population, chi square = 48.7 (significant at .001).

21. The minority designation is used to refer to black and Hispanic persons only.

22. A summary of several empirical studies and estimates of the incidence of handicapping conditions by ethnicity are provided in the SRI International report, David H. Kaskowitz, *Validation of State Counts of Handicapped Children* (Menlo Park, Ca.: SRI International, 1977).

23. Information was obtained from school district records or reports by school district personnel.

24. This estimate was made on the basis of available data on employment of the heads of these households, and the mean rent and house values on their blocks of residence.

Modal incomes associated with residence values equivalent to these blocks was less than $2 thousand; the mean was less than $5 thousand in the 1970 census. All of these seven were single female heads of families.

25. Estimated from weights summarized from extant studies of the incidence of various handicaps by incme in Kaskowitz, *Validation of State Counts*, p. 34.

26. The occupational information used was for male parents in families where they were present and for females when fathers were absent. Omitting unemployed, retired, military, and unknown, n=95. State chi square = 4.88 (not significant at .05); Metropolitan = 4.21 (not significant at .05).

27. For a discussion of the relatively low economic status of female family heads, see United States Dept. of Labor, Employment and Training Administration. "Women Who Head Families: Employment Problems and Perspectives," in *Employment and Training Report of the President* (Washington, D.C., U.S. Government Printing Office 1979).

28. Parents were ranked in three groups: low-income—those known to receive or estimated to qualify for public assistance (n=19); high-income—families in which the head had a high income-ranked occupation and a mean residence block value equivalent to the top 10 percent in the state (n=24); and middle-income, the large remainder (n=102).

29. Because low-income parents were concentrated in just two districts and a large majority of them were from one district where parents won a high proportion of cases, all five districts that had any variation in the income ranking of parents were looked at separately. In all of them, lower ranked parents fared better than higher.

30. None of the chi square tests for the three categories of issues was significant at .05. Status quo = 4.52, Change funding = 4.99, New service = 2.33. Frequencies, however, were quite small. It is the consistency of the direction of the differences that is notable.

31. Low-income parents appealed all of the local decisions that denied them their claim.

32. This contrasts with the findings of Kirp et al. in their review of hearings in Pennsylvania; see Kirp et al., "Legal Reform of Special Education."

33. Omitting decisions not specifically made by the appeal officers and comparing pro-parent vs. prodistrict decisions for parents with attorneys vs. parents without attorneys, chi square = 3.32 (not significant at .05).

	Proparent	*Prodistrict*
Represented	18	7
Not Represented	8	10

34. The number of day school representatives may have been even higher. People at hearings were not always identified by title in written records of the hearings.

35. Comparing proparent vs. prodistrict decisions in local cases in which parents defended current private school services at public expense, chi square = 18.23 (significant at .05). For new funding, chi square = .02 (not significant at .05). For new services, frequences were too small to test.

	Status Quo		New Funding		New Service	
	Proparent	Prodistrict	Proparent	Prodistrict	Proparent	Prodistrict
Represented	39	6	10	11	2	0
Not represented	4	10	8	8	2	5

36. He represented 10 other parents in cases in 30 other districts for a total of 45 out of the 145 other hearings.

37. While the California Master Plan allows for private placements in instances of ex-

ceptional need or when appropriate public programs are not available, in all of the cases reviewed, districts had determined local programs were available. Certainly they may have overestimated their capacity to serve some of these children. But a majority of these cases involved children with learning disabilities, and/or mild handicaps, generally served in special day classes or resource rooms widely available in public school districts.

38. For an example and a discussion of longitudinal designs in the evaluation of public policy, see Michael W. Kirst and Dick Jung, "The Utility of a Longitudinal Approach in Assessing Implementation: A Thirteen-Year View of Title I ESEA" (Monograph printed by the Institute for Research on Educational Finance and Governance, Stanford University, 1980).

39. See Barry Boyer, "Alternatives to Administrative Trial-Type Hearings for Resolving Complex Scientific, Economic, and Social Issues," 71 *Michigan Law Review*. 111 (1972); Jowell, *Law and Bureaucracy*; Mashaw, "The Management Side of Due Process."

40. In this collection of local and appeal hearings, parents were represented by attorneys much more often than school districts, although practices varied among districts.

41. See William T. Hartman, "Estimating the Costs of Educating Handicapped Children: A Resource-Cost Model Approach" (Ph.D. diss.) Stanford University, 1979).

42. Interestingly, there was at least one private school involved in several hearings where tuitions were $3 thousand per year, admittedly less than that district would have spent in comparable public programs.

43. For a discussion of AFDC, see Joel F. Handler and Ellen Hollingsworth, *The Deserving Poor: A Study of Welfare Administration*; also, Jowell, *Law and Bureaucracy*. For Veteran Administration hearings, see Robert Rabin, "Preclusion of Judicial Review in the Processing of Claims for Veterans' Benefits: A Preliminary Analysis," *Stanford Law Review* 27, no. 905 (1975): 911–922.

44. See Kirp et al., "Legal Reform of Special Education," p. 80, for a discussion of discretion in these hearings.

CHAPTER 7 /

Direction: The Coordination of Social Services

GARRY D. BREWER

Introduction

Coordinating social services has become a policy holy grail—many seek it, but success has been elusive. This chapter begins with a general discussion of social service coordination, with particular reference to a number of obstacles that inhibit its success. Attention then turns to the special status of handicapped children, where a particular case is made for this group in terms of its needs for careful and precise coordination of available services. In this regard, the idea of "direction" is presented and recent efforts to transform this idea into a reality are discussed. The chapter concludes with several lessons that these efforts suggest, including general insights about program assessment, social innovations, and the extraordinary problems faced in securing enduring improvements for children.

Be warned: the story is far from encouraging and the matter of "success" is still an open question. However, the issues addressed here are common and persistent ones in social affairs, and that seems reason enough to tell the tale.

Service Coordination

Few would quarrel with a general objective of improving service delivery by blending and balancing specific programs to make them fit an individual's particular needs. Nor could one object to efforts that foster efficiency and effectiveness. Social service coordination has often been sought for just these reasons; however, as desirable as it appears, getting coordination has been problematic. Many reasons contribute to the noticeable lack of success.[1]

The concept of coordination has seldom been scrutinized and pinned down. What does it mean? How does one go about accomplishing it? Rather, in the usual discussion, one finds general agreement that coordination is a "good thing," but not any sense of what a "good thing" really means. The implicit meanings of "coordination" and "good thing" are as varied and contradictory as the diverse individuals who work to bring these conditions about.

To cite a general class of obstacle to coordination, different professions operate as if each possessed special insights about how to provide services best; unfortunately, one profession's preferred methods frequently conflict with another's. Change or moderation, either demanded or implied in the concept of coordination, is fine—just so long as someone else's profession does the changing. Professional norms of specialization, autonomy, and expertise routinely collide with the legitimate needs of those being served, and sometimes interfere with the total operation of the complex systems that professionals serve.[2]

Organizational phenomena get in the way of coordination, too. Changing an institution is seldom cheap but involves multiple costs, uncertainties, and threats, the sum total of which outweigh, or can be perceived to outweigh, conceivable benefits.[3] Intergovernmental frictions likewise contribute to poor and inefficient service provision. Local coordination, for instance, seldom results from federal decree or edict; more sensitive consideration of the matter is needed.[4]

Politics, as usual, infest service coordination. Considered as the broad process by which inconsistent individual and collective goals are sought, politics plays a prominent role in virtually any scheme to rationalize, streamline, or control complex systems. Seeking coordination may very well bring to the surface value conflicts and system contradictions that one has previously overlooked or learned to accept and live with. And while compromise, bargains, and negotiation—primary political tools —are not inherently harmful, they may become so in specific situations in which goal or value inconsistencies are rubbed raw enough to cause social conflict or sharpen social divisions. Common goals here are those associated with efficiency and, equally viable, accountability, increased participation, comprehensiveness, and advocacy. Coordination often implies reducing inefficient, overlapping, or marginal services; however, labels such as these invite political stress whenever a clear consensus about their meaning is open to interpretation and dispute. It usually is.

The real possibility that coordination may be "bad" is usually not considered by its enthusiasts. Duplication and overlap could be positive characteristics of a system, especially if the population being served is diverse in make-up and needs. Too much success in coordination may result, for instance, in reduced choices for a group seeking help—a possibility of some consequence for exceptional children, who by definition do not conform very well to average or normal categories or interventions. Or, zealous coordination that achieves high efficiency through razor-edged evaluation and hard-nosed reduction of "nonessential" or otherwise hard-to-defend programs may have the unwanted consequence of stifling creative or innovative impulses. This is particularly so when efficiency benefits cannot be "proved" for initiatives before or very early in their existence.

At a more general level, it should be remembered that few of mankind's social works are either neat or highly rational; most are not.[5] It takes little effort to discover contradictions in social systems and then to argue for their destruction based on the discovery. It takes enormous effort to create, sustain, or defend them. And, in this regard, coordination efforts themselves seem at least as vulnerable to attack as other activities—perhaps even more so, when one stops and realizes that the constituency for them is usually poorly defined and even less well organized to defend them.

Nevertheless, the quixotic quest for service coordination continues. But, Cervantes notwithstanding, some evidence exists that in this case the occasional windmill can be vanquished—but not without effort and certainly not without careful thought and a measure of good luck.

Many problems thwart efforts at social service coordination, but several stand out especially: confusion about the level at which coordination will be sought; poor specification of the focus for the effort; and poor agreement about what coordination is supposed to accomplish— and what it will not be burdened to do.

It may be possible to attain coordination of all social services in some defined geographical area, such as a state or one of the territories used by federal departments to organize and administer regional programs. It is most certainly the case that overall coordination at the federal level has so far failed to be a productive pastime. The many programs involved in this sort of analysis may be lumped together into aggregate and gross abstractions made of what should be happening; however, neither aggregates nor abstractions have very much meaning or interest to individuals in specific locations with very specific problems. An implication is that service coordination ought to be as close to people with real problems as possible, which means that carefully designated local settings will take precedence over larger scale, less personal ones.

Furthermore, one needs to be very clear about whom service coordination will benefit. If there is confusion about whether the service professional, the administrator in charge of various programs, or the individual consumer should take precedence, the normal outcome is that all will be disappointed. As a practical matter, let us focus only on individual consumers and then consider everything that might improve coordination for these individuals. If others involved also sustain something of value, that is certainly not to be dismissed; however, one must be mindful of the importance of clear and straight specification of beneficiary: a reasonable preference here is for the individual consumer.

As can be surmised from the general discussion of service coordination, many different persons perceive in it a long and inconsistent list of desirable objectives. Professionals expect to see their own interests and specialties advanced and improved; administrators recognize opportunities to get control over errant programs and subordinates; politicians envision symbolic rewards in terms of reduced costs and more extensive services; consumers see coordination as a means to call attention to their plight and to push for more services, needed reform, and other changes in a less-than-ideal status quo. Everyone stands to be disappointed, of course, and most coordination does exactly this—disappoints. A key reason is that objectives are seldom carefully or realistically specified, and no one bothers to seek agreement on a limited and attainable set of them before plunging headlong into coordination activities.

Throughout all of this some essential and difficult truths are lost sight of. "Coordination cannot generate new resources, cannot devise new treatment methods, cannot solve problems of alienation or mistrust, cannot transmute ineffective services systems into effective ones."[6] But, then, what might it be expected to accomplish?

If very clear and limited objectives are defined so as to limit disruption and threats to existing service providers and so as to keep consumer expectations under control, we believe a very special kind of service coordination is not only feasible but highly desirable. Furthermore, if the scope of activities and definition of the spatial unit of analysis are likewise clear and limited, the implementation problems of coordination may also be reduced to manageable proportion. And if, in addition, a compelling target or recipient group can be defined as the beneficiary of coordination, then the entire matter becomes even more plausible.

Handicapped Children and the Idea of Service Coordination

Handicapped children are a reasonably well-defined population within our society, comprising nationwide some 10 million individuals up to age 21 who need special services not required by "normal" children.[7] By definition these children are "exceptional," and many of them require numerous, expensive services to function well or at all. Such services must usually be delicately interrelated in each individual case. No two children necessarily need the same help, in the same amounts, at the same time. Furthermore, an individual child's service requirements change through time in response to past assistance and to the child's evolving needs—a newborn with problems is treated differently than a teenager; and varying causes of handicapping result in widely varying impairments and subsequent demands for help—a mildly retarded youngster has quite different requirements than a severely retarded one, all other things being equal. General prescriptions seldom guarantee general and appropriate benefits to these children; much hand tailoring and fine tuning are required to ensure that exceptional individuals get what they need, in the amounts that do the most good, when they most need it. Careful orchestration of available services is perhaps more essential for handicapped children than for any other group one can imagine.

It is in direct response to these characteristics that a specialized form of service coordination for handicapped children and their families has been created. This effort goes by the label "direction," indicating a continuing requirement to point individuals to specific, available services throughout their lives.

Direction is an information-based activity intended to match an individual's special needs with a mix of services to satisfy those needs. The idea of direction goes beyond simple information and referral and includes efforts to ensure that an individual's needs are reassessed periodically and systematically as services and needs both change through time. Direction strives to make the "best" match possible, where the notion of "best" includes concern for the amount, quality, and costs of all services received.

Direction is not well developed in the vast system servicing handicapped children in this country. Indeed the system has often been characterized as being fragmented, uncoordinated, inhumane, and many other distressing things.[8] Where direction does occasionally occur, it is sporadic and uneven.[9] Information about the overall system, its components, assets, and limitations is simply not normally available to either those who seek services or those who provide them. In this situation, responsibility for matching the client's needs with the available resources falls by default to the children and their families. They are often poorly equipped to know what specific needs are and where to find services; families are at best uninformed consumers; at worst, they are operating under personal, emotional, and financial stress, ignorant of the range of opportunities from which they might choose. Few know enough about what is required, what is available, and how to make the connections between needs and resources.[10]

Poor direction has stark implications for the general operation of services for handicapped children. For example, attempts to evaluate performance are regularly thwarted for lack of basic information. Data exist, but they usually have not been compiled and integrated in ways that allow one to determine what the whole system contains, how its various parts interact, what is happening within any constituent element, and how well services are being provided. Without this information, no one even at the highest management levels can know enough about problems that inevitably exist; certainly no one seeking help at the local level will know enough to make an appropriate match between needs and resources. There are few reliable and available sources of local information for handicapped children and their families, and the results for them are as unsatisfactory as they are for the operation of the system as a whole.

A complete description and discussion of the direction service concept for handicapped children are developed elsewhere.[11] The following list summarizes direction's main functional requirements.

- To serve as a local point of access and source of both general and specific information for those needing services.
- To collect and maintain comprehensive information on each client served by all elements of the system.

- To emphasize the individual, human dimension so as to create specific, realistic programs for each client's particular needs.
- To serve all eligible citizens in the local area of responsibility by developing outreach, identification, and follow-up procedures.
- To serve as a spokesman for the clients, individually and as a group, but such activities are to be confined mainly to existing operational procedures and communication channels and to broad scale public education.
- To operate independently of the existing administrative apparatus to the greatest extent possible.

Merely pulling together information about all the services and programs available in a local area is often a valuable exercise. Few, including those most responsible, have detailed and reliable information about what exists and is needed in given locales.[12] The average consumer seldom knows as much as is required about needs, entitlements, and service availability. Such information would highlight many system limitations and deficiencies. Likewise, there are undoubtedly underused or inappropriate programs and services. Direction is intended to provide such information and thereby foster improved operations.

Currently, a consumer has nowhere to go for help in assessing total needs and in matching these against what is available. A direction service is designed to do this. For instance, client records are usually not well kept and duplication of basic client information exists. Someone needs to collection information from all service providers in one place. Doing so could mean less paperwork and, with forethought, improved confidentiality and privacy.[13]

Direction could also help clients with outreach, diagnostic, planning, referral, and follow-up assistance. The idea is not to duplicate existing efforts, but to make them as responsive, humane, and effective as possible.

Many problems confronting handicapped children are complex and require careful resolution from several different perspectives. Diagnosis of a chronic medical condition, for example, may involve many professional specialties—not all of which are medical in nature. Besides collecting and collating previous diagnoses, assessments, and accounts of a client's current situation, an initial case review by those in a direction service could try to understand as well as possible the nature and extent of the client's total needs—including but not limited to the most obvious or pressing of them. Additional background information is sometimes required, and direction personnel could make supplementary inquiries to see that tests are carried out with a minimum of duplication. When an accurate picture of problem and need is eventually drawn, plans are then set for a step-by-step course of action and then executed to improve the client's overall quality of life. Follow-up, to ensure that plans are carried out as intended, is an integral activity of a direction service; otherwise, all previous information and assessments may well have been for nought. For instance, someone must figure out how a welfare family with a retarded child applies for assorted benefits to which it is entitled, e.g., to receive long-term care, appropriate special education, vocational assistance. Are the child and the family receiving their entitlements? If not, why not, and what can be done about it?

To serve as the independent, local spokesman for its clients, it might be thought that a direction service should be established as a private entity. The concept of private operations accords well with strong currents in American thought: taking care of one's own with a minimum of governmental influence and a maximum of dignity and efficiency. However, in many specific situations a private base of operations may not be feasible. Then great care needs to be taken to position direction within the public administration structure to minimize interference from the agencies it is meant to coordinate. One interesting placement of direction service might be to make it directly responsible to a jurisdiction's chief executive officer—a governor at the state level or a mayor for a city.

From Idea to Reality

The general shape and purpose of direction can thus be imagined. However, moving from "good idea" to tangible programs for improved service coordination has proved to be a very difficult undertaking. Captured in the following discussion are many specific lessons—about coordination and about policy-related research. Several of these figure prominently as our story about direction services for handicapped children unfolds.

Sharpening the Focus on the Idea

During the period from February 1972 to May 1974, a large scale, comprehensive evaluation of programs and services for handicapped children and youth was conducted by the Rand Corporation on behalf of the secretary of Health, Education, and Welfare. That project resulted in the publication of two volumes under Rand sponsorship: *Services for Handicapped Youth* (1973) and *Improving Services to Handicapped Children* (1974).[14] Some five years later, in 1978/79, the project was generalized, updated, and published in a single book for the general public.[15] The project brought together, for the first time, an unbelievably large and diverse body of data and information about the entire service system responsible for care and assistance to America's handicapped children and youth. Besides bringing the total system into focus so that responsible officials might begin to understand and, in time, improve operations, the research described many general problems the existence of which made the system a less-than-ideal one.

One such problem stood out, mainly because it affected *all* handicapped children and their families, and specifically because virtually no one in the system was directly responsible for its solution. The problem was service coordination, a topic singled out for detailed consideration.[16] The following discussion zeroes in on the problem's main elements.

Each major service program is designed to meet rather specialized needs; each has generated special constituencies and nurtured special interests; and each has its own separate budget, often not formulated according to any reasonable assessment of the children's actual needs. Pity the unfortunate child who does not meet the letter or spirit of the law as "interpreted" in a federal or state bureau.

Some services are not a major responsibility of any program. We spend billions of dollars caring for handicapped children, but . . . we have traditionally spent very little on prevention or identification activities. This lack of responsibility for certain services is especially telling with respect to direction.

Direction is the periodic and systematic matching of a child's needs with the proper mix of services to satisfy those needs. Individual needs change, for instance, as the child ages or improves in response to services; a system's capacity to serve is dynamic, too. To put it somewhat differently, then, direction is an information-based service designed to match individual needs and local service system capabilities.

Our society's service system is faced with an urgent need to become child-centered, not speciality-centered. Currently, agencies and professionals are responsible for providing only one or a select few professional services. Even assuming that each agency and professional performs well, the fact still remains that each single service meets only part of the child's overall needs. We must begin to regard our handicapped children less as a faceless statistical group, and more as individual fellow human beings worthy of the utmost in respect and dignity—and attention. What is needed is an institution specialized to the job of looking at the child as a total being.[17]

Our discussion ends with recommendations about direction that include (1) evaluating the then existing partial models of service coordination for handicapped children, to learn their strengths and weaknesses,[18] (2) undertaking a careful feasibility study—or "implementation analysis"—to guide the creation of a small number of prototype regional direction centers around the country, and (3) determining, based on these prototypes, the best design and operational features of direction centers so that these might be used to spread the concept and service nationwide, ending ultimately in a national network of direction centers.

In short, the need was well understood, but our low level of experience with service coordination, coupled with our general appreciation of how difficult coordination had proved to be in a range of other social service settings, urged on us a cautious, measured approach for handicapped children. Both of these considerations joined and made the promotion of the three recommendations just listed extremely difficult. Some of our experiences with these recommendations are summarized next.

Gaining Attention and Moving Ahead

Beginning in the spring of 1975, various efforts were made to gain the attention of interested professionals and responsible officials concerned with programs and services for handicapped children. The idea of prototype direction centers was first broached in April, 1975, at a meeting of the Council for Exceptional Children, an omnibus special interest group for handicapped children. The response from this quarter was very encouraging and resulted in a lengthy series of discussions between Garry Brewer, one of the principal investigators on the Rand project, and interested officials within the Bureau of Education for the Handicapped, the federal office responsible for special education services within the Office of Education. At some point during the early fall of 1975, a decision was reached to carry through with the three direction center recommendations, and a formal call for proposals to implement the prototypes was issued. Adhering strictly to the specifications contained within the Rand research reports, the request for proposal resulted in numerous responses, all of which were considered and 12 of which were finally selected in January, 1976.

One interesting aspect of the decision to try out the prototypes was the direct involvement of Brewer in an advisory and facilitative role. Everyone was aware of the general problems that service coordination efforts had suffered in other well-intended situations, and the specifications for the direction center prototypes were drawn in such a way that many of these would be surmounted or minimized. However, it was also well known that the needs for service coordination for handicapped children varied enormously across the country: no two sites were expected to "look" the same or to be faced with exactly the same particular problems of start-up and operation. Thus, a modest "implementation analysis" contract was provided to ensure direct involvement of the researcher with those willing to try out his institutional innovation.[19]

Facilitation, the key objective sought in the implementation analysis, meant "helpful assistance." The researcher and the two others, hired to do this phase of the work, were not responsible for the operation of any of the prototypes, nor were they to engage in evaluations to determine the worthiness of the total concept or of any specific operational details. What they were asked to do included visiting each site, talking with those directly responsible for the prototypes (in Washington and in the field), and doing whatever else seemed reasonable to ensure that direction centers got off to a good start and demonstrated as well as possible a reasonable means of providing service coordination.

The story so far has omitted an important element. Deciding to move ahead with direction centers not only involved the various parties already mentioned, but also the independent efforts of a private foundation to help focus on the needs for service coordination and the communication of social research. From the fall of 1974 to January, 1976, members of the Russell Sage Foundation of New York City had been taking an interest in the Rand Corporation project on handicapped children. Several of them saw within it an opportunity to call public attention to a particularly compelling social need—service coordination for handicapped children—and to make use of different communication techniques than the usual ones of formal reports and briefings to government research clients. The general sentiment was that the usual dissemination means were certainly appropriate, but that in many circumstances interesting research ideas were simply not attended to.

Accordingly, the foundation decided in late 1974 to think about how the many recommendations in the Rand handicapped study could be presented more forcefully, more effectively, and to a wider audience. In the same approximate period that federal officials were considering the idea of moving ahead with direction centers, a Russell Sage Foundation sponsored documentary film project was also being conducted. This resulted, in February, 1976, in a 30-minute film about direction, *What Do We Do Now? The Need for Direction.* This film became an important, additional ingredient in the total process of moving from concept to reality, in much the same fashion that including the researcher in the early stages of direction center implementation had been.

The Film

A decision was reached to let real families "tell their stories" of what it had been like coming to terms with a handicapped child and then trying to find out what to do in response to their child's special needs. To be sure that the message was delivered as well as possible, a highly respected documentary film company was hired and the foundation also provided for the direct involvement of an Emmy-winning news and documentary producer and for consultation from one of the Rand researchers. The first individual was hired as a foundation staff member and supervised the project in all its aspects; Brewer, the researcher, participated in the same manner. Here again, the unusual opportunity to involve a researcher was appreciated and valued by those in the foundation as one means to ensure as close a replication of the original ideas in the film version of them as possible.

It should also be added that the production of the film, coming when it did, may have had some impact on the way federal officals were thinking about direction. Many of them were consulted directly about the production of the film, and several of them actually appeared on camera discussing the problems of handicapped families and the usual difficulties faced in securing needed services. One of the earliest showings of the film, to continue this point, was to then Secretary of Health, Education, and Welfare David Mathews who, in his own words, "gained a deeper appreciation of some important problems." While not entirely sure of the actual cause and effect links, we are reasonably confident that the film did, on balance, make a positive contribution in getting direction centers started and on the track recommended in the original research.

The film has been used by most of the direction centers in the initial demonstration for outreach and public education—letting the public know about direction and about the existence of a new means to help provide it. Additionally, the foundation turned over all rights to the film along with many copies of it, to the federal government for use through their National Media Center. And, as part of the foundation's own limited dissemination strategy, the film has been shown to hundreds of influential individuals around the country—influential with regard to their care and responsibility for handicapped children. In its own fashion, a private initiative thus helped bridge the gap between research and action in an important area of social services.[20]

The First Year

The initial prototype direction centers were selected with an eye toward diversity: in location, relative abundance of both handicapped children and available services, size of staff to provide direction, and methods of operation. This seemed important for several reasons. As a research concept, direction was reasonably clear (and has been described above); however, equally clear was knowledge that trying to coordinate services for a handicapped child in Los Angeles was going to be a very different proposition than doing the same general thing for children in a farming community in North Carolina or in the vast territory of southern Utah. No one was exactly sure, before gaining essential experience, how much or how little would be needed to provide "adequate" levels of direction. Indeed, the prototypes were selected and operated to help determine this and other basic operational parameters. The concepts of "success" and "efficiency" were thus not foregone at the onset, but were accepted by all as legitimate objects of inquiry during the first year of operations. However, most involved with the project shared the sense of direction ought not be a lavish enterprise—existing information systems would not be duplicated, direction personnel would not take on service responsibilities that were rightfully the province of other individuals and agencies, and aggressive actions to advocate major changes were to be avoided out of concern that doing such might diminish the direction task or earn political enmity that direction and the children served could ill afford.[21]

Because task responsibility had been accepted by the federal Bureau of Education for the Handicapped, the prototypes were not ideally located in the administrative sense. Recall that one desirable design feature of service coordination for the handicapped was to make it as independent of the various agencies it sought to coordinate as possible. Private sponsorship was thought to be a "best" means; linkage directly to a governor or mayor was believed to be nearly as good. However, the practical matter of who would be willing to support the overall concept was settled when the bureau (BEH) took responsibility for it. Additionally, specific provisions of the Education for All Handicapped Children Act, PL 94-142 (noted previously), were also aimed at the same general requirement to coordinate all services for handicapped children; and BEH had, through a number of related legal and program mandates, sufficient funds to get direction centers started. This feature of the prototypes certainly had an effect on their character and operation; however, the alternative of doing absolutely nothing in the absence of BEH interest and support seemed a far more costly outcome.

The sites were located all around the country: Harlem, in New York City; West Lost Angeles; a remote region in southern Utah serving mainly an Indian population; several satellite sites in Alabama and North Carolina. A three-way collaborative project was centered at the University of Oregon in Eugene involving Portland and Vancouver, Washington; and a facility was located in Independence, Missouri. Two sites, in Connecticut and Idaho, were started up and, for a variety of reasons only slightly related to the direction concept, terminated sometime near the end of the first year.[22]

Some direction centers were large—one had 10 full-time equivalents, another nine—but others were very small and were able to function well with only one full-time staff member. On average, the service could be provided with about two to three staff members, if these were augmented by parents and other volunteers, such as students or interns. Variations in staff size related directly to variations in the number of children served—and this ranged from urban catchments having more than 1.5 million total population to rural ones having as few as 15 thousand. On average, the catchment population served by the "typical" direction center is about 250 to 300 thousand total population, and the average number of handicapped clients served is somewhere in the neighborhood of 100 to 200 each year. Diversity is normal, however; several sites serve as the headquarters, where records are kept and detailed information about local services is centered, and which operate much smaller, remote service centers that are closer to the children and their families.

The outreach and awareness function of direction services is handled by all centers, but they have adopted specific approaches that work best in their own settings. Advisory boards, composed of representatives from the various handicapped service agencies, parents, and direction center personnel, are one common feature, and these have been important educational devices. In addition to having these boards, several direction centers have worked closely with professional associations, e.g., medical associations, rehabilitation and educational societies, and others, to inform them of direction's existence and actual purposes (and to keep everyone as clear as possible about what direction does *not* do). An imaginative public education component is evident in the sum total of all prototype activities: some have used local radio and television extensively; most have information pamphlets and brochures; one has a quarterly newsletter of highest professional quality that informs the total handicapped service community; and so forth.[23]

One general feature of the early stage of direction centers stands out. It would have been impossible to anticipate all the specific needs and aspects presented in each of the diverse settings where the prototypes were established, hence it would have been impossible to specify one "best" way to implement direction. Diversity of situation, in this regard, necessarily means that there will be great diversity in the ways service coordination is provided. This is common sense, but for one interested in a rigid specification against which individual performance in the sites can be assessed, the commonsensical experience presents formidable research problems. Indeed, our experience suggests strongly that specific contextual details should weigh more heavily in one's implementation efforts than slavish adherence to any list of abstract, non-site-specific performance criteria. What's "right" and "works" in Portland may be entirely "wrong" in Blanding, Utah.[24]

The "batting average" or success rate for the 12 initial sites is impressively high. Ten remained intact, functioning well, and providing coordination services valued by handicapped children and their families at the end of 1977.[25] Federal officials and others were sufficiently impressed to continue to support the project and, indeed, to expand it in various ways. By the end of 1979, 25 direction centers were working around the country in a loose confederation as a newly defined service specialty—service coordination for handicapped children.

For a researcher interested in a variety of social policy issues, the direction experience has provided untold insights and several strong lessons. Of course, the appropriateness of these must be appraised in light of other specific settings and details—no claims are here made as to their generality.

First and foremost is the fact that a distinctive problem could be identified and, with careful design, an appropriate mechanism to contend with that problem could be created. A great deal of time and attention were expended to both understand the problem and to devise a feasible solution for it. In this aspect of the work, the direct involvement of the policy analyst in helping to bridge the usually considerable gap between research and action seemed to play an important, if not essential, role. In this regard, paying specific attention to organizational realities such as trying not to duplicate what others were already doing (and thus to minimize problems of "turf," and other, sensibilities) was important. Working to temper direction staff members in their over-zealous pursuit of services they, as individuals, believed to be essential but missing or inadequately provided, helped to dampen political antagonisms that otherwise might well have drawn adverse reaction to the direction institution. Throughout the project's first year, the distinction between service coordination—making do with what was available—and advocacy was repeatedly stressed.

Another strong lesson learned is that each of the multiple professional specialities involved in caring for handicapped children has something valuable to contribute; however, for a variety of complex reasons, each profession tends to believe that its own specialized perspective has (or should have) the lead role to play in helping the handicapped client. This is a fact of social service life. Direction offers a different perspective, one that starts with the child and then asks the key operational question: "What does this specific individual *actually* need, when, in what amounts, and for what length of time?" It is an important change of perspective that helps to reduce the unfortunate and wasteful consequences of a client's being "captured" by one or another service or professional specialty. It is, in many circumstances, about the only time that the child is considered as a total entity, not merely as one needing this or that specialized care.

On a more prosaic level, our earlier concern to make the direction centers as independent as possible of existing administrative structures and systems still seems valid. Linking the prototype of demonstration to the educational system was done simply because it was the one place where some action could take place; but this linkage appears to have almost jeopardized the entire operation. We are not particularly concerned here with day-to-day influences emanating from higher educational authorities as these might affect direction's functioning; rather, we stress the vulnerability of direction's funding in these times of budget stringency and retrogression at the federal level with respect to all educational endeavors. The entire federal educational establishment is, of course, threatened in this, the winter of 1981. Direction services, to the extent they rely on federal sources of support, are no more immune than any other program—regardless of their utility, importance, or "worthiness." Certainly change is the only permanent feature of life, and current conditions strongly suggest that the five-year experiment with service coordination for the handicapped is about to enter a new phase. Whether or not all of the existing centers survive is less of a question than how quickly they will be able to adapt to the current, Draconian measures affecting social services in America. As compared with large scale and very expensive government programs, direction services are admirably situated to harness private energies for their survival and continuing development. They are relatively inexpensive, they do provide a needed service valued by the hundreds who have received it, and they have already shown themselves to be both adaptive (the diversity point stressed earlier) and resilient.

Several specific observations point to promise for the future:

- Direction services are ideally configured to be sustained by private initiative and voluntary support.
- When connected to a professional education program (e.g., as at the University of Oregon), direction provides an invaluable teaching and training opportunity for budding social service workers and researchers.
- In an era of contracting resources for all social services, the need to make the very best use of what remains creates an additional demand for something very much like direction to exist at the local delivery level.

As a group, the parents of handicapped children are generally among the most energetic in our society. The particular problems they face often allow them to draw deeply from resources within themselves that "ordinary" parents simply never have to tap. This energy has been channeled into many of the existing direction centers to positive advantage. In Boston, for instance, one center is operated almost entirely by parents who have been trained and supervised by a few direction specialists. The results are encouraging and suggest one survival strategy for other centers (existing and yet to be established) interested in insulating themselves from the vagaries of official funding. Private funding initiatives have been tapped somewhat, but much more could easily be done here to secure a more stable, diverse financial base. The minimum essential support needed for an average direction service is probably on the order of $75 thousand per year, a figure within the reach of most communities in terms of private charitable support. Anything in addition to this minimum figure would, of course, mean even greater service coordination; and here federal, state, and other government dollars could be used for incremental improvement.

The fragmented character of most professional specialties has been noted throughout this discussion and is well known to anyone who has had even the slightest acquaintance with those in the helping or social service professions. Because of its unique perspective on the child as a total entity, direction offers an important partial corrective to the piecemeal, fragmented view of children often imparted, albeit unwittingly, in regular training programs around the country. In this matter, a lively opportunity exists to link direction centers to these programs for internship and other instructional purposes. Such an opportunity has been realized only slightly so far, and much more could readily be done to expand on this initial base of experience.[26]

Finally, in a period when many social services are threatened by budgetary and political maneuvers, the need for effective coordination of what remains implies that direction will be more, not less, important in coming years. This is at once a very difficult and at the same time a perfectly rational argument to make: difficult when everyone's level of anxiety is reaching unheard-of heights, but rational from the point of view of "making do" with what remains in the interest of continuing services to the handicapped. Cutting the budget will not reduce the number of handicapped children (it may, indeed, add to their number as preventive and other programs to lessen their incidence are cut back). As a society—and as human beings—we owe it to our children to provide the best possible services, in the amounts realistically required; and direction is precisely aimed at this end.

It must be stressed, however, that direction and advocacy are entirely different matters. In a period of fiscal stringency, such as that envisioned for the coming years, there will be strong impulses to confuse the two, as we encounter situations of receding resources and diminishing services. Direction is too important, in its own right, to be subjected to the political buffeting advocates routinely encounter. The functions of direction and advocacy are complementary, but different. The primary rationale underlying direction is to improve management control and operations of existing agencies, and to do so with skilled professionals working within the constraints of present capacity on behalf of the consumer. The best idea here is "make the system work." The rationale and operational objectives of community-based advocacy are to build a more complete and humane system through educational and other direct political activities.[27] The best idea here is to "create and enhance the system." Advocacy is a laudable concept, often misunderstood and abused in our society. To be an advocate means, simply, to be in support or in favor of someone or something; the term also implies that one will do whatever is necessary to support an individual or cause in a public way. The thrust of advocacy is toward the political arena, which, in times of cutbacks, becomes a hostile place indeed.[28] Mistakenly likening direction to advocacy carries the grave risk of putting our handicapped children on the battlefront—a place they can ill afford to be.

Notes

1. My thinking about these matters has been enriched by conversations with Janet A. Weiss, a Yale colleague. See her, "Substance vs. Symbol in Administrative Reform," *Policy Analysis* 7, no. 1 (1981): 21–45, for a detailed exploration of the general topic.

2. Martin Landau, "Redundancy, Rationality, and the Problem of Duplication and Overlap," *Public Administration Review* 29 (July/August 1969): 346–358.

3. Garry D. Brewer, "On the Theory and Practice of Innovation," *Technology in Society* 2, no. 3 (1980): 269–279, treats this problem in more detail.

4. See for example, Jeffrey Pressman and Aaron Wildavsky, *Implementation: How Great Expectations in Washington Are Dashed* (Berkeley: University of California Press, 1973).

5. William Barrett, *The Illusion of Technique* (Garden City, N.Y.: Doubleday-Anchor, 1978), provides important illumination here.

6. Weiss, "Substance vs. Symbol in Administrative Reform," p. 43.

7. Garry D. Brewer and James S. Kakalik, *Handicapped Children: Strategies for Improving Services* (New York: McGraw-Hill, 1979), chaps. 1 and 2, supply the definitions and the numbers.

8. Nicholas Hobbs, *The Futures of Children* (San Francisco: Jossey-Bass, 1975), is illustrative of a large literature on this topic.

9. James S. Kakalik, Garry D. Brewer, L. A. Dougherty, P. D. Fleichauer, and S. M. Genensky, *Services for Handicapped Youth: A Program Overview* (Santa Monica, Ca.: Rand Corporation, chaps. 1–4.

10. Alfred J. Kahn, "Public Social Services: The Next Phase—Policy and Delivery Strategies," *Public Welfare* 30, no. 1 (1972): 15–24, takes this as a main theme.

11. Brewer and Kakalik, *Handicapped Children*, chap. 8.

12. Martin Rein, "Decentralization and Citizen Participation in Social Services," *Public Administration Review* 32 (1972): 687–700.

13. Alan F. Westin, *Privacy and Freedom* (New York: Atheneum, 1967). The point here is to limit the number of places holding privileged information and then to impose strong disclosure and privacy restrictions and standards on these.

14. Kakalik, et al., *Services for Handicapped Youth*; and idem, *Improving Services to Handicapped Children* (Santa Monica, Ca.: Rand Corporation, 1974).

15. Brewer and Kakalik, *Handicapped Children*. Specific attention was given here to the Education for All Handicapped Children Act, PL 94-142, and other important changes up to 1979.

16. Kakalik et al., *Improving Services to Handicapped Children*, chap. 3 ("Direction").

17. Ibid., pp. 58–59.

18. A relative handful of partial examples of direction had been identified, but no studies did this as a matter of course and all of those identified were inadequate to the full requirements specified in the research.

19. A small contract was given to the Policy Science Center, Inc. of New York City for this purpose. Brewer served as the principal investigator and was assisted by two junior colleagues, both of whom had had experiences with social services, children, and demonstration projects. All three visited each of the demonstration sites to assist with design and early implementation problems, and Brewer then made subsequent visits as the project unfolded during its first year. Additionally, frequent telephone contacts, to resolve specific problems, highlighted this one-year project.

20. The film was recognized and its producers were awarded a CINÉ "Golden Eagle" for the best documentary of 1977 stressing the theme of social responsibility. As a result, the film was entered as an official United States entry in various foreign film festivals during 1978. It has also been catalogued by Time-Life Films and distributed through the Modern Talking Pictures network (as well as through the National Media Center, as noted).

21. This practical issue helped keep direction centers out of the political fray—thus avoiding a general failing of many other service coordination efforts (noted in the opening segment of this chapter).

22. Lack of commitment on the part of state officials has been implicated, as has harmful turnover of direction center personnel during the early, start-up period when the demonstrations were most vulnerable to upset.

23. All details of the program are recorded in National Association of State Directors of Special Education, *Direction Service: From Concept to Reality* (Washington, D.C.: National Association of State Directors of Special Education, 1979). Names, addresses, and other operational details of the 25 sites that existed in November, 1979, are produced in this report, which is available from NASDSE, 1201 16th Street, Washington, D.C. 20036. Telephone: (202) 833-4193.

24. This finding squares well with a theoretical point made by Paul Berman in his "The Study of Macro- and Micro-Implementation," *Public Policy* 26, no. 2 (1978): 158. It does not, however, conform neatly to the rigid evaluation requirements that underlie many experimental and quasi-experimental assessment designs.

25. At the conclusion of the first year of effort, Brewer, the Russell Sage Foundation,

and the Policy Sciences Center all decided to end their direct involvement in direction services. A general feeling was that the large effort necessary to get something in place and in operation had been successful; growth and improvement of direction services was, in the future, the responsibility of those entrusted with them. If the idea were to thrive it had to be able to stand on its own.

26. One of the more successful of the prototype direction centers was linked to the School of Education at the University of Oregon. For any interested in this innovative program, contact with its director, Dr. Richard Zeller in Eugene, Oregon, is highly recommended. Dr. Richard Zeller, Lane County Direction Services, 1736½ Moss Street, Eugene, Or. 97403. Telephone: (503) 686-3598.

27. Elizabeth Berger, "The Compleat Advocate," *Policy Sciences* 8; no. 1 (1977): 69–78, is a very clear statement of what advocacy is and what an advocate does. It is essential reading for anyone interested in the key distinctions stressed in this part of the chapter.

28. Termination politics are just like "regular" politics except that the level of intensity and the emotions run white hot. See Garry D. Brewer, "Termination: Hard Choices— Harder Questions," *Public Administration Review* 38, no. 4 (1978): 338–344, for a discussion.

PART IV

Financing Special Education

A Resource-Cost-Based Approach to the Funding of Educational Programs: An Application to Special Education

Jay G. Chambers and

William T. Hartman

Introduction

Over the last 15 years, the federal government and many states have established a variety of categorical funding programs to serve the various special need (e.g., disadvantaged, non-English-speaking, and handicapped) populations among school-aged children. Each of these categorical programs has generated its own state and federal level bureaucracies in order to provide the mechanisms for funding and service delivery to local educational agencies. There has been little, if any, coordination at the federal and state levels with regard to service delivery or funding of these various programs.

Concurrent to the development of these categorical programs, there has been a growing movement to reform state school finance systems. Efforts in the courts and the legislatures have focused on reducing or eliminating the effects of variations in local property wealth on the patterns of local spending for education. More recently, there has also been attention devoted to determining ways of adjusting state aid distributions for differences in the purchasing power of local educational dollars due to differences in the prices of school resources across local school districts. Despite the fact that the development of categorical programs and the school finance reform movement have occurred concurrently, each has developed independently of the other.

For the purpose of improving the equity of school finance systems and increasing the efficiency with which educational funds are distributed and services delivered, a more appropriate strategy would be to consider the development of categorical programs and the reform of school finance systems within the context of a common conceptual framework. It is the purpose of this chapter to offer such a common framework that could provide the basis for funding educational services and to demonstrate how that framework might be applied specifically to the funding of special education services. We are proposing a cost-based funding approach that provides equal access to educational resources across local districts serving similar student populations, and also provides for systematic differences in access to resources for districts serving students with specified differences in programmatic needs. That is, the model we propose addresses differences in educational costs arising out of both differences in pupil needs and differences in the prices paid for educational resources.

The first two sections of this chapter set the stage for analysis by reviewing state categorical funding mechanisms and the previous literature on need-based cost adjustments in education. The third section provides a conceptual framework for addressing programmatic cost differences, while the fourth section presents an empirical application of the model to special education funding. The final section offers some policy implications and concluding remarks.

It should be emphasized at this point that the conceptual framework proposed for funding educational programs is not limited to special education. It can readily be generalized to all types of educational programs and could be developed into a comprehensive educational funding system.

A Review of State Programs for Need-Based Cost Adjustment

Five basic types of programs that employ need-based cost adjustments are found across the states:

- Special education—programs for handicapped and gifted students.
- Compensatory education—programs for educationally disadvantaged students.
- Bilingual education—programs for non- or limited-English-speaking students.

- Vocational education—programs for training students for employment.
- Grade level differentials—different funding levels for different grades of otherwise regular students.

These programs focus on specified categories of students, and their funding is usually separate from funds for regular school programs. Their characteristics include the following: they serve a specific, limited population whose educational needs are felt to be different from the regular school population; the delivery systems (in terms of the types, organization, and mix of resources) used to provide these services vary from the regular school programs; because of their differing characteristics, these programs generally cost more than the regular school program due to the special resources employed and/or due to the smaller class sizes; and, to compensate for these legitimate cost differences, funds are earmarked specifically for these programs through various categorical funding arrangements. The differing technologies for these programs arise out of differing programmatic needs of certain students. Since the composition of such programmatic needs of pupils is beyond district control, funding adjustments are required to account for these programmatic cost differences.

A variety of different categorical funding approaches are used by states to provide the programmatic cost adjustments.[1]

1) *Pupil weighting*. The funding amount is based on a multiple of the regular per-pupil funding amount. The weights vary by type of program or type of pupil (e.g., compensatory education, educable mentally retarded, visually handicapped, non-English-speaking).

2) *Flat grants*. These are fixed per-pupil funding amounts provided for specific categories of students. The categories may be broad (e.g., handicapped, Title I, low achievers) or narrow (e.g., educable mentally retarded, trainable mentally retarded).

3) *Units*. The funding base is a defined teacher unit or unit of instruction where specified numbers of students define the unit. Funding is to cover all or a portion of the costs of the unit (e.g., teacher salary, aide salary, benefits, instructional materials and equipment, maintenance and operation). The costs may be either standardized or actual.

4) *Personnel*. In this approach, direct funding is provided for special kinds of approved personnel associated with the categorical programs. By funding only personnel, this approach is a specific case of the more general unit funding approach.

5) *Excess costs*. The excess costs are those that are above and beyond the

costs of educating regular students. This funding approach provides a reimbursement for all or for a portion of these costs.

6) *Percentage*. With this approach, a specified percentage of program costs are reimbursed. The percentage may vary by type of program and the cost base may be last year's, current, or projected expenditures.

7) *Approved programs*. The costs of approved programs for special populations are reimbursed in full or in part under this approach. In operation, this method requires the submission and review of a program application specifying the expenditures for reimbursement.[2]

In each case, the formulas provide additional funds to districts because of the greater educational needs of students in the categorical programs. To match the funding levels with the necessary cost increases due to these programs, it is necessary to identify the composition of the programs in terms of the resources that go into them. That is, the cost of each program is determined by the selection, quantities, arrangements, and prices of the various resources that it utilizes. Therefore, to calculate the costs of the categorical programs and consequently the cost adjustment for programmatic need, it is necessary to specify the resources that comprise the programs. This can be done explicitly by program (as in the unit formula approach), in aggregate for a total program (often the case with excess costs), or implicitly (as in pupil weighting where an outside calculation based on needs, resources, and prices is used to arrive at the weights). In any case, the estimation of the costs of meeting the educational needs of students in these programs is done through the specification of the input resource configurations of the programs.

Note, however, that these approaches do not include cost adjustments for variations across local districts in the supply prices of school resources. Specifically, none of the approaches presently in use incorporate adjustments for the differences in the resource prices that local districts have to pay for comparable school resources. Only two states (Florida and Alaska) have employed geographic consumer price level indices that are directed at adjusting state aid distributions for variations in the cost of living across local districts and, presumably, the wage levels paid by these districts for school personnel. However, a consumer price index is not the same thing as a cost-of-education index. Consumer price level variations are but one component of work choice decisions facing school personnel. The attractiveness of the district and the region as a place to work and live also effect personnel employment decisions.[3] Moreover, school districts purchase different kinds and combinations of goods and services than consumers. Thus, the market basket of consumer goods priced out in a consumer price level index is different from that employed by school districts. Thus, for a thorough correction, it may be necessary to combine the programmatic and resource price adjustments for categorical programs. The programmatic adjustments will account for the effects of student characteristics that are beyond district control, while the resource price adjustments will do the same for the prices of the various resources used in the programs.

In general, a fundamental problem in establishing programmatic cost adjustments is determining the basic level of services to be provided or the appropriate outcomes of the special programs. For example, it is especially difficult to determine objectively or scientifically just what a handicapped pupil "needs" to attain a level of educational quality comparable to that of regular students. We could set a standard of attaining the average reading level of regular students and evaluate the costs of reaching this goal for a physically disabled student. But such a goal may be unreasonable, perhaps impossible, for a mentally handicapped student. What is the appropriate set of services for the latter student in the reading area, if programmatic funding were to be this specific? Moreover, even comparability of educational "quality" between the regular and physically disabled student quickly loses its meaning when one considers the other than intellectual dimensions to the preparation of the two kinds of students for their respective places in the labor force or other aspects of life. Studies that have attempted to address some of these issues in determining appropriate cost adjustments for funding these programs are reviewed in the next section.

A Review of Previous Literature on Cost Differences

The empirical studies of the costs of categorical programs tend to be of three types: an examination of the average per-pupil expenditure patterns (cost per student); determination of supplemental, replacement, and common costs of the program; and the specification and costing out of the components that make up the program (resource-cost model).[4]

The cost-per-student approach has taken several different forms. First, the average dollar cost per student has been calculated by simply (*a*) summing over all the costs directly associated with programs for a particular type of student and those indirect costs that may be allocated to the programs, and (*b*) dividing the total program costs by the number of students involved. An example of this approach is found in a study by Kakalik and others in which the average reported costs by category of handicapped student were determined.[5] While providing summary per-pupil expenditure data, this approach places serious limitations on the use of the results for analytical or funding purposes. The average cost by type of student masks a significant variation among individual student costs; in fact, another recent study of special education has shown that there is less variation in the cost per student by the type of delivery system (e.g., special class, resource room, itinerant instruction) than by type of handicapped student.[6] The use of the average cost figure also obscures the cost differences due to educational need. The differences in selection, quantity, and organization of resources that cause the programmatic cost differences are not specified and their effects are unknown.

Another, and perhaps the most prevalent, form of the cost-per-student approach has been the development of "cost factors" for categorical and grade level programs. The general procedure in the cost-factor approach was used in the special education component of the National Education Finance Project (NEFP) by Rossmiller and others in 1968/69.[7] A cost factor, which is the ratio of the cost per student of a special education program to the cost per student of the regular education program, was calculated for each special education program. A ratio greater than one indicated the degree to which the estimated total cost of a special education program was greater than that of the regular education program. The overall cost index averaged about 2.0 for all special education students, but there were wide variations among categories within a single district and among districts with similar categories.

The cost-factor approach, however, presents a number of problems for cost analysis and funding applications. Rossmiller has noted some of the primary limitations to using these "cost factors."

A cost index generally is expressed as either a statewide average or a median. . . . Provision must be made . . . to deal adequately with the fiscal needs of individual districts which deviate from the state average for good and sufficient reasons. . . . They reflect only what is currently being done, not what could be done (or should be done) in the way of educational programming for specific pupils. . . . Cost indices show the relative cost of educating pupils in regular programs. . . . It is possible that a given special education program could be offered to an equal number of students, could provide the same educational services, and could cost the same amount per pupil in two school districts but the cost indexes in the two districts could differ because of differences in the cost of the regular program in each district. . . . A cost index which lumps together all programs for educating a particular category of handicapped children without regard to the way in which educational services are delivered to such children will mask a great deal of cost variation within these programs. . . . Finally . . . for a variety of reasons, costs will vary between districts for identical programs . . . the cost of transporting pupils involved in special programs, . . . pupil/teacher ratio, . . . differences in salaries and in the cost of educational supplies and materials, . . . and these differences will be reflected in educational program cost and in cost indices.[8]

Subsequent to the original NEFP study, there have been many individual state studies conducted using the cost-factor methodology; these have included studies in Delaware, Florida, Idaho, Illinois, Indiana, Kentucky, Mississippi, South Dakota, and Texas. Additionally, cost studies using this approach have been reported by Bentley, Snell, Mc-Clure et al., and Clemmons.[9] These studies followed the specific cost-factor methodology developed by the NEFP study and they generally found the same results—and overall median index of approximately 2.0 with much variation among districts and among categories.

A second methodology that can be used to recognize the costs of programmatic needs of categorical programs focuses on specifying the supplemental, replacement, and common costs for the overall programs. The analytical emphasis is on specifying which activities, resources, and costs are appropriate for each classification, and making subsequent adjustments to the regular and categorical program costs to reflect these changes.[10]

Supplemental services and costs are those that are in addition to the regular education program (e.g., special education resource room, vocational education counseling). The students who receive supplemental programs and services obtain the bulk of their education from the regular education program. The supplemental programs and services can be considered completely additional, since the students receive them while also attending the regular education program. Therefore, the costs of these programs are totally in addition to those of the regular program.

Replacement costs are for those programs and services that, in whole or in part, are substituted for the regular education program. The general procedure for determining these costs is to total the direct costs of the replacement education programs, but then to deduct the costs of the regular education programs and services that are replaced. This net cost is then the additional costs of the programmatic needs of students served by these programs. Such deductions may range from only the instructional component (for a separate categorical program classroom within a school) to the entire regular education cost (for programs provided by other agencies). The common costs for general services that are provided to all students (e.g., district administration, debt service) are generally allocated to all students or programs in a district on a pro rata basis.

The major difficulties in this approach to cost adjustment are with the replacement costs. The supplemental costs are additional by definition and would need to be included in any adjustment. With the common costs, care must be taken not to double-count (include them in both the regular program and in the cost adjustments for special programs) or omit them (not include them in either program costs). The initial and nontrivial problem with calculating replacement costs is deciding specifically which program components and services are being replaced in the regular program. Further, deduction of the average per-student replacement costs can be a misleading calculation. Many of the costs on a classroom level are fixed over the range of a few students per class and the reduction of several students would not appreciably change the costs of that regular classroom. Similarly, school-wide and district-wide service costs are not greatly affected by the reduction of a relatively small number of students. Rather than deducting the average costs per student of these components (which are relatively easy to calculate from student and financial records), the marginal costs per student would be the correct deduction. Unfortunately, marginal costs per student are generally unknown since they are not collected or reported by financial accounting systems in education. They will, however, certainly be much smaller than the average costs per student.

The final cost methodology used in studies of categorical programs is that of the resource-cost model (RCM). The focus of this approach is on the specification in programmatic terms of the educational program to be provided, i.e., the total special education types and numbers of students to be served, definition of programs in terms of resources, allocation of eligible students to various programs, student/teacher ratios, etc. Consequently, the program costs are explicitly derived from the structure of the educational program. It is this resource-cost model that is more fully developed in the next section.

A Conceptual Framework for Addressing Programmatic Cost Differences in Education

Equity and Cost Adjustments in School Finance

In recent years policymakers have come to believe that school finance equalization should not be limited to improving the distribution of nominal differences in school spending, but rather should be directed toward improving the distribution of "real" educational services. Indeed, from this perspective, some nominal variations in school spending may be justified on the basis of uncontrollable variations in the prices of school resources, differing needs of student populations, variations in the scale of school district operations, and variations in other locational, geographic, or demographic characteristics of school districts that affect the organization, coordination, and allocation of school resources. This justification for allowing differences in school spending suggests a concept of equity in school finance that extends beyond the more narrow conceptualization that has focused on distributions of general fund aid to local school systems and the relationship of this aid to fiscal and cost disparities for regular education programs. The extension involves simultaneous consideration of all sources of differences in educational costs that have traditionally been addressed through the development of categorical programs, whether these arise out of differences in resource prices or differences in pupil needs.

This section presents a systematic approach to the determination of the variations in the costs of providing educational services to different kinds and numbers of children. The analytical framework set out below may be used to examine differences in costs associated with serving students from different backgrounds, with varying language capabilities, with various handicapping conditions, of different grade/age levels, or with different vocational or educational aspirations. The model represents a systematic approach to costing out special education, compensatory education, vocational education, and bilingual education as well as elementary versus secondary education programs. In addition, the model provides an explicit mechanism for making adjustments for the systematic differences in the prices paid for school resources employed in these various programs. Moreover, the approach adopted below provides policymakers with a framework within which to examine the cost savings associated with different tradeoffs among resources, as well as a basis for considering tradeoffs among programs. (Unless otherwise indicated, policymakers generally refers here to state and federal level legislators or administrators.)

Although the model is general, many of the examples used to illustrate the various elements of the model focus on special education, and the empirical example presented will develop more explicitly how the model could be used for costing out special education programs for funding purposes.

The Resource-Cost Model (RCM)

Conventional wisdom suggests that different kinds and combinations of school resources will be required to provide educational services for pupils with varying educational needs. Unfortunately, the assessment of differences in educational costs associated with serving various student populations is not straightforward. If one could measure educational quality (outcomes) easily, and if the concept of educational quality were identical across the different student populations served (e.g., regular versus special education), there would be no difficulty in assessing educational cost differences across programs or across local school districts. However, neither of these conditions is easily satisfied. Educational quality is not easily measured and is likely to differ substantially across student populations served. The questions that need to be addressed in assessing the programmatic cost differences are:

- What characteristics of students reflect different educational needs?
- How do we objectively identify these characteristics among populations of students?
- How do we translate these educational needs of students into the resource requirements that define the programs necessary to ameliorate the particular problem?
- How do we determine the variations across local school districts in the prices of the resources of which these programs are composed?

Because of the difficulty in making any kind of objective comparison of the relative merits of these different pupil needs from the point of view of the larger society in which we live, some judgment will be necessary on the part of educational policymakers as to the relative priorities that these different student needs should be assigned. Moreover, it is likely, given the state of the art in understanding educational input-output relations, that there will be a considerable element of judgment by policymakers in determining what educational programs will look like. It is the purpose of this model to set out a conceptual framework that will facilitate the kinds of decisions that educational policymakers will have to make regarding the nature of educational programs directed toward different student populations.

There are three components in specification of the RCM: (1) assessment of student needs and program assignment; (2) specification of the input configurations corresponding to: (*a*) instructional programs and program units (*b*) instructional administration and operation of programs and (*c*) general administration and operations; and (3) determination of resource prices and total district costs.

School decision makers begin with an exogenously determined set of pupils to serve. This set of pupils is exogenous in the sense that both their numbers and their compositions with respect to certain observable characteristics are outside the control of the local school district. The objective of the school district in these circumstances is to assess pupil needs in some fashion (e.g., through testing or observation of behavior) and to determine some scheme by which to assign these pupils, classified according to some set of observable characteristics, to educational programs that meet their individual educational needs. There is not necessarily a one-to-one correspondence between the set of observable pupil characteristics and the combinations of programs to which children might be assigned, and any one pupil might be assigned to more than one program.

An educational program in this context is defined as a type of educational delivery system that involves a designated input configuration for the delivery of educational services. While the "program" defines the general nature of the delivery system, the "program unit" is simply one such representative educational setting or location such as a self-contained elementary or a special education classroom. For our purposes, it is important to point out that by "program" we do not mean the process or curriculum by which educational services are produced. Program and program units are defined only in terms of the levels of the inputs assigned to them, but not according to the way in which the inputs themselves are used to produce educational outcomes. For example, a program unit might specify the number of teachers, teachers' aides, desks, books, and other materials used in a special education classroom, but it does not necessarily imply what methods are employed in the classroom to develop cognitive or affective skills. This is not to deny the importance of process and curriculum for ultimate educational outcomes, but rather simply to admit that such a refined specification of programs is beyond the scope of the present research effort.

Figure 8-1 illustrates the components and steps in the process of assembling the data required for the implementation of the RCM approach. The boxes are numbered in the order of the decision process. What is described in Figure 8-1 is the process necessary to cost out the educational services provided by a given district. Some of the information presented will be unique to the district (e.g., student counts in different categories), while other information such as program configurations represent standardizations that must be imposed on all districts within a state for the purposes of funding and perhaps service delivery. The relationship between funding and service delivery and the implications for equity in school finance are discussed more extensively in a subsequent section of this paper. The discussion below provides a description of each of the boxes contained in Figure 8-1 in the order that they appear in the diagram.

Box (1). The process of program specification begins with box (1), which contains the actual distribution of pupils in a given district according to some set of observable "need" characteristics. This step is intended to identify the number of pupils who possess a particular combination of characteristics. These characteristics are referred to as "need" characteristics because they are intended to reflect, or at least be related to, some specific dimensions of educational need, and will ultimately be relevant in identifying program assignments. While the counts themselves are unique to the district, it will be the responsibility of the state, or perhaps federal level policymakers, to identify precisely which characteristics of students are important for this purpose. For example, in considering funding for special education, one would begin the process by identifying children according to various handicapping conditions, while for consideration of funding for compensatory education, one would want to identify children who are low achievers or are from families eligible for AFDC payments. While these particular "need" characteristics may not reveal all the necessary information about programmatic needs, they are sufficiently objective that they may be counted fairly readily, and they do bear some relationship to educational needs.

Box (2). This step describes the assignment process that allocates students in the various need categories to educational programs or service delivery systems. Box (2) represents a matrix whose elements indicate the proportion of pupils with any given combination of need characteristics that are assigned to a particular instructional program (e.g., a special class or a resource room both of which are uniquely described by some combination of resources). From the standpoint of building the cost model, this matrix of assignment patterns may represent actual assignment patterns in the district or some standardized pattern of assignments imposed by the state. In the former case, the model incorporates data derived from local school district sources to determine the actual assignments of children to programs. In this particular instance one may actually begin the determination of district costs in box (3), described below. While using district information on student assignment to programs would provide a more accurate basis for the determination of educational costs, procedures for allocating children among programs are not likely to be uniform across districts. That is, two districts may well assign children who are virtually identical to different instructional programs as a result of different procedures for assignment or differences in perceptions of those responsible for making program assignments. Moreover, use of such district information would require some auditing of district counts in order to ensure that they do not reflect higher proportions of assignments to "high cost" programs than actually exist. The district could actually profit (i.e., be overfunded) from such an arrangement.

An alternative to using actual district data on program assignments is the establishment of a standardized assignment pattern. Based on state-wide averages or some other conventional wisdom about assignment patterns, policymakers could develop a standardized matrix that would be used to allocate students in particular need categories among instructional programs. Alternatively stated, this standardized matrix would be used in conjunction with actual district counts on the numbers of pupils in various need categories (box 1) to determine the number of pupils for which the district will be funded in each instructional program. While

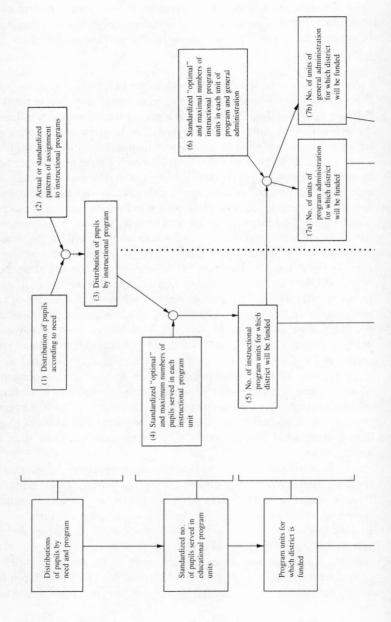

Figure 8-1. Diagram of the Resource-Cost Model

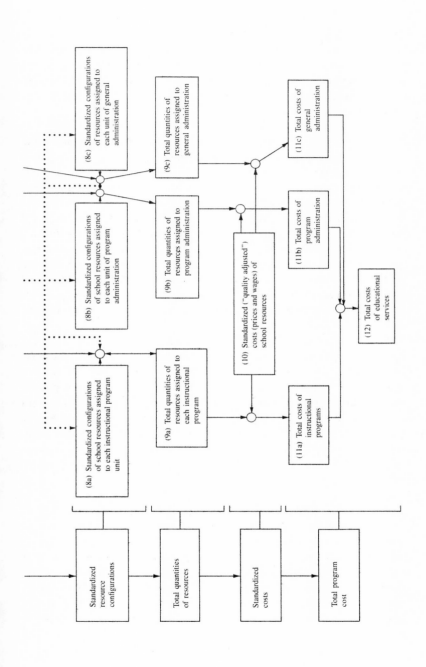

the standardized assignment matrix reduces the accuracy of educational costs to the extent that the actual assignment patterns differ across districts, it is based on procedures for identifying children in various need categories that are likely to be more uniform across districts than the varying procedures individual districts actually use for allocating children to programs.

Box (3). Combining boxes (1) and (2) through multiplication results in box (3), which contains the distribution of pupils across instructional programs for which the district will be funded. Note that this is a duplicated count since pupils may be assigned to more than one program. For example, in the case of special education, some children will spend part of their school days in mainstreamed classrooms and part in resource rooms or supplementary instructional programs. Thus, any one student, because he/she may be served in more than one program, will contribute to the determination of the number of instructional program units to be funded for each program. The time (proportionately) a student must spend in a program before he/she is counted as being served by the program is a necessary policy decision in the implementation of this step.

Box (4). Step 4 in the process of building this cost model involves specification by educational policymakers of the "optimal" and maximum numbers of pupils that may be served in each instructional program unit. "Optimal" is used in this context to represent the policymakers perceived ideal number of students to be served in each program unit (e.g., classroom or therapy session). The maximum number of pupils permitted (for funding purposes) to be served is provided for in order to allow policymakers to establish some upper limit on the number of pupils that may "adequately" be served within a given classroom or other instructional situation.

Box (5). The total number of pupils in a given program (box 3) combines with the optimal and maximum numbers of pupils (box 4) to determine the number of instructional program units for which the district will be funded (box 5). It is at this stage of the process that the role of the optimal and maximum numbers of pupils permitted in an instructional unit becomes apparent. First, one determines how many instructional units would be necessary to serve all children assigned to any given program in the optimal size unit. This is determined by simply dividing the total number of pupils assigned to a program by the optimal unit (class) size. Second, since the result of this division may not yield an even number of units, this number will have to be rounded off to the whole number of units that provides the fewest program units to be funded while ensuring that no unit would have to exceed the maximum size.

Note that while the number of pupils is instrumental in the determination of the number of instructional program units, the emphasis for purposes of funding of educational programs is on the number of program units rather than on the number of pupils served per se. The advantage of this approach is that it recognizes the discontinuous nature of costs with respect to the numbers of students. In many cases, adding an additional student to a particular classroom has virtually no significant impact on programmatic costs. By the same token, this approach also explicitly recognizes the fact that as the number of students served within a particular program expands, there is going to come a point when another entire classroom (program) unit will have to be added—in particular at the point where at least one of the units is forced above the maximum students allowed in a program unit.

Box (6). This step in the process involves the specification of the "optimal" and maximum numbers of instructional program units necessary to define a unit of program or general district administration. Program administration refers not only to supervisors and directors involved in program development and operations, but also to personnel involved in support of direct instructional activities (e.g., psychologists and specialists in curriculum). General administration refers to support and administrative services that apply across all programs within a school or throughout the district. From these brief descriptions, the diagrammatic representation of this step in the process is quite simplified since there are likely to be a variety of kinds of program or general administrative units that would apply (e.g., support services for speech programs, special education administration, school site administration, the office of the superintendent).

In actual practice the relationship between instructional program units or resources and the level of administrative and support services is likely to be nonlinear. This nonlinear relationship would result from the recognition that districts of relatively small size will have greater administrative burdens than larger districts, simply because of the diseconomies of small scale operation. There are a number of alternative approaches to building the recognition of these kinds of diseconomies into the RCM. The numerical example developed later in this paper, however, ignores these issues to simplify the exposition.

Boxes (7a) and (7b). In a manner comparable to the way boxes (3) and (4) combined to determine (5), box (5)—the number of instructional program units for which the district will be funded—and box (6)—the optimal and maximum numbers of instructional units per unit of program and general administration—combine to determine the number of units of program administration (box 7a) and the number of units of general administration (box 7b) for which the district will be funded.

Boxes (8a), (8b), and (8c). These boxes represent the decisions of educational policymakers regarding the standardized configurations of various kinds of personnel and nonpersonnel resources required to define each instructional program unit and each unit of program and general administration. The resource configurations themselves will specify on a per-unit basis (whether we are referring to an instructional or administrative unit) the numbers of full-time equivalent personnel of different types (e.g., teachers, teachers' aides, special education coordinators, curriculum specialists), the quantities of various pieces of specialized equipment or materials, and the dollar amounts allocated to other less specific categories of school resources (e.g., supplies). Decisions about resource configurations for each of the various educational programs will be based on some concept of "best practice" within the confines of state and local budget constraints for educational services. This determination of what constitutes "best practice" (not necessarily the same as "current practice") will likely be a complex process of interaction between the state level educational policymakers, the educational professionals who provide the services, parents, and other major interest groups that have specific knowledge and concern about effective and equitable education. It is important to stress that these resource configurations are not likely to be done independently of overall constraints on educational budgets. As will be seen as we proceed through the diagram, if the total educational costs exceed available revenues, some modifications of these standard resource configurations will be necessary in order to bring costs in line with budgets. However, the starting point for this analysis could well be policymakers' concept of the ideal programs for serving all children.

Note that a dotted line has been drawn from box (3), reflecting the numbers of students in the various programs, to boxes (8a), (8b), and (8c). The purpose of this line is to indicate that the model can explicitly take account of the number of students actually served in the specification of the resource configurations. Where there are sufficient numbers of students served in each program, this line would be irrelevant and resource configurations would be done on a per-unit basis only. However, in districts serving very small numbers of pupils, either in terms of total district size or with respect to certain programs, the model explicitly recognizes the fact that resource configurations may well have to be modified to reflect the smaller numbers of students. For example, a special class for special education children might normally take 10 children and would include a teacher and a teacher's aide as well as other resources. However, suppose that the district only had three pupils in total that would be served by such a program. Even though a normal unit of this kind of program might include the teacher's aide, in the special circumstance of this district with so few pupils, one might want to exclude the teacher's aide from the standard configuration. Similarly, a very small school may not require a full-time principal, but rather might do fine with a part-time principal who taught during the remainder of the day. In essence, the RCM approach may be easily adapted to circumstances to account for diseconomies resulting from small scale operations.

The RCM can also be designed to offer local school districts alternative ways (delivery systems) for providing the same basic set of services. As an example of the ways such flexibility might be incorporated into the program structure and student assignment procedures of the RCM, students in "home and hospital" programs are being served in at least two alternative ways in Florida school districts. In one approach, children are being served in the usual way by traveling teachers who visit children and provide instruction in their own homes or hospitals. Each such teacher is assigned a specific caseload to serve. Clearly, this is a very expensive program relative to the standard self-contained, or departmentalized, modes of instruction in which the children would be placed under normal circumstances in the district. However, in another approach, children in the home and hospital programs are being served by transmitting regular instruction from a central location via television connections that are installed in the homes or hospital rooms for these children. The cost of this alternative technology is considerably lower. Nevertheless, it may turn out that some districts will have more limited access to such technologies than other districts and would not have the choice. The RCM offers the flexibility to allow districts the alternative approaches to serving these home and hospital children while, at the same time, providing a more accurate representation of the costs of the alternative technologies to these different school districts. Thus, the RCM can provide for a variety of alternative ways in which local districts might offer instructional services to children, depending on local conditions as well as local preferences that the state would consider legitimate.

Boxes (9a), (9b), and (9c). Having defined the per-program unit resource configurations in boxes (8), one need only multiply these requirements by the total number of instructional or administrative program units to determine the total quantities of instructional and administrative resources for which the district will be funded.

Box (10). Having determined the total quantities of resources for which the district will be funded, we now need to translate the information into programmatic costs. For this step in the process, we will need to define and specify some standardized wage and price levels of the personnel and nonpersonnel resources, respectively. The importance of standardizing wages arises out of the fact that not all districts are equally effective, for reasons quite beyond their control, in attracting school personnel.[11] Previous studies of resource price differences in education have shown that in order to attract the same kinds ("qualities") of teachers, districts located in regions exhibiting relatively higher costs of living or a poorer quality of life (e.g., poorer climate or higher crime rates), or districts serving relatively high proportions of low ability or disadvantaged pupils, have to pay relatively higher salaries than districts located in regions with low costs of living, with a better quality of life, and serving a more attractive pupil clientele.[12] Similar patterns of wage differentials have also been shown to hold with respect to virtually all categories of school personnel.

In addition to the differential costs of personnel, districts located in different regions of a state might also have to pay different prices for other resources such as energy to heat, cool, and light classrooms.

Moreover, they may require greater levels of energy consumption to compensate for climatic differences.

With the addition of box (10) to the model, one can see that the RCM not only accounts for the differences in educational costs arising out of differences in the combinations of resources required to serve various student populations, but also for those differences in costs arising out of the differences in the wages and prices necessary to employ similar kinds and qualities of educational resources. The simulated wages and prices used in the RCM arise out of the analysis of the development of a "cost-of-education index". The RCM integrates this analysis of educational cost differences into the analysis of programmatic cost differences associated with differential pupil needs.

Boxes (11a), (11b), and (11c). This step simply involves multiplying the total quantities of resources by the standardized wages and prices to arrive at the total costs of instructional programs.

Box (12). Summing these individual components of cost finally brings us to the figure representing the total costs of educational services for the district. As one can see, there is a good deal of standardization involved in this ultimate calculation, and it is possible to prepare computer programs that, while being tedious, are relatively straightforward conceptually. Such programs would permit policymakers to replicate this procedure for every school district or local educational agency within the state. Summing over the results of such a computation will provide state policymakers with an estimate of the total costs of educational services throughout the state. It is at this stage of the analysis that comparisons of costs and state budgets can occur and decisions can be made regarding tradeoffs of the education budget with other components of state services (e.g., welfare, transportation, health), or tradeoffs of resources within the educational budget that might reduce the overall costs.

It should be emphasized that the model primarily provides a decision-making structure for educational policymakers that will allow them to conduct sensitivity analyses of alternative policies for the provision of adequate educational programs to alternative student populations. From a funding perspective, policy decisions could enter the model in any one of the following places:

- Definitions of student eligibility for various need categories.
- The assignment process described in box (2).
- The determination of the optimal and maximum numbers of pupils served in instructional units and the optimal and maximum numbers of instructional units that define units of program and general administration (boxes 4 and 6).
- The formula that determines the number of program units for which districts will be funded (boxes 5, 7a, and 7b).
- The resource configurations for instructional programs, program administration, and general administration (boxes 8a, b, and c).

The model does not require precise knowledge about the educational effects of any of the alternative specifications. It does require policymakers to be specific and clear about their judgments regarding the appropriateness of particular instructional programs and, at the same time, provides them with detailed information on precisely what their judgments and policy decisions will cost.

An Empirical Illustration of the Resource-Cost Model

The purpose of this section is to illustrate the process of constructing an estimate of the cost of educational services as prescribed by the resource-cost model. We have chosen to illustrate these calculations for a single hypothetical school district providing only special education and regular education programs. This simplification should facilitate the explanation of the application of the RCM without losing any of the generality of the concept and approach as it might be applied in circumstances involving a wider variety of educational settings and programs. Extension of the model to these other programs, across all school districts, could be used to establish a cost-based funding approach for educational services.

The purpose of this process is to determine the funding to be provided to the district for various educational programs. The underlying tenet of this approach is that funding amounts should be based on the costs to the district of providing the instructional programs. Consequently, the RCM process concentrates on student and program characteristics and related policy choices that influence costs and funding levels. In this example, the steps necessary to determine the RCM funding system, including the basic data requirements and necessary policy decisions, are presented for a sample district. Although the specific data in the example are hypothetical, they have been drawn from actual district and state data and are representative of a district special education program.

The first step in the process is for the state to establish a scheme of student classification to be used to identify handicapped students and determine their educational needs. This takes the form of a set of categories of handicapping or exceptional conditions recognized by the state and generally formalized in statutes and/or regulations. This step has been completed in practically all states, although it may be appropriate to review the existing categories for possible modifications. For the most part, all that will be necessary in this step is to specify what categories are in use, and to recognize that this will be an important dimension along which data will need to be collected and reported. The categories selected for our example include: educable mentally retarded (EMR); trainable mentally retarded (TMR); physically handicapped (Phy Hc); speech impaired; deaf; visually handicapped (Vis Hc); seriously emotionally disturbed (SED); specific learning disabilities (SLD); profoundly handicapped; gifted; and homebound and hospitalized (Home/Hosp). All other students in the district were considered to be regular students for the purposes of this sample.

The second step is to specify the number of students currently served (i.e., to be funded) for each of these categoires at the district level. These data are usually readily available from existing district records and/or frequently required reports to the state and federal education agencies. The student numbers can either be in enrollments (membership, average daily attendance) or full-time equivalents (FTE), but whichever is chosen must remain consistent throughout the remainder of the funding calculation process (e.g., number of teachers, students served in one program unit). District enrollments of exceptional students and regular students in the example are shown in Table 8-1 in the student unduplicated count column.

The third step involves establishing a standard set of instructional programs in which exceptional children will be served. This should be done at the state level and made sufficiently general to apply across all districts. This represents an important policy decision, as the funding to districts will be based on this set of programs. For this example, four basic types of programs were established based on the amount of time students spend in each program, the particular set of resources utilized

Table 8-1. Category/Program Placement Matrix
(figures in parentheses indicate proportion of unduplicated student count)

Students	Unduplicated student count	Instructional Programs										
		Self-contained class				Special class			Resource room		Supplemental instruction	
		Regular class	Basic special education configuration	Physically hc or profound	Emotionally disturbed	Basic special education configuration	Physically hc or profound	Emotionally disturbed	Basic special education configuration	Gifted	Basic special education configuration	Home and hospital
Exceptional												
EMR	181					181 (1.0)						
TMR	42		42 (1.0)									
Physically handicapped	54			20 (0.37)			34 (0.63)					
Speech	356	356 (1.0)									356 (1.0)	

Classification	Deaf	Visually handicapped	Emotionally disturbed	Specific learning disabilities	Profoundly handicapped	Gifted	Home and hospital	Subtotal	Regular (and all other)	District Total
Deaf	24 (0.83)								5 (0.17)	29
Visually handicapped		6 (0.55)							5 (0.45)	11
Emotionally disturbed			33 (0.33)				10 (0.10)		56 (0.57)	99
Specific learning disabilities				35 (0.14)					221 (0.86)	256
Profoundly handicapped					17 (1.0)					17
Gifted						212 (1.0)				212
Home and hospital							17 (1.0)			17
Subtotal	47	37	10	246	34	33	282	212	850	1,274
Regular (and all other)								356	12,004 (1.0)	12,004
District Total	47	37	10	246	34	33	282	212	12,854	13,278

in each program, and the number of students per unit in each program. These programs are (1) self-contained class (greater than 20 hours per week); (2) special class (from 12 to 20 hours per week); (3) resource room (from five to twelve hours per week); and (4) supplemental instruction (less than five hours per week). In fact, these four basic programs are extended to 11 different program configurations to reflect the special resources required to meet the educational needs of certain categories of handicapped children.

The next step involves identifying the program placements for each student category. This is done through the use of a matrix with the categories as the rows and the instructional programs as the columns. Working down the matrix one category at a time, the district would specify or report to the state the number of students in that category in each of the programs. Table 8-1 shows the results of this process for this example. Not all programs are appropriate for all categories and empty cells indicate that there are no students of that category placed in that program. For example, EMR students were reported only in the special class program, specific learning disability students were reported in the regular self-contained class, special class and resource room programs, and the regular students were all assumed to be in regular self-contained classes.

Note that the sums of the proportions of students in various need categories assigned to educational programs exceeds one in some cases. This reflects the fact that students are assigned to more than one educational program during any given day. For example, five of the students listed as visually handicapped are shown to spend a portion of their day in a regular education self-contained classroom, while the other portion of their day is spent in a resource room. These students are, for the purpose of program assignments, counted twice.

Our example assumes the use of the actual district placements of exceptional children in instructional programs. To reduce district incentives to choose placements for revenue maximization rather than student need, it may be necessary to place state controls or limits on the distribution patterns of students to programs. An alternative would be to establish a single statewide pattern for *funding* purposes only. This standard pattern would be applied to all districts' exceptional student populations to establish a standardized distribution of students among program placements on which to calculate state aid. Given the present requirements that districts prepare an individual education program

(IEP) for each special education student, the goal of obtaining data on actual student placements in instructional programs is probably more reasonable than the standardized assignment approach.

The next step requires the specification of the input configurations for each of the instructional programs. It is the critical policymaking step in the process since the results determine the funding levels for the programs. In actual practice, it would be appropriate for the specification of the input configurations to be done at the state level with consultation from district personnel and to be based on available cost and student data.

The specification process focuses on defining a "unit" of each program, which is the basic instruction module, and is usually centered around a single teacher. Two separate, but related, components are involved. First is the establishment of the number of students that can be served by one unit of each program. In order to allow for some flexibility in student assignment within districts, it is necessary to specify an optimal (or ideal) number of students per unit. These represent judgments by the policymakers on what the appropriate values should be and can be aided by knowledge of current and exemplary practices, state regulations, experience, and the fiscal effects of different values. The second component of this step is the specification of what resources make up one unit of each program. This requires identification of both the personnel and nonpersonnel resources that comprise the different units. This specification includes the type of resources, their characteristics, and quantities in the units. For example, types of resources may include teachers of various qualifications, instructional aides, other support personnel, materials and supplies, travel, classroom operation and maintenance. In specifying the students per unit and the resource configurations of the various programs, one further consideration is important—the time period for the program. By this is meant the shortest period of time in which the full number of students specified are served by the unit. In the four basic programs in the example this would mean:

1) Self-contained class—one day, since this is a full day, every day program for students placed here.
2) Special class—one day, again, students in this placement receive instruction every day in this program.
3) Resource room—one week, since this is a part-time program for stu-

Table 8-2. Specification of Input Configurations

| | Resource Quantities | | | | | | | No. of students per unit | |
| | Personnel (units) | | | Nonpersonnel ($) | | | | | |
Instructional programs	Teacher	Aide	Other professionals	Purchased services	Materials and supplies	Other	Equipment	Optimal	Maximum
Self-contained class									
Basic configuration	1.0	1.0	0.15	100	700	150	200	8	10
Physically or profoundly handicapped	1.0	2.0	0.20	200	1000	200	500	8	10
Emotionally disturbed	1.0	1.5	0.30	150	700	150	200	6	9
Regular class	1.0	—	0.05	50	500	100	100	26	28
Special class									
Basic configuration	1.0	1.0	—	100	600	150	100	11	14
Physically or profoundly handicapped	1.0	1.5	0.05	200	900	200	300	9	11
Emotionally disturbed	1.0	1.0	0.20	150	600	150	100	10	12
Resource room									
Basic configuration	1.0	—	—	50	600	100	100	20	25
Gifted	1.0	—	—	100	600	100	100	40	50
Supplemental instruction									
Basic configuration	1.0	—	—	100	500	250	50	50	60
Home and hospital	1.0	—	—	50	200	200	50	10	12

dents and they do not necessarily receive room services daily, it is assumed that the teacher will see all students assigned to this program within the course of one week.

4) Supplemental instruction—also a part-time program with a one week cycle of instruction for the teacher to serve the assigned number of students.

The example of this specification process is given in Table 8-2. For each of the four instructional programs the basic input configuration is specified in terms of quantities for appropriate teachers, aides, and other professional personnel, and the amounts of other nonpersonnel resources in the given unit. To illustrate with Table 8-2: the basic configuration of the self-contained class is defined as having one teacher, one aide, the equivalent of 15 percent of a support person (a more detailed breakdown would reveal that this fraction is composed of .10 FTE school social worker and .05 FTE counselor), and standardized amounts of nonpersonnel resources ($100 for purchased services, $700 for materials and supplies, etc.). Additionally, the optimal and maximum number of students that can be served by one self-contained class are given as eight and ten, respectively. By contrast, the basic configuration of the resource room provides for one teacher, no other personnel resources, and smaller standardized amounts per week, of 20 and 25 respectively, represent the number of students served by a resource room teacher during the course of one week.

Each of the four major instructional programs has more than one basic configuration specified, however. All in all there are actually 11 programs for which input configurations were specified in the example. For the self-contained class, separate specifications have been made for physically handicapped or profoundly handicapped, for emotionally disturbed (ED), and for regular students. The reason for this is that the needs of the various types of students placed in this basic type of program may be sufficiently different from one another to necessitate different input specifications. In comparison to the basic configuration, the physically handicapped self-contained class has an additional aide, slightly more allocation of other professionals, and higher amounts of nonpersonnel resources, particularly equipment, in order to accommodate the needs of these students. The other reason for a separate specification would be the use of different numbers of students per unit values. In the resource room specifications, for example, the basic and the

Table 8-3. Calculation of Instructional Units

Instructional program	Category	No. of students	Optimal students per unit	Average units	Rounded down units	Students (rounded down units)	Maximum students per unit	Below maximum?	Allowable units
Self-contained	TMR	42	8	5.2	5	8.4	10	Yes	5
	Phys. hc.	20	8	2.5	2	10.0	10	Yes	2
	Deaf	5	8	.6	0	—	10	No	1
	ED	10	6	1.7	1	10.0	9	No	2
	Profound	17	8	2.1	2	8.5	10	Yes	2
	Regular	12,854	26	494.4	494	26.0	28	Yes	494
Special class	EMR	181	11	16.5	16	12.9	14	Yes	16
	Phys. hc.	34	9	3.8	3	11.3	11	No	4
	Deaf	24	11	2.2	2	12.0	14	Yes	2
	Vis. hc.	6	11	0.5	0	—	14	No	1
	ED	33	10	3.3	3	11.0	12	Yes	3
	SLD	35	11	3.2	3	11.7	14	Yes	3
Resource room	Vis. hc.	5	20	0.25	0	—	25	Yes	0
	ED	56	20	2.8	2	28.0	25	No	3
	SLD	221	20	11.0	11	20.1	25	Yes	11
	All hc.	*282*	*20*	*14.1*	*14*	*20.1*	*25*	*Yes*	*14*
	Gifted	212	40	5.3	5	42.4	50	Yes	5
Supplemental instruction	Speech	356	50	7.1	7	50.9	60	Yes	7
	H & h	17	10	1.7	1	17	12	No	2

gifted configurations have almost the same resource quantities specified, but the number of students per unit is doubled in the resource room for gifted students. In the language of the general RCM model, each of these separate specifications represents a different program.

The next step is to determine the number of program units that the district is allowed for funding purposes. Ideally, each unit would be of optimal size, but this is not likely to be possible in an actual district because of uneven distributions of students. Therefore, the procedures have been designed to allow for the fewest number of program units while ensuring that no single unit exceeds the maximum.

The calculation of the number of allowable program units involves the number of students in the category/program matrix (Table 8-1) and the optimal amd maximum numbers of students per unit for the program (from Table 8-2). The calculation process is demonstrated in Table 8-3. First, the number of students of a given category in a given program placement (e.g., TMR in self-contained class = 42) is divided by the optimal number of students in a unit of that program (e.g., 8 for the basic configuration which applies to TMR). The resulting number of units (e.g., 5.2) is rounded down to a whole number of units (e.g., 5 units) since it is assumed for the example that only complete units will be funded. A check is then performed to see if the rounding down results in the number of students divided by the rounded down number of units yielding an average number of students per unit (e.g., 42 ÷ 5 = 8.4) greater than the maximum number of students per unit allowed (e.g., 10 for TMR in a self-contained class). If it does not, then the allowable units are equal to the rounded down number of units (e.g., 5 units). If it does exceed the maximum, then one is added to the rounded down number of units to obtain the allowable units (e.g., physically handicapped in a special class goes from a rounded down number of units of 4 to meet this criterion).

It is important to emphasize at this point the focus on program units as the basis for cost and funding determination rather than on a per-student basis. This approach more closely approximates the actual district situation in which the marginal cost of one additional pupil, in general, is close to zero, until the maximum class size is exceeded. At that time, there is a large increase in costs as a full additional unit is added.

There may arise instances in which the district has too few students in a certain category to qualify for even one unit of a given program; that is, there are fewer students than the optimal number of students per unit. There are several alternatives when this occurs: (*a*) always allow one unit of the program if there are any students in the category/ program combination; (*b*) allow one unit of the program if the number of students equals, say, half or more of the optimal number and disallow a unit with fewer students than this number; (*c*) disallow a unit if the program has fewer than the optimal number of students and expect the students to be placed with students of different handicaps in the requested program (e.g., deaf with profoundly handicapped in self-contained classes), or to be placed with students of the same handicap in a different program (e.g., deaf from self-contained in with deaf in special classes); or (*d*) modify the specification of the input configuration to adjust for fewer students. Different decision rules may be appropriate for different categories and programs, or to fit different state or district preferences. In the example, the second alternative was used for simplicity. The numbers of both the deaf students in the self-contained class and the visually handicapped students in the special class exceeded half of the optimal number of students per unit for these programs, so one unit was allowed for each. On the other hand, the number of visually handicapped students in the resource room was only 25 percent of the optimal number of students per unit for this program, so no unit was allowed. It is assumed that the visually handicapped students will be placed with students of other handicapping categories in the resource room units that the district operates. In fact, this is a common practice for this program.

The generic nature of the resource room, in which it is often possible for a given resource room teacher to serve most categories of mildly handicapped students in a single setting, provides another alternative for calculating the number of allowable units. If it is felt that it is feasible to mix different categories of mildly handicapped students in a given resource room, then there is no need to calculate the number of program units by separate category. Rather, it would be easier and more realistic to calculate the number of allowable units based on the total number of handicapped students in the resource room program. This alternative calculation in which the handicapped students are summed is shown in parentheses in the example. The total number of allowable units is identical in this case, although this is not necessarily always the case. In fact, if there is a difference, separate calculations by handicap will yield a higher number of allowable units.

In a similar fashion, it is now necessary to specify and determine the requirements for supervision and administration of the instructional programs. This involves the same process of establishing the supervision and administrative programs (or functions) that are to be provided and funded, specifying the input configurations of each of these programs, and calculating the number of allowable units of each program. For the sake of the example, these activities have been simplified into only two functions—administration of instructional programs and general administration. In actual practice, a much more detailed identification would be made and would include in program administration functions all of the supervisory, support, curriculum, and coordination activities necessary to operate and direct the instructional programs; and in the general administration functions all of the overall district activities and services such as executive administration, fiscal services, personnel administration, health services, and planning and evaluation.

Table 8-4 provides the example specification of both the program and general administration activities. In each, the personnel and nonpersonnel resources are specified in terms of one unit of administration. Analogous to the instructional program unit, the administrative unit is centered around a manager and identifies the support personnel and services that are thought to be required for the unit to operate adequately. One unit of program administration, for example, has been specified to include a manager (e.g., supervisor, program coordinator), half-time clerical support, and half-time from another professional (e.g., school psychologist, curriculum specialist, school social worker, assessment person) for personnel resources, and dollar amounts for the various nonpersonnel resources totaling $3,400 per unit. In the example, the number of administrative units is a function only of the number of program units allowed the district. For every 12 instructional program units for special education, one exceptional administrative unit is allowed, with a maximum number of program units to exceptional administrative units of 14. Regular education program administration has an optimal program unit to administrative unit ratio of 15 and a maximum of 18. A more precise specification might also consider the number of students in the district by both category and program placement as well.

The calculation of the required number of program and general administration units for the district example is shown in Table 8-5. In an identical procedure to that of instructional programs, the allowable administrative units are determined by dividing the number of instructional program units by the optimal program unit to administrative unit

Table 8-4. Program and General Administration Specification

| | Resource Quantities | | | | | | | | |
| | Personnel (units) | | | Nonpersonnel ($) | | | | Program units per administrative unit | |
Administrative unit	Manager	Clerical	Other pro-fessionals	Purchased services	Materials and supplies	Other	Equipment	Optimal	Maximum
Program administration									
Special	1.0	0.5	0.5	2,000	1,000	200	200	12	14
Regular	1.0	0.5	0	1,000	700	200	100	15	18
General administration									
Special	1.0	1.0	1.0	3,000	1,000	300	200	60	70
Regular	1.0	1.0	0	2,000	1,000	300	200	75	85

Table 8-5. Calculation of Program and Generation Administration Units

Administrative unit	No. of program units	Optimal ratio	Average units	Rounded down units	Program units per rounded down units	Maximum ratio	Below maximum?	Allowable units
Program Administration								
Special	69	12	5.75	5	13.8	14	Yes	5
Regular	494	15	32.9	32	15.4	18	Yes	32
General Administration								
Special	69	60	1.15	1	69.0	70	Yes	1
Regular	494	75	6.6	6	82.3	85	Yes	6

ratio, rounding the result down to the nearest whole number, and checking to see if this rounding down results in an average ratio exceeding the maximum. The outcomes indicate that for the overall exceptional program, five program administration units and one general administration unit will be allowed.

With the resource specification and the allowable number of units for the instructional programs, program administration, and general administration established, it is now possible to determine the district costs for each of these areas. In order to calculate the different program and total costs, it is necessary to establish the prices of each of the resources identified in the input configuration. For example, this includes personnel costs (salaries and benefits) for each of the different types of personnel specified. The nonpersonnel resource costs were originally specified in dollar amounts and these amounts can be used directly in the cost calculations. The process of establishing the personnel costs is illustrated in Table 8-6. For each personnel type a basic salary is determined; this amount would be specified by the state, after a thorough analysis of the average cost of the specified position given a standardized set of personal characteristics. It is at this point that the resource-cost indices are used to adjust the average salary figures. The teacher or other personnel cost indices are used to adjust salary levels for variations in the cost of attracting and employing personnel with similar personal characteristics to any particular job assignment. An example of the impact of such a wage adjustment is subsequently presented.

Note that a difference in average base salary is shown between special education teachers and regular education teachers. It was derived by examining the differences in salaries paid to special education teachers

Table 8-6. Examples of Personnel Costs

Type of personnel	Base salary	Benefits (20% of salary)	Personnel cost
Special education teacher	$16,320	$3,260	$19,580
Regular education teacher	16,000	3,200	19,200
Instructional aide	6,000	1,200	7,200
Other professional personnel	20,000	4,000	24,000
Program administrator			
Exceptional	24,000	4,800	28,800
Regular	25,000	5,000	30,000
General administrator	28,000	5,600	33,600
Clerical	10,000	2,000	12,000

versus regular education teachers, holding constant other characteristics such as years of experience, age, sex, race, degree level, personal circumstances related to mobility, district working conditions, and general district and regional characteristics relating to attractiveness and cost of living. The result indicated that on average the added cost of a special education versus regular classroom teacher was 2 percent. This is reflected in the $16,320 salary used for special education teachers and the $16 thousand salary for regular education teachers. To the base salaries, an amount equal to 20 percent was added to account for benefits. The sum of the base salary and benefits were used as the personnel costs by type of personnel.

To calculate the separate program costs, it is necessary to determine the number of various types of resources required by the allowed program units and multiply these amounts by the price of the resource. This procedure is shown in Table 8-7. For instructional programs for special education, the various allowable program units are arrayed by type of program and by category. The number of each of the types of personnel resources associated with the number of allowable program units is tallied along with the amount for nonpersonnel resources. For example, for TMR students in self-contained classes, five program units are allowed. This in turn requires five special education teachers, five aides, .75 (FTE) other professional personnel, and $5,750 in nonpersonnel resources (5 × $1,150/unit). The requirements for all of the special education programs are totaled; the example shows totals of 69 special education teachers, 48 aides, 3.10 other professional personnel, and $70,900 in nonpersonnel resources. These quantities are then multiplied by their respective prices to obtain the cost of instructional programs for special education—$1,842,000 in the example. Similar calculations are carried out for regular instructional programs, program administration, and general administration. The results from each program are then summed to arrive at the total district cost of $14,185,000. Thus, the example shows how district cost estimates are determined from student needs, program specification, and prices of resources.

It is important to reiterate at this point that the RCM funding system, which the example illustrates, is not only designed to establish district funding based on student needs, but to provide for differences in funding levels of districts with differing student needs. First, it should be clear that another district with the same number and mix of students and facing the same prices for resources would have calculated the same costs and received the same amount of funding.

Let us now extend the example to examine what would happen if there are differences between two districts in either the number and mix of students and/or price of resources. First, let us vary the students. For simplicity, only one category of exceptional students will be considered. Assume that: (*a*) a second district has the same total number of students and an identical student composition, except for the specific learning disability (SLD) category; (*b*) that instead of 256 SLD students, the second district has 400 (or 144 more SLD students); and (*c*) that 50 SLD students are assigned to special classes and 350 to resource rooms. What differences would this make in district costs?

To determine the effect of the greater number of SLD students on costs, it is first necessary to recalculate the allowable number of instructional program units for this category. Following the same procedure shown in Table 8-3, the allowable number of units for the special classes and resource rooms for SLD students increase by one and six respectively. The additional program units cause a cost increase of \$150,310. These additional program units also have an impact on the units required for program and general administration; the specific situation in the example causes both the program and general administration units to increase by one, which causes an additional \$124,300 in these costs. Therefore, the total district special education cost increase, because of the differences in the number of SLD students and their placements, is \$274,610. However, the placement of 15 additional students into special classes for SLD and out of regular education classrooms has a potential effect on regular education costs as well. (The SLD students in resource rooms are assumed to be already in regular education classrooms as their primary placement.) The reduction in the number of regular education students causes a reduction of one in the allowable units for instructional programs. Program administration and general administration units are not affected in this situation. The net cost reduction associated with the loss of one program unit is \$21,150 from the regular education costs. The net effect for the district for the increase in SLD students is a cost increase of \$253,460. Table 8-8 shows these calculations.

Next, the effect of changing the prices of resources between districts will be examined. Assume in this case: (*a*) that a second district has an

Table 8-7. Calculation of District Funding

Funding unit	Allocated units	Teachers		Aides		Managers		Clerical		Other professionals		Price of nonpersonnel resources ($)	Total Price ($)
		No.	Price ($)	No.	Price ($)	No.	Price ($)	No.	Price ($)	No.	Price ($)		
Instructional programs													
Special													
Self-contained													
TMR	5	5	97,900	5	36,000					.75	18,000	5,750	157,650
Phys. hc.	2	2	39,160	4	28,800					.40	9,600	3,800	81,360
Deaf	1	1	19,580	1	7,200					.15	3,600	1,150	31,530
ED	2	2	39,160	3	21,600					.60	14,400	2,400	77,560
Profound	2	2	39,160	4	28,800					.40	9,600	3,800	81,360
Special class													
EMR	16	16	313,280	16	115,200							15,200	443,680
Phys. hc.	4	4	78,320	6	43,200					.20	4,800	6,400	132,720
Deaf	2	2	39,160	2	14,400							1,900	55,460
Vis. hc.	1	1	19,580	1	7,200							950	27,730
ED	3	3	58,740	3	21,600					.60	14,400	3,000	97,740
SLD	3	3	58,740	3	21,600							2,850	83,190
Resource room													
Vis. hc.													
ED	3	3	58,740									2,550	61,290
SLD	11	11	215,380									9,350	224,730
Gifted	5	5	97,900									4,500	102,400

Supplemental instruction													
Speech	7	7	137,060									6,300	143,360
Home and hosp.	2	2	39,160									1,000	40,160
Price per resource			19,580		7,200								
Regular instruction													
Self-contained	494	494	9,484,800						24,000	24.7	592,800	370,500	9,855,300
Price per resource			19,200						24,000				
Program administration													
Special						5	144,000	2.5	30,000	2.5	60,000	17,000	251,000
Price per resource							28,800		12,000		24,000		
Regular						32	960,000	16	192,000			64,000	1,216,000
Price per resource							30,000		12,000				
General administration													
Special						1	33,600	1	12,000	1	24,000	4,000	73,600
Regular						6	201,600	6	72,000			21,000	294,600
Price per resource							33,600		12,000		24,000		
Total													
Special	75	69	1,351,020	48	345,600	6	204,000	3.5	42,000	6.6	158,400	91,900	2,166,520
Regular	532	494	9,484,800			38	1,161,600	22	264,000	24.7	592,800	455,500	11,958,700
District	607	563	10,853,820	48	345,600	44	1,543,200	25.5	306,000	31.3	751,200	547,400	14,125,220

Table 8-8. Cost Differences

	Number of students	Due to Additional SLD Students					Due to Lower Personnel Costs	Total
		Allowable units	1st District units	Difference	Cost per unit	Cost change*	Cost change*	
Special education								
Instructional programs								
Special class	50	4	3	+1	$27,730	$27,730	($35,420)	
Resource room	350	17	11	+6	$20,430	$122,580		
Subtotal						$150,310	($35,420)	$114,890
Program administration	76	6	5	+1	$50,200	$50,200	($4,680)	$45,520
General administration	76	2	1	+1	$74,100	$74,100	($1,400)	$72,700
Subtotal						$124,300	($6,080)	$117,220
Total special education cost difference						$274,610	($41,500)	$233,110
Regular education								
Instructional programs	12,839	493	494	−1	$21,150	($21,150)	($201,560)	($222,710)
Program administration	493	32	32	0			($23,040)	
General administration	494	6	6	0			($5,480)	
Total regular education cost difference						($21,150)	($230,080)	($251,230)
Total district cost difference						$253,460	($271,580)	($22,900)

*Negative numbers are in parentheses.

identical composition of students as the example district; (*b*) that the second district is in a different portion of the state and faces different wage requirements due to differences in cost of living or other factors which affect the ability of the district to attract similar personnel— specifically, that the salary costs for personnel with similar characteristics is 2 percent lower in the second district; and (*c*) that the nonpersonnel resource costs are the same for both districts. This 2 percent cost differential is derived from simulating the salaries required to attract similar kinds of personnel between the two districts, based on an econometric analysis of the patterns of variation in personnel compensation across local school districts within a state. Personnel cost indices would be used to adjust the wages paid to school personnel across all districts.[13] Now let's consider what the effect on total district costs would be of the lower personnel resource costs.

To determine the impact of wage differentials between the two districts, it is necessary to reduce personnel costs calculated for the first district by 2 percent. (An alternative procedure would be to recalculate the example district costs [Table 8-7], but include a wage index of .98 applied against personnel costs and calculate the difference between the two districts' total costs.) The results of this procedure are shown in Table 8-8. The calculations indicate that the impact of a 2 percent differential for the prices of personnel resources would reduce the total costs in the second district by $271,580 with the greatest effect in the regular education program.

As a final example, let us consider the two effects together—a comparison district facing both a different number and mix of students (SLD example) and a different price of resources (2 percent lower personnel costs). In this case, not only the cost implications of the individual effects must be determined, but additionally the joint effect of the differences in pupil needs and resource prices. The results of this process are shown in Table 8-8. The cost implications of the individual changes have already been presented in the two previous tables and they are simply repeated here. However, the joint effect is slightly more complicated. They involve the 2 percent wage adjustments to the personnel cost changes caused by the additional SLD students. First, the personnel costs in the additional special education units (instructional programs) also have to be reduced by 2 percent of the personnel costs, or $420. When combined with the two individual effects, the net cost difference for a district with the differences in student number and mix and in the prices of the personnel resources is a reduction of $22,900 from the example district.

Implications of the Model and Some Concluding Remarks

What we have proposed in the preceding pages is a model designed for the purpose of funding educational services provided by local school districts. The model emphasizes a resource-cost-based funding approach that explicitly recognizes systematic differences not only in the prices of schooling resources employed across districts in different locations, but also in the patterns of employing various school resources necessary to provide the kinds of educational programs directed at the different combinations of pupil needs. It implies that state and federal policymakers will need to take account explicitly of both differences in resource costs (prices) and programmatic differences in service costs in the distribution of state aid to local educational agencies. It also provides a rational basis for making fiscal decisions at the state level regarding the provision of funding for any given educational program or the entire package of educational programs to be offered by the state and provided by the local schooling organizations. With these issues in mind, let us now explore some of the virtues and limitations of the approach by examining its relationship to equity and efficiency considerations in school funding.

Equity Issues

The ultimate effort of school reform, whether limited to general education programs or extended to include categorical programs directed at special needs, is to improve the equity in the distribution of state aid to local districts for the provision of educational services. Would equal dollars to all districts provide an equitable distribution of state and/or federal funds to local districts? The answer to this rhetorical question is obviously no, on at least two counts. First, any two districts might be serving students with different educational needs and thus require different combinations of school resources and incur differential costs accordingly. Second, even if the two districts served the same combinations of children with respect to educational needs, one might find that they confront differences in the prices they have to pay to attract similar kinds of school resources (e.g., teachers or other school personnel).

234

Thus, it seems reasonable to conclude that a more equitable solution to the inequity of the school finance system would be to provide enough additional dollars to compensate for the higher costs incurred by districts serving pupils with special educational needs or districts located in regions exhibiting higher prices for school resources.

The proposed resource-cost model does just this. It provides an estimate of the additional costs of providing for special programmatic needs of pupils, and can incorporate into the cost and funding calculations the differences in resource prices paid by districts in different locations. It forces policymakers, at least at the state level, to think systematically about what an adequate educational program should look like for different kinds of children; and once they have defined what they believe is an adequate program, it requires a systematic distribution of resources according to pupil needs across districts serving various combinations of pupils. Districts in similar circumstances with respect to the combination of pupils according to educational needs, and the prices of school resources they face, are treated similarly; while districts serving different combinations of pupils and facing different resource prices are treated systematically differently.

Once we have accepted as reasonable the standardized resource configurations associated with serving the various programmatic needs of different pupils, then we can say that the resource-cost model treats districts, and ultimately the children they serve, equitably. However, there are serious and important limitations to this conception of equity that ought to be recognized by the state and/or federal policymakers considering such a funding approach. While it does provide a systematic framework within which one might consider relationships between educational inputs and outcomes, it in no way ensures that the distributions of resources to different districts or to different kinds of pupils will result in similar "life chances," or even similar educational outcomes. Obviously, this problem goes right to the heart of how one defines the concept of equity. At best, the model ensures that with respect to funding, similar students will be treated similarly and different students will be treated differently, where the differences have been identified and defined in terms of the perceptions of educational policymakers. It is the responsibility of these policymakers to identify (*a*) the kinds of differences in pupil needs that will be recognized, and (*b*) the differences in the program configurations that are "adequate" to meet these different needs. Whether or not the identification of students or specification of their needs is coincident with some more basic concept of educational outcomes or life chances is not essential to the development or implementation of the resource-cost model. Moreover, the resource-cost model does not imply any kind of attention paid to how programs are actually implemented. At one level, this means that no specification of curriculum and curriculum materials is included in the definition of a program, and there is no attempt to define what goes on inside programs in terms of instructional technology. Moreover, this resource-cost model approach could be implemented as strictly a funding mechanism with no required link to service delivery. Districts could be given a lump sum grant which simply accounts for the differences in resource prices and program configurations, and permitted to spend the funds as they please. Alternatively, districts might be given funds based on the RCM, but portions of which are earmarked for particular programs, and be told they could spend within programs in any way they please. Or finally, districts might be given funds and told to spend them according to the resource configurations specified in the construction of the funding allocations. In this last case, the delivery of services would simply mirror the resource configurations specified in the RCM.

If the RCM is used exclusively for funding purposes and there is no link to the actual delivery systems for educational services, the relationship between equity in funding and service delivery is obviously mitigated to some degree. The use of standardized patterns of student assignment among programs would further reduce the linkage of this funding mechanism to equity. Without accurate headcounts of students in programs by districts, it is not possible to tie costs to actual service delivery, and therefore a standardized matrix would be required indicating the proportion of different combinations of children (e.g., AFDC, non-English-speaking, educable mentally retarded) who are assigned to specific programs. This may or may not actually reflect the patterns of service delivery within a given district.

Efficiency Issues

The RCM provides a solid foundation for educational policymakers to make rational decisions regarding funding of educational services in local school districts. It provides a framework for specifying what policymakers regard as adequate educational programs to serve various pupil needs and provides a systematic mechanism for distributing funds across local districts. It also can serve as a planning device that can be used to make projections into the future as well as to evaluate current options for tradeoffs both within and between programs, to examine the cost of alternative delivery systems, and/or to reduce costs. To see how this tool might be used, it is useful to describe how the approach could be used to determine the funding for educational services within the state.

The state would specify all of the appropriate programs, count up the students served (or predicted to be served) by each of these programs within each of these districts, and price out the appropriate combinations of resources to arrive at not only a dollar figure required for each district, but also a total dollar figure required to provide the various programs for the state. This figure may be used by policymakers to trace out the relationships between potential patterns of service delivery and costs. This information could be used to arrive at final budget figures based on the willingness of policymakers to spend money to provide certain kinds of services. Policymakers are forced to think systematically about what the appropriate input configurations are to provide adequate educational services, and to make comparisons against alternative uses both within and across programs. From this perspective, it is clear that one cannot consider the funding of various programs in isolation from one another; they must be considered simultaneously. Policymakers will have to confront two facets of the comparisons across programs and the tradeoffs within programs. First, they will have to make some judgments about relationships between educational outcomes and inputs. Clearly, there is not likely to be much objective information upon which to base such judgments. Nevertheless, some perceptions of what the educational process yields in terms of outcomes for these various programs will have to be considered seriously in the debate. Professional judgments, perhaps based on observations of programs over time and discussions with educational professionals providing the services, will have to be made in order to begin to specify these programs.

Second, some value judgments will have to be made not only with respect to the various component outcomes associated wtih various educational programs (e.g., achievement test scores, or the acquisition of self-help skills by a mentally handicapped child), but also with respect to the importance of meeting the overall educational needs of different kinds of children (e.g., handicapped, disadvantaged, or those without special needs). Without more objective information about educational technologies and input-output kinds of relations (if such information is indeed obtainable), it will be virtually impossible to distinguish between the professional judgments about educational outcomes being produced versus the relative priorities placed on them.

Despite all of these difficulties, it still seems clear that the RCM provides a systematic framework within which these issues may be explicitly addressed. However, that in itself may present another difficulty. Policymakers (particularly elected officials) may not want these kinds of tradeoffs made so apparent to "outsiders," who might evalute their judgments. In the case of the RCM, any changes in the resource configurations, etc. from one year to the next, or from one proposed budget to the next within a given year, reveals quite explicitly the nature of the tradeoffs that have been made, not just in dollar terms (as is currently possible), *but also in terms of the specific resources devoted to children.* It frankly may not be that attractive to make these kinds of tradeoffs so apparent. Without more objective information on the educational effects of these tradeoffs, the numbers become open to widely varying interpretations by various interest groups and create potential difficulties for legislators considering budget allocations.

This does not mean that the RCM cannot be used in this context. Some policymakers may welcome this kind of framework for decision making. However, it may be well to suggest that the stage of the budgetary process at which this model gets implemented be carefully considered and that the ultimate funding decision made by a legislative body be simplified so as to avoid some of the technical arguments over educational program specification and political difficulties that could arise from these decisions. As an example, the state of Florida uses full-time equivalent (FTE) counts of pupils assigned to various "programs" in the funding of the state educational system. While the Florida funding approach differs in some important respects from the RCM, there is an interesting facet of the way in which it is implemented. Each FTE pupil receives a weight according to the "program" in which the pupil is served. This weight is in fact a per-pupil "cost factor." (For the purposes of this discussion it is not important how the "cost factor" is derived.) Therefore, the state can determine both unweighted and weighted FTE counts of pupils. A regular pupil in grades 4–9 is counted as one (1.0), while a deaf pupil is given a weight of 3.92. The legislature is then asked to attach a dollar figure to one FTE. In other words, the legislature attaches a dollar figure indicating the amount they are willing to spend on a per-pupil basis to educate a regular pupil in grades 4–9. The allocations among the various categorical programs may then be determined by simply looking at the weights associated with each type of educational program and the number of weighted FTE pupils assigned to each by district and for the state as a whole. Since the weights are based on "cost factors," the legislature never has to consider these tradeoffs (at least not on a year-to-year basis).

Some kind of similar technique could well be devised for the RCM, only it would more likely be based on a standardized unit of service rather than on a per-pupil basis.

Notes

1. See M. A. Thomas, "Finances: Without Which There Is No Special Education," *Exceptional Children* 39 (1972): 475–480; C. D. Bernstein, William T. Hartman, Michael W. Kirst, and R. S. Marshall, *Financing Educational Services for the Handicapped: An Analysis of Current Research and Practice* (Reston, Va.: Council for Exceptional Children, 1976).

2. For a detailed discussion of the advantages and disadvantages of these alternative funding approaches, see William T. Hartman, *Estimating the Costs of Educating Handicapped Children: A Resource-Cost Model Approach* (Ph.D. diss., Stanford University, 1979).

3. See Jay G. Chambers, "The Development of a Cost of Education Index: Some Empirical Estimates and Policy Issues," *Journal of Education Finance* 5 (Winter 1980): 262–281 and idem. "The Hedonic Wage Technique as a Tool for Estimating the Costs of School Personnel: A Theoretical Exposition with Implications for Empirical Analysis," *Journal of Education Finance* Vol. 6, No. 3 (Winter 1981).

4. Hartman, "Estimating the Costs of Educating Handicapped Children," chap. 4.

5. James S. Kakalik, Garry D. Brewer, L. A. Dougherty, P. D. Fleischauer, and S. M. Genensky, "Services for Handicapped Youth: A Program Overview," Report R-1210-HEW (Santa Monica, Ca.: Rand Corporation, 1972).

6. William T. Hartman, "Policy Effects of Special Education Funding Formulas," *Journal of Education Finance* 6 (Fall, 1980), 135–159.

7. Richard A. Rossmiller, James A. Hale, and Lloyd E. Frohreich, *Educational Programs for Exceptional Children: Resource Configurations and Costs* (Madison, Wisc.: Department of Educational Administration, University of Wisconsin, 1970).

8. Richard A. Rossmiller, "Financing Educational Programs for Handicapped Children," *Financing Educational Programs for Handicapped Children*, ed. Nancy Cain (Denver, Colo.: Education Commission of the States, 1974), p. 14.

9. For states mentioned, see Richard A. Rossmiller and Thomas Moran, "Programmatic Cost Differentials for Delaware School Districts" (Gainesville, Fla.: National Education Finance Project, 1973); Philip Jones and William Wilkerson, "Special Education Program Cost Analysis" (Bloomington, Ind.: Department of School Administration, Indiana University, 1972); National Education Finance Project, "Financing the Public Schools of Kentucky" (Gainesville, Fla.: National Education Finance Project, 1974); Governor's School Finance Study Group, "Mississippi Public School Finance" (Jackson, Miss.: Governor's School Finance Study Group, 1973); National Education Finance Project, "Fi-

nancing the Public Schools of South Dakota" (Gainesville, Fla.: National Education Finance Project, 1973); Tish Newman Busselle, "The Texas Weighted Pupil Study" (Austin, Texas: Texas Education Agency, 1973). For general studies, see Ronald W. Bentley, "An Exploration of the Relationships between Expenditures for Educational Programs for Exceptional Children and Expenditures for Regular Education Programs" (Ph.D. diss., University of Wisconsin, 1970); Dwayne E. Snell, "Special Education Program Cost Analysis for Three Selected School Corporations in Indiana" (Ph.D. diss., Indiana University, 1973); William P. McClure, Robert A. Barnham, and Robert A. Henderson, "Special Education: Needs—Costs—Methods of Financing" (Urbana: Bureau of Educational Research, College of Education, University of Illinois at Urbana-Champaign, 1975); Alfred L. Clemmons, "An Assessment of Cost Variations in Selected Exemplary Special Education Programs in Six Selected Minnesota School Districts" (Ph.D. diss., University of New Mexico, 1974).

10. Leigh S. Marriner, "The Cost of Educating Handicapped Pupils in New York City," *Journal of Education Finance* 3 (Summer 1977): 82–97.

11. For a more comprehensive theoretical discussion of the issues related to the development of resource price differences, see Chambers, "The Hedonic Wage Technique."

12. See Joseph R. Antos and Sherwin Rosen, "Discrimination in the Market for Public School Teachers," *Journal of Econometrics* 3, no. 3 (1975): 123–150; Chambers, "The Development of a Cost of Education Index"; and Lawrence W. Kenny, David Denslow Jr., and Irving J. Goffman, "Determination of Teacher Cost Differentials among School Districts in the State of Florida," *Selected Papers in School Finance 1975* (Washington, D.C.: Office of Education, U.S. Department of Health, Education, and Welfare, 1975).

13. See for example, Chambers, "The Development of a Cost of Education Index."

CHAPTER 9/

Projecting Special Education Costs

WILLIAM T. HARTMAN

Introduction

How much will it cost to implement PL 94-142, the Education for All Handicapped Children Act, of 1975, and similar state legislation that mandated an appropriate education for all handicapped children? This is a question that received curiously little attention from policymakers involved in the passage of special education legislation.[1] Similarly, the courts did not concern themselves greatly with the costs of carrying out their decisions, which have opened and expanded educational opportunities for handicapped children.[2] This is certainly understandable given the civil rights context in which successful judicial and legislative efforts to establish the educational rights of handicapped children were framed. These rights were not considered to have a price tag attached to them.

Compliance with the new laws, coupled with the prevailing legal and humanitarian attitudes, has resulted in very rapid growth of special education budgets in recent years.[3] However, the new and growing levels of special education funding are attracting greater attention from policymakers concerned with increasing costs. Education budgets are under strong pressures from tax and expenditure constraints (or threats of their passage), negative voter attitudes in school finance elections, and reduced federal funding. The luxury of spending "whatever it takes" for special education may well be gone. It is becoming increasingly important to understand the fiscal implications of special education laws at all government levels when planning future needs for funds and their allocation.

Estimation of the costs of educating handicapped children, particularly at the national level is a difficult and uncertain process. To begin, definitions of the eligible populations are not consistent among states. Differences in state laws and regulations include the handicapping conditions to be served, the specific requirements for eligibility, and the age ranges mandated or allowed.[4] These differences lead to wide ranges in the estimates of the relative occurrence of handicapping conditions (usually expressed as an incidence rate or percentage of the total population expected to be classified as handicapped) and in the number of handicapped children thought to need special education services.

A second difficulty is the lack of commonly accepted national standards for special education programs and services. This void stems from an inadequate theory of education and from disagreement among special education experts over appropriate treatments. The difficulty is compounded by an absence of reliable and generalizable data on the effectiveness of various educational programs and services for different types of handicapped students. This results in great variation in actual program practices at the local level. Consequently, even at the state level, it is often difficult to obtain commonality in the availability of various special education programs and services, the placement patterns of students in special education programs and services, and key operating measures such as the student/teacher ratios and the use of instructional aides in each of the special education programs and services. Further, educational accounting and reporting systems used by local education agencies are not designed to provide detailed programmatic information for special education on a regular basis.[5]

A third difficulty occurs with the use of reported special education cost data as the basis for future cost projections. As reported by school districts and aggregated by state education agencies, the reported costs are generally prepared for other purposes than cost analysis and contain many hidden and inconsistent treatments of cost data that can materially affect their validity.[6] Further, not all costs of special education may be reported by districts if they do not receive reimbursement for them, and accounting systems may not be able to identify special education costs adequately. A particular difficulty occurs with the common form of average cost per student. For example, a figure of $1,750 as an average cost per handicapped student in a given state probably conceals as much information as it provides. Within that average, costs for various types of students in different programs may vary from $250 for speech and language therapy to over $15 thousand for a residential program. The average figure gives no information on what types of students are being provided with what mix of programs and services. Further, because of price level differences among states, average costs for identical programs and services could vary substantially. Finally, even if the above difficulties could be resolved, the reported costs are historical data—a record of what costs were, not what they are expected to be. To be used for cost projection purposes, it must be assumed that the student population, program practices, and price levels that prevailed at the time the cost data were collected will continue essentially unchanged in the future. Otherwise, ajdustments to the historical cost data must be made to account for anticipated student program, and/or price changes—a difficult task when the historical composition of these elements is unknown. In sum, reported costs for special education, and particularly average cost per student figures, provide interesting, but incomplete information for cost estimation purposes.

As a result of these problems, there have been relatively few cost studies in special education and even fewer efforts to project the national costs of special education—for either the actual number of handicapped students served or for an estimate of the total handicapped population in need of special education.[7] For purposes of cost estimation and projection, past cost studies of special education have several shortcomings. Actual program practices were either obscured or unidentified in the methodological procedures. Past program practices and costs were extrapolated to project future costs. Use of aggregated average costs per student by type of handicap (the most common approach) hid large cost variations in actual practice. Neither future changes in special education practices nor the uncertainty associated with their happening were recognized. Consequently, the usefulness of either their methodology or empirical results is limited.

In order to deal with the difficulties inherent in estimating costs of special education and to avoid the limitations of previous studies, a resource-cost model (RCM) approach, as described in the previous chapter, was employed to develop national projections of the current and future costs of educating all school-aged handicapped children. A previous study by the author had demonstrated the feasibility of utilizing the RCM in this manner.[8] The results indicated a wide range of possible costs due to varying assumptions about student and program characteristics.

This chapter presents a detailed application of the RCM methodology to special education costs. The overall organization and process of special education formed the basis of the model used. The key student, program, resource, and price variables affecting special education costs

243

were developed from results of 28 states that had used the RCM for individual state special education cost projections. Values for each of these variables (e.g., incidence rates of handicapping conditions, student/teacher ratios, available instructional placements and related services, student placement patterns, use of instructional aides, non-personnel resources) were specified as an integral part of the analyses. Based on these data, most likely estimates of future special education costs were projected. In addition, a series of sensitivity analyses were conducted to determine those variables the magnitude and future uncertainty of which had the greatest impact on estimated costs. The results of the sensitivity analyses were then used to reestimate alternative low and high projections of special education costs in order to narrow the range of probable cost estimates to a more meaningful and useful variation for policymakers.

The policy implications of the study were considered along two dimensions: the policy uses of the results of the projections; and the policy uses of the RCM methodology. First, the effects of the magnitude of the projected costs were analyzed. In particular, the large increase in funds needed to implement fully the special education legislation and the possible sources of those funds were reviewed. Additionally, through the results of the sensitivity analyses, those aspects of the special education process that are both important to costs and that can be influenced or controlled by policymakers were identified as potential points of intervention in order to modify future costs. Second, the potential policy applications of the RCM methodology were explored. The applications are broader than special education, or even education, and extend to all governmental levels. Examples illustrating the possible uses of the RCM methodology are presented. They include: cost estimation for proposed programs, cost analyses for existing programs, state and federal funding of various social programs, program planning, evaluation of cost tradeoffs among different program practices, budget preparation, and cost-effectiveness analyses.

Resource-Cost Model Methodology

As described in the previous chapter, the resource-cost model is a methodology in which the student characteristics and program configurations form the basis for estimating the costs of special education. The procedures require specification of the student population to be served, description of the instructional programs and services to be offered and the resources which comprise each program (e.g., teacher, aide, materials and supplies, travel allowance, classroom operating and maintenance expense), a price for each resource, determination of the distribution of students across the various programs and services, and the student/personnel ratios of the programs.

The data used in the present projections are of two types: actual values for current operations (e.g., actual number of students served according to type of handicap, present percentage of students in each instructional program, current salary and price levels); and planned or estimated future values (e.g., maximum percentage of handicapped students in the total student population, future percentage of students in each instructional program, inflation rate). The RCM is used in this context as a planning model that utilizes actual values to initiate the planning process with current practice, and employs assumptions about expected student needs and programming practices to estimate future costs. As a result, the cost projections are derived from specific and explicit expectations about the future special education operations and are not necessarily an extrapolation of past practices or costs. The model also projects future special student education enrollments as well as the number of special education personnel required to serve them.

Figure 9-1 shows the input data requirements, calculation process, and resultant projections of the RCM for special education. This model is known as the Special Education Planning Model (SEPM)[9] and its calculation steps are described below.

1) The *total population* in which handicapped students are found is specified (e.g., the K–12 enrollment in public and private schools).
2) The *classification system* to be used to identify handicapped students is selected along with an *expected incidence rate* for each category (e.g., educable mentally retarded (EMR): 2.00%; visually handicapped: 0.10%). The classification system specified may be other than by type of handicap, for instance by type of learning needs.
3) The *number of students in each handicapping category* expected to need special education services is then calculated (total population x incidence rates).
4) The *percentage of handicapped students that are to receive each special education program* are estimated by type of handicap (e.g., for EMR: 20% in consulting teacher program, 40% in resource rooms, and 40% in special classes).
5) The *number in each category of handicapped students to receive each*

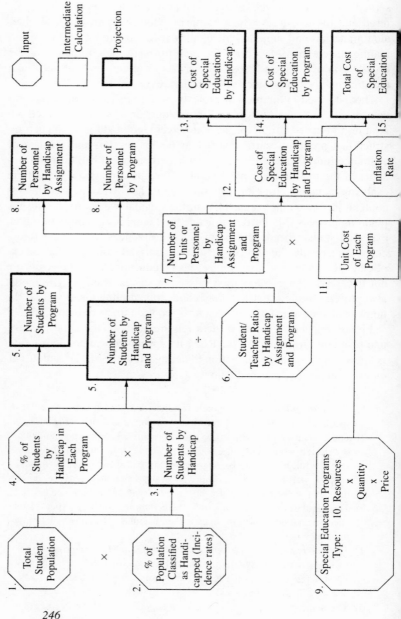

Figure 9-1. Schematic Diagram of the Special Education Planning Model

246

program is then calculated (step 3 x step 4). The total *number of handicapped students in each program* is also calculated.

6) The *number of students per unit* in each special education program for each category of handicapped student is specified (e.g., for EMR: 45 in consulting teacher program; 25 in resource rooms; 12 in special classes).

7) The *number of units* (and personnel) of each program required for each handicapping category is then calculated (step 5 ÷ step 6).

8) The *number of personnel to serve each handicapping category* and the *number of personnel required for each program* are than calculated by summing across programs for each handicapping category and across handicapping categories for each program, respectively.

9) The set of *special education programs* to be provided to handicapped students is determined (e.g., consulting teacher program, resource room, special class).

10) For each program the *type and quantity of resources* required in the program are selected along with a *price* for each resource (e.g., one teacher at $12 thousand, instructional materials at $500 per class).

11) The *unit price* for each program is then calculated by summing the quantity times the price for each resource in the program.

12) The *cost of special education for each handicapping category in each program* is then calculated from the number of units required times the unit cost (step 7 x step 10).

13) The *cost of special education for each handicapping category* is then calculated by summing the costs of each category across all programs. Both constant and inflated costs are calculated.

14) The *cost of special education for each program* is then calculated by summing the costs of each program across all handicapping categories. Both constant and inflated costs are calculated.

15) The *total cost of special education* is obtained by summing the costs of all handicapping categories (Σ step 13) or by summing the costs of all programs (Σ step 14). Both constant and inflated costs are calculated.

Several aspects of this approach differentiate it from previous cost studies in special education. While the model establishes a generalized structure of the special education instruction process—the essential variables, and their relationships—the user of the model specifies the values of the variables. This provides substantial flexibility since the SEPM can be tailored to replicate special education programs at all levels of operation. Use of the model requires specifying the critical programmatic aspects of special education, both on a current and future basis, and cost projections are derived directly from these programmatic variables and relationships. Finally, because the SEPM is a planning approach, its orientation is toward the future; the projections that are developed are based on expectations of future special education students and programs.

There are, however, several limitations to this approach that should be noted. Foremost is the dependence of SEPM results on the quality of the data used in its operation. Without accurate data for the values of the model's variables, the subsequent cost projections can be erroneous and misleading. An additional problem can be the unavailability in some areas of certain data required by the model. While the SEPM is designed to function with data that are generally available, all educational agencies may not collect data in the form required by the model. Also, the assumptions concerning the future programmatic aspects of special education are not verifiable since they concern events which have not yet occurred. These values are generally based on the professional judgment of special educators and administrators and, as such, are subject to their biases. However, since the approach utilizes a model, alternative values can easily be substituted to test their impact.

Data Analysis

To operate the SEPM, it was necessary to establish values for each of the variables in the model shown as an input in Figure 9-1. Primary among the data sources utilized were 28 states that had used the SEPM to develop their own state projections. These states represented a wide diversity in size, population, geography, demographic characteristics, special education philosophy, and programming practices. The values of the SEPM variables that they had established for their current and future special education programs provided the basis for the bulk of the programmatic data for the model. This grounded the model's projections in the actual and expected state special education program practices. Other data required by the model were of an aggregate or national total nature (e.g., total student population in grades K – 12 in the United States); these data were obtained from other sources that provided them in summary form.

The data obtained from the selected sample states were first grouped by type of variable. On a variable-by-variable basis, the individual state values were analyzed and, where necessary, made comparable (e.g., combining data for two different handicapping categories—blind and partially sighted—into a single category—visually impaired). To facili-tate nationwide use and comparability of the projections, standardized groupings for the two major qualitative variables—handicapping condi-tion and special education programs—were established. Based on the analysis of the states' reported data, most likely, low, and high values for each of the other SEPM variables were derived. Additionally, aggre-gate national estimates of the school-aged population were obtained from census sources. The process of establishing the values for each of the major variables is discussed below in further detail.

Total Student Population

The total student population is an estimate of the number of students, both nonhandicapped and handicapped, in a particular age group. This population is estimated for each year of the planning period. The latest enrollment projections from the National Center for Educational Statis-tics (NCES) were used to estimate the future grade K–12 enrollments. Three different birthrate assumptions were used in their basic popula-tion projections. Series II was selected to represent the most likely esti-mate of future public and private school enrollments, since the com-plete cohort fertility assumption most closely approximated the latest expected fertility data. Series I and Series III provided the high and low alternative values, respectively. In addition, the NCES enrollment pro-jections were increased by the estimated enrollments in residential schools for handicapped children (approximately 133 thousand stu-dents) to arrive at an adjusted enrollment projection.[10] The results are shown in Table 9-1.

Classification Categories

The classification categories are used to identify those students be-lieved to need special education programs and services, and to indicate the handicapping conditions that require special assistance. While other groupings could have been chosen, the categories selected by the states using the SEPM were generally the traditional disability categories. An analysis of their choices indicated much overall similarity, although many individual differences did occur. An effort was made to use the federal reporting categories specified in PL 94-142 as the standardized categories in these projections. In all but three cases this approach was feasible: mentally retarded students were commonly reported in two categories, educable and trainable; deaf and hard of hearing students

Table 9-1. Projected Enrollments in Grades K–12
for Regular Day and Residential Schools

Year	Enrollments (in thousands)		
	Series I (High)	Series II (Most Likely)	Series III (Low)
1976*	49,335	49,335	49,335
1977	48,820	48,820	48,820
1978	47,973	47,973	47,973
1979	47,067	47,063	47,061
1980	46,259	46,227	46,209

*actual enrollment

Source: National Center for Educational Statistics, *Projections of Educational Statistics: 1986–87*, p. 16–17.

were more frequently combined into a single category; and a separate category was necessary for multiple handicapped students. Based on these data, 10 standard categories were selected for the projections; they were educable mentally retarded (EMR), trainable mentally retarded (TMR), hearing handicapped, speech impaired, visually handicapped, seriously emotionally disturbed (SED), orthopedically handicapped (Ortho), other health impaired (OHI), specific learning disabilities (SLD), and multiple handicapped.

Incidence Rate

The incidence rate is an estimate of the expected percentage of children with a certain handicap to be found in the total population; it includes both those handicapped children presently identified and those anticipated to be found and served. Since these values determine the size of the population to be served, their values are critical to the cost projections. In fact, a prior study found that incidence rates were the single most important variable in estimating the costs of special education.[11]

The SEPM group of states used a variety of methods to estimate incidence rates. Some chose theoretical rates; some chose "prevalence" rates based on the number of handicapped students actually identified; and other states chose modified rates based on the number actually identified and on their professional judgment of the number of unidentified-unserved handicapped students needing special education services. Numerous analyses of incidence rates were conducted to discover possible relationships between states' estimated categorical and total incidence rates and other logically connected state characteristics for which data were available from other sources. No consistent statistical relationship was found between the states' estimated incidence rates and geographic location, per capita school expenditures, size of the school-aged population, or percentage of the population in metropolitan areas.

Failing to find any statistical relationships upon which to base national incidence rate estimates, two other approaches were utilized to develop possible values. First, values were derived by calculating the weighted average incidence rate for each category from the data reported by the SEPM group of states. (The weighting was based on the total school-aged population in each state.) Initial calculations included all 28 states, while subsequent ones eliminated extreme values reported by states (i.e., incidence rates of less than half or more than double the mean of the category). The weighted average values calculated from all states' data were selected as the most likely values of the categorical incidence rates, since dropping the extreme values from the calculations had little effect (e.g., total incidence rate [sum of the rates for each category] calculated from all states' data was equal to 10.48 percent versus 10.33 percent calculated by eliminating extreme state values).

An analysis of federal data provided the low and high alternative values for the incidence rates. A lower bound on incidence rates was established as the percentage of school-aged children served in 1977/78, the latest year for which data were available. The theoretical expected rates were used as the upper bound. All of these incidence rates are shown in Table 9-2.

Number of Students Served in Beginning Year

Operating the model requires information on the number of students served by each classification category in the beginning year of the planning period (i.e., 1976/77). These data were obtained from the Bureau of Education for the Handicapped (BEH), U.S. Office of Education reports, which contained national totals of the number of handicapped students served in both public and private schools and institutions as of February, 1977. These reports were based on federally mandated child counting procedures in all states and provided the most comprehensive summary information on students in special education. The reported numbers of students in certain categories were rearranged to be compatible with the standard categories. The adjustments were: (1) the

Table 9-2. Estimated Handicap Incidence Rates and Total Number of Students Served

| Handicapping Category | Estimated Incidence Rates | | | Total Number of Handicapped Students served 1976–1977[§] |
| | Low Values[†] | Most Likely Values | High Values[‡] | |
	Actual percentage Served	Weighted Average (percentage)	Federal Estimates (percentage)	
EMR	1.54	1.81	1.88*	761,429
TMR	.41	.40	.42*	202,405
Hearing	.19	.29	.58	91,366
Speech	2.72	3.56	3.50	1,341,152
Vision	.08	.10	.10	40,166
SED	.60	1.03	2.00	294,461
Ortho	.18	.20	.18*	88,623
OHI	.27	.36	.32*	134,173
SLD	1.66	2.56	3.00	818,206
Multiple	.13	.17	.06	65,401
Total	7.78	10.48	12.04	3,837,382

* Values starred were reported as combined numbers and separated in proportion to the existing ratios between, those categories most likely values.

[†] Source: U.S. Department of HEW (OE). *Progress Toward A Free Appropriate Education*. January, 1979, p. 162. (Adjusted to reflect differences in student population).

[‡] Source: Kaskowitz, David. *Validation of States Counts of Handicapped Children*, Volume 2: S.R.I. Menlo Park, Ca. 1977, p. 32.

[§] Source: Statistics reported by the Bureau of Education for the Handicapped, U.S.O.E. for the purpose of PL 94-142.

mentally retarded category was divided between educable mentally retarded students (EMR) and trainable mentally retarded students (TMR) in proportion to the number of students in each category identified by the SEPM states using the EMR and TMR categories (EMR: 79 percent; TMR: 21 percent); (2) deaf and hard of hearing categories were summed to form a single category; and (3) a fraction of the students from all categories, except speech, was allocated to a multiple category (2.62 percent). The results are also shown in Table 9-2.

Types of Instructional Programs

This variable specifies all of the types of instructional programs to be provided to handicapped students. A standardized set of eight instructional programs for the national projections was established based on a review and analysis of programs utilized by the SEPM group of states. Overall, there was a general similarity of programs offered among these states, although individual states differed in their specific sets of instructional programs. All states did offer a range of possible placements for handicapped students—from supplemental assistance to full-time special education to residential schools. This range was reflected in the standard set of instructional programs, which is shown in the list below, together with examples of corresponding states' programs.

Placement Pattern

Placement pattern refers to the distribution of handicapped students across instructional programs, and is expressed for each handicapping category as a percentage of the total number of handicapped students served by each instructional program. The SEPM uses two such matrices—beginning placement pattern (in the initial year of the planning period), and expected placement pattern (in the final year of the planning period). This allows the model to begin with an actual situation and then show movements of students among programs to reflect anticipated future programmatic trends.

For each handicapping category, the unduplicated number of students reported by the states using the SEPM was summed. These totals were used as a base and divided into the total number of students for the given handicapping category in each instructional program—both primary placement and additional (duplicated) services—to arrive at a percentage of students by type of handicap in each program. These calculations yielded weighted average placement patterns for the SEPM states. This procedure was used for both the beginning (1976/77) and expected (1980/81) years, using the states' data from each of these years in turn. The results are shown in Table 9-3.

- Indirect Services (Ind Svc): Aide in Regular Classroom, Consultive Services, Consultant Teacher, Consultive-Diagnostic

- Speech and Language Instruction (S & L): Speech and Language, Supplemental Instruction, Itinerant Instruction, Communication Disorder Specialist

- Other Direct Services (ODS): Itinerant Consultant, Itinerant Instruction, Individual Instruction, Tutor, Supplemental Instruction

- Resource Room (Res Rm): Resource Room, Resource Services, Special Resource, Teacher-Consultant

- Special Class (Sp Class): Self-Contained Classroom (Part or Full-Time), Special Class, District Center, Public Day School

Table 9-3. Current and Most Likely Student Placement Pattern (in decimal percentages)

		Ind Svc	S&L	ODS	Res Rm	Sp Class	OA Day	Resident	Hosp/Hbd
EMR	Beginning	0.031	0.038	0.021	0.394	0.569	0.012	0.013	0.0
	Expected	0.042	0.059	0.055	0.464	0.491	0.017	0.006	0.0
TMR	Beginning	0.020	0.060	0.005	0.017	0.802	0.039	0.132	0.009
	Expected	0.022	0.077	0.014	0.026	0.819	0.047	0.100	0.008
Hearing	Beginning	0.024	0.330	0.152	0.185	0.366	0.086	0.170	0.037
	Expected	0.041	0.225	0.234	0.199	0.252	0.193	0.086	0.023
Speech	Beginning	0.001	0.972	0.001	0.009	0.017	0.0	0.0	0.0
	Expected	0.002	0.978	0.001	0.010	0.009	0.0	0.0	0.0
Vision	Beginning	0.021	0.003	0.216	0.203	0.350	0.057	0.092	0.070
	Expected	0.030	0.004	0.224	0.241	0.348	0.058	0.070	0.063
SED	Beginning	0.047	0.038	0.026	0.264	0.543	0.082	0.063	0.028
	Expected	0.030	0.033	0.056	0.360	0.423	0.097	0.038	0.055
Ortho	Beginning	0.016	0.086	0.300	0.194	0.320	0.012	0.051	0.142
	Expected	0.042	0.117	0.274	0.243	0.293	0.013	0.034	0.156
OHI	Beginning	0.032	0.006	0.023	0.125	0.564	0.008	0.068	0.215
	Expected	0.033	0.017	0.029	0.207	0.416	0.010	0.062	0.283
SLD	Beginning	0.056	0.030	0.071	0.698	0.190	0.022	0.001	0.0
	Expected	0.073	0.053	0.099	0.703	0.173	0.018	0.001	0.0
Multiple	Beginning	0.049	0.035	0.034	0.033	0.630	0.041	0.287	0.002
	Expected	0.039	0.079	0.041	0.056	0.695	0.024	0.214	0.006

- Other Agency Day School (OA Day): Tuition/Contract, Private Agency, Private School, Special Day School, Out-of-District

- Residential School (Resident): Residential School, Public Agency, State School, State School for Deaf or Blind, State Institution, Private Residential

- Hospital and Homebound (Hosp/Hbd): Hospital, Homebound, Home and Hospital

Alternative placement patterns were only needed for 1980/81 since the 1976/77 pattern represented current practice. The wide variety of placement patterns utilized by the SEPM states, and their incompatibility when reported as percentages of students in different programs, made a detailed statistical analysis of the variations in state placement patterns difficult. Rather, the major programmatic trend of mainstreaming was used as the basis for establishing alternative 1980/81 placement patterns. A more conservative future placement pattern than the most likely pattern was selected as the high alternative. In this alternative, the 1980/81 placement percentages equaled 1976/77 placement percentages (i.e., no change in the present placement pattern was assumed). On the other side of the most likely values, a low alternative placement pattern was established that incorporated a greater shift of students into programs considered less restrictive and a greater use of additional services, primarily speech and language instruction. These values are shown in Table 9-4.

Number of Students per Unit

The number of students per unit variable represents the average number of pupils in one unit of an instructional program; since most programs are specified in classroom units, this amounts to a student/teacher ratio for each handicapping category and instructional program combination.

To establish the most likely values for the projections, the mean number of students per unit for each instructional program and handicapping category was calculated from the responses of the SEPM group of states. Alternative low and high values were obtained by subtracting and adding one standard deviation from the mean value of the number of students per unit. These values are shown in Table 9-5. To check the reasonableness of these data, a comparison was made with the results of a recent study of state regulations governing the number of students per

Table 9-4. Current and Greater Mainstreaming Student Placement Pattern (in decimal percentages)

		Ind Svc	S&L	ODS	Res Rm	Sp Class	OA Day	Resident	Hosp/Hbd
EMR	Beginning	0.031	0.038	0.021	0.394	0.569	0.012	0.013	0.0
	Expected	0.080	0.120	0.060	0.550	0.400	0.0	0.0	0.0
TMR	Beginning	0.020	0.060	0.005	0.017	0.802	0.039	0.132	0.009
	Expected	0.040	0.150	0.030	0.030	0.890	0.020	0.055	0.005
Hearing	Beginning	0.024	0.330	0.152	0.185	0.366	0.086	0.170	0.037
	Expected	0.050	0.300	0.300	0.250	0.300	0.100	0.050	0.010
Speech	Beginning	0.001	0.972	0.001	0.009	0.017	0.0	0.0	0.0
	Expected	0.005	0.985	0.0	0.005	0.005	0.0	0.0	0.0
Vision	Beginning	0.021	0.003	0.216	0.203	0.350	0.057	0.092	0.070
	Expected	0.060	0.010	0.300	0.300	0.300	0.050	0.050	0.0
SED	Beginning	0.047	0.038	0.026	0.264	0.543	0.082	0.063	0.028
	Expected	0.050	0.100	0.100	0.450	0.350	0.050	0.020	0.030
Ortho	Beginning	0.016	0.086	0.300	0.194	0.320	0.012	0.051	0.142
	Expected	0.080	0.150	0.300	0.330	0.250	0.010	0.010	0.100
OHI	Beginning	0.032	0.006	0.023	0.125	0.564	0.008	0.068	0.215
	Expected	0.070	0.050	0.050	0.300	0.350	0.0	0.050	0.250
SLD	Beginning	0.056	0.030	0.071	0.698	0.190	0.022	0.001	0.0
	Expected	0.150	0.100	0.100	0.750	0.140	0.010	0.0	0.0
Multiple	Beginning	0.049	0.035	0.034	0.033	0.630	0.041	0.287	0.002
	Expected	0.050	0.150	0.080	0.100	0.650	0.015	0.200	0.005

Table 9-5. Estimated Number of Students per Unit

Category	Esti-mate	Ind Svc	S & L	ODS	Res Rm	Sp Class	OA Day	Resi-dent	Hosp/Hbd
							Program		
EMR	ML	88	67	33	22	14	1	1	6
	High	40*	49	21	15	11	1	1	6
	Low	140	85	45	29	17	1	1	5
TMR	ML	88	60	24	20	11	1	1	6
	High	40*	39	16	10	9	1	1	5
	Low	140	81	32*	30	13	1	1	7
Hearing	ML	79	65	21	15	9	1	1	8
	High	35*	47	10	7	6	1	1	8
	Low	98	83	32	23	12	1	1	8
Speech	ML	75	67	25	20	9	1	0	0
	High	40*	51	25	11	6	1	0	0
	Low	110*	83	25	29	12	1	0	0
Vision	ML	86	72	24	17	9	1	1	4
	High	32	51	12	9	6	1	1	4
	Low	140	93	36	25	12	1	1	5
SED	ML	69	73	26	20	10	1	1	7
	High	32*	56	16*	12	7	1	1	3*
	Low	118	90	36	28	13	1	1	11
Ortho	ML	76	65	22	17	11	1	1	6
	High	20*	46	18	9	8	1	1	4
	Low	140	84	26	25	14	1	1	8
OHI	ML	78	54	24	19	12	1	1	8
	High	20*	43*	18	12	9	1	1	4
	Low	140	65	30	26	15	1	1	12
SLD	ML	75	66	28	24	12	1	1	10
	High	32*	55	19*	17	9	1	1	5
	Low	120	77	37	31	15	1	1	15
Multiple	ML	130	70	18	23	7	1	1	8
	High	110*	51	12	13	5	1	1	6
	Low	150*	89	24	33	9	1	1	10

*In some instances, due to the small number of observations, plus or minus one standard deviation from the mean value exceeded the range of values found among the reported state data. In these cases, the end value in the range was used to avoid an input value more extreme than was present in the base data.

unit.[12] The most likely, low, and high values calculated for the projections were reviewed to ensure that they were within the range of reported state regulations. In the few cases where a calculated value was outside the reported range, the value was changed to the endpoint of the range.

Resources, Quantities, and
Prices for Instructional Programs

In the resource-cost model methodology used by the SEPM, each instructional program is specified in terms of selected, identifiable resources, each present in the specific quantity with an associated price. Combined, these resources, quantities, and prices yield a unit price for each instructional program. To establish the resources, quantities, and prices for the projections, a review and analysis of the corresponding data from the states using the SEPM was conducted. Resources used most frequently were selected as the most likely resources for each respective instructional program. Other resources, which were used by some, though not most, states, were included in the alternative low and high formulations of the resources for the programs.

To establish prices, resources were divided into three groups—personnel, nonpersonnel, and cost per student. The personnel related resources consisted of teacher salaries, aide salaries, and fringe benefits. Due to the great variability in reported salaries from the SEPM states, a National Educational Association (NEA) estimate of the national average teacher salary ($13,312 in 1976/77) was used as the most likely value.[13] Alternative values for teacher salaries were established at plus and minus 10 percent of the most likely value. Aide salaries were established as proportions of the most likely teacher salary, using the relationships between aide and teacher salaries in the SEPM states' data. The mean aide salary to teacher salary ratio (.45) was used to calculate the most likely value for aide salary, and the low and high aide/teacher salary ratios (.29 and .64) to calculate the alternative values. Similarly, fringe benefits were calculated based on the benefit levels reported by the SEPM states (most likely of 13 percent, low of 7 percent, and high of 20 percent applied against the respective salaries).

For the nonpersonnel resources—instructional materials, travel, and maintenance and operation expenses—specified for a given instructional program, the most likely values for the prices were taken to be the average of the prices reported by states for those resources. Low and high alternative values for prices for these resources were established by reviewing the number of states using a resource in a specific instructional program, the likelihood of the generalized use of this resource by other states, the range of reported prices, and the distribution of the reported prices.

258

The final type of resource used by the SEPM group of states was an average cost per student in a particular instructional program. This designation was most common in programs the budgets and operations of which were controlled by agencies other than the public schools—other agency day schools and residential schools. For these programs, the most likely value for the price was established as the mean value of the average cost per student for those states reporting. The alternative values were determined through an analysis of the range and distribution of the reported costs per student for these programs. The resulting most likely and alternative values for the resources, quantities, and prices for all programs are shown in Table 9-6.

Inflation Factor

In order to reflect changes in the price levels in future years, the SEPM uses an inflation factor that specifies the average annual rate of inflation of the initial prices expected over the planning period. The most likely value for this variable was established as the weighted average inflation factor (weighted by the total student population of each state) for the SEPM group of states. Alternative low and high values of plus and minus one standard deviation from the unweighted average inflation factor for these states were also calculated. These results are shown in Table 9-7.

There was some concern that the rates of inflation selected by the states did not accurately reflect the actual changes in price levels between 1976/77 and 1980/81. To investigate this potential problem, the rate of actual salary increases were compared with the assumed inflation rates. It was found that the average annual rate of increase in teachers' salaries from 1976 through 1979 was 6.2 percent, while the most likely inflation factor used in the projections was 6.65 percent.[14] Since teacher salaries comprised the bulk of the projected costs, and since it is probable that the other cost items had higher rates of cost increases, the most likely inflation rate appeared to be reasonable.

Related Services

Related services are those services of a developmental, corrective, or supportive nature that are provided to help handicapped students to benefit from the instructional programs in which they are enrolled.[15] The SEPM distinguishes between two types of related services. The first type is specific related services, which are those associated with a cer-

Table 9-6. Resources and Prices for Instructional Programs

Program	Resource	Most Likely	Low	High
Ind Svc	Teacher	$13,312	$11,981	$14,643
	Benefits	1,731	839	2,929
	Materials	305	200	400
	Travel	837	670	1,000
	Maintenance & Operation	0	0	236
	Total	$16,185	$13,690	$19,208
S&L	Teacher	$13,312	$11,981	$14,643
	Benefits	1,731	839	2,929
	Materials	582	300	1,000
	Travel	855	627	1,000
	Maintenance & Operation	0	0	261
	Total	$16,480	$13,747	$19,833
ODS	Teacher	$13,312	$11,981	$14,643
	Benefits	1,731	839	2,929
	Materials	622	300	1,000
	Travel	913	730	1,000
	Maintenance & Operation	0	0	168
	Total	$16,578	$13,850	$19,740
Res Rm	Teacher	$13,312	$11,981	$14,643
	Aide (quantity)	(.33/unit)	(0/unit)	(1.0/unit)
	(price)	($5,990)	($3,860)	($8,520)
	cost	1,977	0	($8,520)
	Benefits	1,988	839	4,633
	Materials	603	400	1,000
	Maintenance & Operation	645	0	1,474
	Total	$18,525	$13,220	$30,270
Sp Class	Teacher	$13,312	$11,981	$14,643
	Aide (quantity)	(.51/unit)	(.25/unit)	(1.0/unit)
	(price)	($5,990)	($3,860)	($8,520)
	cost	3,055	965	8,520
	Benefits	2,128	907	4,633
	Materials	769	500	1,000
	Maintenance & Operation	810	0	1,737
	Total	$20,074	$14,353	$30,533
OA Day	Average Cost per Student	$ 3,618	$ 2,500	$ 5,000
Resident	Average Cost per Student	$10,390	$ 8,000	$14,000
Hosp/Hbd	Teacher	$13,312	$11,981	$14,643
	Benefits	1,731	839	2,929
	Materials	378	226	500
	Travel	689	482	1,000
	Total	$16,110	$13,528	$19,072

Table 9-7. Inflation Factors

Most Likely (weighted average rate)	6.65%
Low Alternative (minus one standard deviation)	5.58%
High Alternative (plus one standard de- viation)	7.96%

tain handicapping category (e.g., special transportation for TMR students). The second type is nonspecific related services, which are those provided to benefit more than one category of handicapped students (e.g., in-service training for teachers, supervision).

Related services data provided by the states using the SEPM were much less comprehensive than those for the instructional programs. Of the 28 sample states, only nine reported specific related services data, while only 13 reported nonspecific related services data. There was, therefore, a shortage of data on which to base national projections. However, since related services are an important part of special education and they are explicitly included in PL 94-142 and many state statutes, their costs should not be forgotten. Therefore, projections of related services were developed to provide some indication of the general magnitude of the costs involved.

The most commonly reported specific related services were selected for inclusion in the projections. These were special transportation for five different categories of handicapped students, and physical therapy for orthopedically handicapped students. Calculations from the states' data of the estimated cost per student and the percentages of students receiving these services are shown in Table 9-8. Nonspecific related services estimates were based on data reported by all 50 states to the Bureau of Education for the Handicapped. The data utilized for these projections included estimates of the numbers of several types of support personnel who were: (*a*) employed in 1976/77, (*b*) needed in 1977/78, and (*c*) needed in 1978/79. These were utilized in the cost projections as the low, most likely, and high values, respectively. These personnel estimates were combined with salary levels that were estimated relative to the most likely teachers' salaries to project the costs for nonspecific related services. These data are also given in Table 9-8.

261

Table 9-8. Related Services Data

Related Service	Category	Cost	1980 Service Level		
			Low	Most Likely	High
Specific					
Special transportation	TMR	$777/student		55% of students	
	Hearing	$596/student		37% of students	
	Vision	$571/student		49% of students	
	Ortho	$769/student		64% of students	
	Multiple	$521/student		85% of students	
Physical therapy	Ortho	$572/student		34% of students	
Nonspecific					
In-service training		$303/teacher		223,940 teachers	
Psychologists		$14,000/staff	17,730 staff	21,713 staff	25,659 staff
Noninstructional staff		$13,312/staff	17,478 staff	21,257 staff	23,756 staff
Supervisors		$14,500/staff	10,161 staff	12,026 staff	13,676 staff
Work-study Coordinator		$14,500/staff	6,854 staff	8,900 staff	11,111 staff
Social workers		$14,000/staff	5,880 staff	7,975 staff	10,218 staff
Physical education therapist		$13,312/staff	5,014 staff	6,852 staff	8,430 staff
Occupational & recreational therapist		$13,750/staff	1,903 staff	3,349 staff	4,618 staff

Most Likely Cost Projections

National cost projections for both instructional programs and related services were developed utilizing the most likely values of each of the model's variables. For instructional programs, this produced a most likely cost estimate to serve all school-aged handicapped children in 1980/81 of $7.2 billion (inflated), an increase of approximately $2.3 billion (50 percent) from 1976/77 estimates. Inflation, however, accounted for the bulk of that increase with only a $777 million (16 percent) increase projected in constant dollars. Table 9-9 presents these cost estimates by type of handicapping classification. Over the five-year period, the largest cost increases appeared in the specific learning disabilities ($353 million or 43 percent) and severely emotionally disturbed categories ($299 million or 43 percent). Both of these projected costs increases stemmed primarily from the relatively large increases in the estimated number of students to be served by 1980/81 (365 thousand or 45 percent for SLD and 182 thousand or 62 percent for SED). These estimates, in turn, were derived from the incidence rate assumptions used in the most likely projections. It is worth noting that these two classifications are among the most difficult to define and diagnose precisely.

These most likely cost projections are also presented by type of instructional program in Table 9-10. These estimates indicate that the resource room program had the largest expected cost increase ($408 million or 48 percent), while other programs with large projected cost increases were other agency day schools ($180 million or 67 percent), special classes ($126 million or 6 percent), and speech and language instruction ($94 million or 27 percent). On the other hand, the costs of residential schools are estimated to decline (-205 million or 18 percent) due to the shift of students into less restrictive settings (i.e., other agency day schools and special classes).

For related services, the most likely cost projections yielded an estimate of $1.8 billion for 1980/81. The bulk of these projected costs were for the support personnel—psychologists, other noninstructional staff, supervisors, work-study coordinators, school social workers, physical education instructors, and occupational and recreational therapists. The remainder of the estimated costs were for specific related services and for in-service training. Table 9-11 presents these results.

Supplemental projections were also developed for the estimated total

Table 9-9. Costs by Classification and Year (in thousands of dollars)

Classification	Year				
	76–77	77–78	78–79	79–80	80–81
EMR	1,029,213	1,029,674	1,033,197	1,043,517	1,061,281
TMR	615,217	602,157	578,774	548,905	514,772
Hearing	311,141	318,531	331,775	347,911	361,449
Speech	383,869	389,538	401,420	420,326	445,973
Vision	104,436	104,832	105,886	107,792	110,504
SED	702,676	737,031	802,627	894,135	1,002,311
Ortho	177,341	176,286	174,662	173,248	172,299
OHI	302,983	308,435	319,870	337,992	362,768
SLD	824,885	859,550	929,282	1,035,427	1,177,601
Multiple	327,868	329,656	333,585	339,854	347,469
Total (constant $)	4,779,629	4,855,690	5,011,078	5,249,107	5,556,427
Total (inflated $)	4,779,629	5,178,591	5,699,708	6,367,478	7,188,504

number of students to be served and the instructional personnel that would be needed. The unduplicated special education enrollment projections showed an increase of approximately one million handicapped students in special education programs (26 percent by 1980/81, to reach full service with the largest increases in the categories of SLD, SED, and speech impaired (305 thousand students). The projected duplicated student enrollments (in which students were counted in each program they received) showed an increase of 1.2 million handicapped students (29 percent). Students in other instructional programs who were also receiving additional speech and language instruction accounted for the majority of the double counting by program. The programs with the largest projected enrollment increases by 1980/81 were resource rooms (486 thousand students or 47 percent) and speech and language instruction (380 thousand students or 27 percent). Corresponding projections of the required number of personnel by 1980/81 indicated an estimated increase of 45 thousand teachers (25 percent) and 10,500 aides (16 percent) to serve the projected most likely number of handicapped student. The largest areas of increase by category were teachers of SLD students (18 thousand teachers or 46 percent) and SED students (12 thousand teachers or 56 percent). By type of program, the greatest increase was projected for the resource room teachers (22 thousand or 48 percent).

At this point it is useful to consider the combined effects of the projected increases in costs and students on the average cost per handicapped student. As Table 9-12 shows, except for the effects of inflation,

Table 9-10. Costs by Instructional Program and Year (in thousands of dollars)

Type of Program	Price per Unit	76–77	77–78	78–79	79–80	80–81
Indirect Services	16,185	20,732	21,882	24,309	28,161	33,648
Speech & Language Instruction	15,480	350,150	358,505	376,007	404,171	443,888
Other Direct Services	16,578	90,101	96,616	110,624	134,082	169,675
Resource Room	18,524	846,380	883,168	959,543	1,081,153	1,254,167
Special Class	20,073	1,951,677	1,967,234	1,997,423	2,038,794	2,078,257
Other Agency Day School	3,618	268,242	283,792	316,491	369,654	447,571
Residential School	10,390	1,118,234	1,103,791	1,071,624	1,013,710	912,553
Hospital & Homebound	16,110	134,147	140,736	155,090	179,417	216,695
Total (constant $)		4,779,663	4,855,724	5,011,111	5,249,142	5,556,454
Total (inflated $)		4,779,663	5,178,628	5,699,745	6,367,521	7,188,539

Table 9-11. Costs for Related Servies (in thousands of dollars)

Classification and Service	Year				
	76–77	77–78	78–79	79–80	80–81
TMR					
Special Transportation Costs	72,343	72,805	73,916	75,954	79,020
Hearing					
Special Transportation Costs	16,880	17,991	20,316	24,076	29,562
Vision					
Special Transportation Costs	6,879	7,404	8,506	10,297	12,933
Orthopedic					
Physical Therapy Costs	6,274	7,074	8,706	11,251	14,836
Special Transportation Costs	19,081	21,551	26,586	34,438	45,501
Multiple					
Special Transportation Costs	16,695	18,236	21,491	26,836	34,801
In-service Costs	27,150	31,220	39,361	51,572	67,853
Psychologists Costs	248,220	253,796	264,948	281,677	303,981
Other Staff Costs	232,667	237,697	247,758	262,850	282,973
Supervisors Costs	147,334	150,038	155,447	163,559	174,376
Work-Study Coordinators					
Students	0	0	0	0	0
Personnel	6,854	7,059	7,468	8,082	8,900
Costs	99,382	102,349	108,283	117,183	129,050
School Social Workers Costs	82,320	85,252	91,118	99,917	111,650
Physical Education Therapists Costs	66,746	69,193	74,086	81,426	91,213
Occupatonal-Recreational Therapists Costs	26,166	28,154	32,130	38,095	46,048
Total (constant $)	1,068,137	1,102,760	1,172,652	1,279,131	1,423,797
Total (inflated $)	1,068,137	1,176,093	1,333,799	1,551,661	1,842,005

Table 9-12. Average Cost for Special Education per Handicapped Student (in dollars)

	1976/77		1977/78		1978/79		1979/80		1980/81	
	constant	inflated	constant	inflated	constant	inflated	constant	inflated	constant	inflated
Instructional program	1,246	1,246	1,236	1,318	1,216	1,386	1,187	1,439	1,147	1,484
Related service	278	278	281	299	284	324	289	350	293	380
Total	1,524	1,524	1,517	1,617	1,500	1,710	1,476	1,789	1,440	1,864

the average cost of serving a handicapped student is estimated to decrease from 1976/77 to 1980/81. This decrease is the net result of several key assumptions in the most likely projections: (1) the majority of the new students will tend to be mildly handicapped and consequently will be assigned to relatively low cost programs; (2) there will be some shift of existing students toward less restrictive (and lower cost) programs; and (3) there will be a greater use of additional services (rising from 5.6 percent to 8.1 percent of the unduplicated enrollment).

Now that the most likely cost estimates have been presented, it is important to review their limitations. First, the cost projections are based completely on the data and assumptions underlying each of the SEPM variables. Changes in the most likely values of any of the model variables would cause changes in the most likely cost projections. (The next two sections of this paper discuss the uncertainty associated with each of the variables and the impact on the projected costs.) Second, the projections for instructional programs are the more reliable due to their extensive state data base, while those for related services are much more speculative. Third, the projections are for the special education costs of school-aged children only. Cost estimates for instructional programs and related services for preschool and postschool-aged handicapped students are not included, which means that the total special education costs for all handicapped children ages 3–21 (the mandated ages in PL 94-142 and many state statutes) would be higher than those shown in the study. Fourth, the 1980/81 projections are not actual costs; rather they are estimates of what the costs would be if all school-aged handicapped children were to be served in an appropriate manner. Finally, the cost projections are of the specifically identifiable special education costs; they are not excess costs, since the equivalent costs of providing a regular education for handicapped students in separate instructional settings have not been deducted; nor are they the total costs of educating handicapped students, since the costs of regular education programs and services provided for these children have not been included.

Sensitivity Analyses

To show the effects of the uncertainty associated with each model variable, a series of sensitivity analyses were conducted. These analyses involved substituting first the low and then high values for the most likely value of each variable, one variable at a time, and then reprojecting the costs. The difference between the new cost projections and the original most likely cost projection gave the cost impact of the low and high alternative values of each variable. The results for both the instructional programs and related services are shown in Table 9-13.

The variable with the largest effect on costs was the assumed total incidence rate. The most likely value of this variable of 10.48 percent was established from the weighted average incidence rate for the states using the SEPM. The low (7.78 percent) and high (12.04 percent) values represented the most recently available percentage of students served (1977/78) and the theoretical federal percentage, respectively. If, instead of the most likely incidence rate, the total percentage of school-aged students ultimately served in special education turned out to be the low value (i.e., no growth in special education enrollments), then the reduction in cost projections would be about $1.4 billion (assuming all other variables remain at their most likely values). Conversely, if the high value was the better estimate for the incidence rate, then the increased costs would be about $1.3 billion. These differences represent approximately minus and plus 25 percent of the most likely cost projections for this one variable alone.

The student/teacher ratios for instructional programs were the variables with the second greatest impact on projected costs. The most likely values in the category/program matrix specified for student/teacher ratios (Table 9-5) yielded a weighted average student/teacher ratio of 22 students per unit. While this value was not used in the projections, it was calculated for Table 9-13 (along with the analogous alternative values) in order to provide a single index number to represent the values in the full matrix. The single weighted average values for the low cost and high cost projections were 27 and 16, respectively. Of particular interest were the values resulting in the high cost projections (which were actually the lower numerical values of the variable), which caused the largest single cost difference of $1.8 billion by reducing the average student/teacher ratio from 22 to 16. This indicated that the cost projections were extremely sensitive to lowering the student/teacher ratio, a common change proposed for special education programs.

The results of the sensitivity analyses for the other model variables are discussed below in order of their cost impact:

(1) For personnel salaries and benefits, a 10 percent change in teacher salaries, combined with larger changes in aide salaries and personnel benefits, resulted in a $700–800 million cost difference

Table 9-13. Results of Sensitivity Analyses

Variable	Most Likely Value	Alternative Type	Alternative Value	Cost Difference (in millions)	Percentage Difference
Incidence Rate	Total = 10.48%	Low	7.78%	−$1,420	−25.5
		High	12.04%	+$1,285	+23.1
Student/Teacher Ratio	Average = 22	Low	27	−$ 633	−11.4
		High	16	+$1,814	+32.6
Salaries and Benefits	Teacher $13,312	Low	$11,981	−$ 696	−12.5
		High	$14,643	+$ 827	+14.9
Placement Patterns	Future Most Likely Pattern	Low	More Mainstreaming	−$ 639	−11.5
		High	Current Pattern	+$ 469	+ 8.4
Use of Aides (aide/teacher)	Resource Room = .33 Special Class = .51	Low	RR = 0; SC = .25	−$ 333	− 6.0
		High	RR = 1.0; SC = 1.0	+$ 576	+10.4
Cost per Student in Other Agency Programs	$10,390 for Residential $3,618 for Day School	Low	$8,000; $2,500	+$ 348	− 6.3
		High	$14,000; $5,000	+$ 488	+ 8.8
Inflation Rate	6.65%	Low	5.58%	−$ 285	− 4.0
		High	7.96%	+$ 359	+ 5.0
Nonpersonnel Resources	$1,403 per Unit	Low	$661 per Unit	−$ 193	− 3.5
		High	$2401 per Unit	+$ 239	+ 4.3
Total Student Population in 1980	46,227,000 Students	Low	46,209,000	−$ 2	− 0.1
		High	46,529,000	+$ 4	+ 0.1
Related Services	82,072 Personnel	Low	65,020 Personnel	−$ 306	−16.6
		High	97,468 Personnel	+$ 277	+15.1

(2) Maintaining the current placement pattern of students in instructional programs in 1980/81 would cause a $470 million increase when compared to the expected shifts toward least restrictive environments; and a further shift toward greater use of mainstreaming placements could reduce costs by over $600 million

(3) Increasing the use of aides to one full aide for each teacher in the resource room and special class programs would raise costs by almost $600 million, and eliminating aides from resource rooms and halving their frequency in special classes would reduce costs by over $300 million

(4) If the average cost per student in other agency day school and residential programs were lower by approximately 25 percent, the projected cost would be reduced by $350 million; and if the average cost per student were higher by approximately 35 percent, the projected costs would increase by almost $500 million

(5) A change of approximately one percent on the annual rate of inflation resulted in cost differences of from almost $300 million to over $350 million in the fifth year

(6) A change of approximately $1,000 per unit in nonpersonnel resources caused cost differences of approximately $200 million

(7) Finally, the small differences in the projected K–12 enrollment for the total student population had a negligible effect on the cost projections.

Only a single sensitivity analysis was conducted for related services, given the limitations of the data base. The changes in the projected number of personnel engaged in related service activities of approximately 16 thousand resulted in cost differences of about $300 million.

Alternative Cost Projections

Given the uncertainty associated with the values of the underlying variables in the most likely cost projections, it would be more realistic to use a range of feasible cost estimates than a single point estimate. To do this, sets of low and high alternative values were established around the most likely values using the results of the sensitivity analyses, knowledge of current trends in special education and the national economic conditions, and reasonable assessments by the author. The sets of low and high values are intended to represent the lower and upper bounds on the combination of events that may occur. It was necessary to consider all of the variables concurrently in establishing values for the alternative cost projections in order to avoid compounding a series of possible, but not probable, events into a final, highly unlikely set of joint occurrences. Each of the low and high values utilized in the sensitivity analyses was established separately, and represented a more extreme possibility for that individual variable. As a result, it is not appropriate to sum the individual cost differences from the most likely projections, nor to utilize all of the low or high values in a single cost projection. To illustrate the point, cost projections for 1980/81 based on only the low values of the variables (including the effects of inflation) totaled approximately half of the 1976/77 reported costs of special education.

The low and high combinations of values to estimate the range of probable costs of special education are shown in the list below. The values are indicated in terms of the previously developed model values for the sensitivity analyses.

Variable	Low projection values	High projection values
Total Student Population	Most Likely	Most Likely
Incidence Rate (Total)	Low + 1%	Most Likely + 0.5%
Salaries and Benefits	Most Likely	High
Non-personnel Resources	Low	High
Cost/Student in Other Agency Programs	Most Likely	High
Use of Aides	Most Likely	Most Likely
Placement Patterns	Current (No Change)	More Mainstreaming
Student/Teacher Ratio	Most Likely + 10%	Most Likely − 10%
Inflation Rates	Most Likely	High
Related Services	Low	High

The model variables in which there were important variations for the alternative values were:

(1) Incidence rate, where the low value was selected as one additional percentage point over the most recent percentage of students served (7.78% + 1.00% = 8.78%) to allow for some growth in the population to be served (13% by 1980/81); and the high value was selected as one half percentage point over the most likely value (10.48% + 0.50% = 10.98%), which provided an increase of 40 percent in the proportion of students served in special education.

(2) The economic variables (salaries and benefits, the cost per student in other agency programs, and inflation rate), where the high values previously developed were chosen for the high cost projections and the most likely values chosen for the low cost projections, in order to reflect the current national economic and price level trends.

(3) Placement patterns, where a reversal of the previous low and high was selected. The more mainstreaming placement pattern was combined with the high incidence rate to reflect the assumption that the increased number of students would be more mildly handicapped and go into mainstreaming placements. The current placement pattern was combined with the lower incidence rate since it was assumed that, with fewer students in special education, they will tend to be more seriously handicapped and their placement pattern will resemble the present pattern.

(4) Student/teacher ratios, where plus and minus 10 percent around the most likely values were selected for the high and low cost projections. The primary effect of this change was to eliminate the extreme differences between the most likely values and the alternative values that were found in the previously developed values.

These combinations were used in the SEPM to develop cost projections for a low alternative estimate and a high alternative estimate of the national costs of educating all school-aged handicapped students. These cost estimates are shown, together with the most likely cost estimates, in Table 9-14. Estimated costs range from a low estimate of $7.3 billion to a high estimate of $12.4 billion, a difference of $5.1 billion. While this range is still substantial, it is considerably less than the $17.2 billion that would have resulted from cost estimates using all of the separate low or the high values in single projections without consideration of probable combinations of different values of the variables.

Policy Implications

There are two types of issues that come out of this study that are relevant for policymakers. The first group of issues concerns the policy uses of the results of the study and the second group of issues centers around the policy uses of the RCM methodology. Each will be discussed in turn.

Table 9-14. Range of Estimates for Special Education Costs to Serve All School-aged Handicapped Students in 1980–81 (in billions of dollars)

Type of Cost	Low Alternative	Most Likely Estimate	High Alternative
Instructional Programs	5.761	7.189	10.113
Related Services	1.534	1.842	2.239
Total Special Education Costs	7.295	9.031	12.352

Policy Uses of Results

The most likely cost projections indicate that approximately $9 billion would be required in 1980 if all school-aged handicapped children were to receive an appropriate education. As a reference point, the comparable reported local, state, and federal special education costs in 1976/77 were $4.5 billion ($4.1 billion from state and local sources and $0.4 billion from federal sources).[16] While the projected figure is only an estimate, it does point out that a significant increase in funding would be required to reach the most likely service levels. However, the necessary cost increases for special education are likely to be even higher when a more complete utilization of related services is considered and when the costs for preschool and postschool-aged handicapped students are included.

Certainly one of the most important policy questions raised by these cost projections is from what sources will the potential $4.5 billion increase in funding come—local, state, federal? How much will each level have to provide, and what will be the impact on the relative share of the funds provided by each? To show the range of possible outcomes, Table 9-15 illustrates three different alternatives under differing assumptions for federal participation. At one end of the range, PL 94-142 would be fully funded to its authorization level of $3.2 billion. The large federal increase would cover much of the increased funding requirements, although the local and state governments would still face a $1.3 billion increase. The federal share would rise to 40 percent from its 1976/77 share of 9 percent. At the other end of the range, the federal funding amount would remain at approximately the actual fiscal year 1981 appropriation level. In this event, state and local sources would be required to fund an additional $3.9 billion, or almost double their

Table 9-15. Alternative Proportions of Special Education Funding by Government Level

Government level	Current $ billion	Current %	Addition $ billion	Future $ billion	Future %
Alternative 1: (full funding of PL94-142)					
Local and state	4.1	91	1.3	5.4	60
Federal	0.4	9	3.2	3.6	40
Total	4.5	100	4.5	9.0	100
Alternative 2: (maintain fiscal year 1981 funding level)					
State and local	4.1	91	3.9	8.0	89
Federal	0.4	9	0.6	1.0	11
Total	4.5	100	4.5	9.0	100
Alternative 3: (equal contribution for additional amount)					
Local and state	4.1	91	2.2	6.3	70
Federal	0.4	9	2.3	2.7	30
Total	4.5	100	4.5	9.0	100

1976/77 amount. A compromise alternative would be one in which the additional costs would be shared equally, with the local and state sources and the federal sources each funding an additional $2.3 billion. This would shift the state and local share to 70 percent and the federal share to 30 percent.

Associated with the program funding is often program control. Already, through new laws and regulations, there have been many shifts of program and fiscal control away from the local level to the state level, and, more recently, away from the state level to the federal level. In this situation of increasing federal influence and control, an important policy concern is the balance between the federal (and state) agencies' tasks of carrying out their legislated duties and the local districts' needs for flexibility in program implementation to meet individual circumstances. The situations found in different districts are too varied to establish a single national (or even state) set of detailed program standards to which all must conform.

The sensitivity analyses, also, provide useful information for policy-makers. In estimating costs and, consequently, funding requirements, the choice of an incidence rate (or individual incidence rates for the various handicapping categories) is critical because, as shown, incidence rates are the major determinant of the projected costs. The wide range of incidence rates estimated by the states, as well as the statistical analyses performed on these data, confirm what is commonly known about incidence rate estimates; that is, they are primarily educated guesses and not scientifically derived from educational theory or research. As such, they are defined differently from state to state, and estimates for the same nominal categories may vary considerably. Furthermore, in addition to educational considerations, these estimates are influenced by many political, social, and historical factors. Also, they are used for many other purposes in addition to estimating the number of unserved handicapped children; and these other purposes— lobbying for additional funds, building public support, projecting personnel needs—may affect the magnitude of the estimated incidence rates. In sum, incidence rates should be viewed with caution, especially those rates that deviate substantially from actual counts of handicapped children. This is particularly true now, given the intensive efforts of locating, identifying, and assessing all handicapped children that have been undertaken in the states over the past few years. The \$9 billion most likely cost estimate was predicated upon the assumption that 10.48 percent (most likely value) of the school-aged enrollments would receive some type of special education services. This assumed value represents an increase of approximately one million students, or 26 percent, over the most recent actual service level of 7.78 percent. For policy purposes, it may be more useful to develop a rule of thumb for roughly estimating what the impact would be of specified increases over present service levels. This estimate could then apply to whatever increase in the number or proportion of students to be served was under consideration. Using the SEPM program and varying the incidence rates, the cost difference of one percentage point in the assumed incidence rate was calculated. It was found that raising the incidence rate from 7.78 percent to 8.78 percent (with all other variables kept at the most likely values) increased the projected costs by \$708 million, the estimated number of students by 470 thousand, and the required number of teachers by 22 thousand.

The selection of the number of students per unit is also a policy decision with potentially significant implications for costs. This variable is very cost sensitive, particularly to a reduction of the number of students per unit. However, as this variable is usually specified in state regulations, it is also largely under the control of policymakers. Therefore, before initiating changes in the student per unit regulations, policymakers may wish to estimate carefully the costs of the proposed changes.

A programmatic trend and legal requirement in special education is the placement of handicapped students in the least restrictive environment appropriate to their needs. The sensitivity analyses support this movement as cost efficient for special education as well. In these analyses, the most likely placement patterns showed a shift of students toward the less restrictive settings. If the 1976/77 placement patterns had been maintained in 1980/81, there would have been an increase in the 1980/81 cost estimate of over $500 million as a result of greater proportions of students in more restrictive placements. These cost savings may be overstated to the extent that shifting students out of separate special education programs and into some (or substantial) participation in regular education would cause an increase in the costs of regular education. In general, however, the marginal cost savings in special education will outweigh the marginal cost increases in regular education. Further, the shifts of students to less restrictive placements within separate special education programs represent significant cost reduction possibilities, particularly if the number of students involved is large enough for the marginal cost savings per student to approach the average cost per student in these placements (i.e., from residential schools averaging $10,390 per student, to day schools averaging $3,618 per student, to special classes averaging $1,755 per student). These results suggest that policymakers should reinforce the current least restrictive setting trend for cost reasons as well as programmatic ones. They indicate that by minimizing restrictive placements and encouraging less restrictive alternatives (subject to the needs of individual children), policymakers may have a substantial influence on special education costs.

In contrast, although teachers' and aides' salary and benefits levels were also shown to have a significant influence on special education costs, these items are most often tied to the general salary levels for all instructional personnel and, consequently, are largely out of direct control of special education. Therefore, while salary and benefit levels are certainly major policy issues, they are ones for all of education, not special education alone.

An important cost area in special education, about which little is known, is related services. The incomplete state data base on which this study had to draw suggests that information on student needs and current practices is limited. The potential for large expenditures in this area exists since the cost impact of state and federal laws and regulations requiring related and support services to be provided to handicapped students is largely unknown. Additional research needs to be carried out to define what related services should be included, the extent of student needs for various related services, and the costs of related services. This is also an area with important intergovernmental and interagency cost implications. Greater federal support for handicapped students may be available through other program areas, such as Rehabilitation, Health, and Social Security, than through PL 94-142 appropriations, which appear to have leveled off. Coordinating services from different social agencies, establishing the appropriate interagency agreements, and utilizing all available sources of funding for handicapped children will become increasingly important as the pressure on educational budgets grows.

Policy Uses of the RCM Methodology

The RCM methodology utilized in this study to estimate the national costs of educating all school-aged handicapped children has a much wider applicability than this single use. It is not limited to special education. It can function as a useful tool in providing relevant information on policymakers for a variety of purposes. The procedures of defining student populations to be served, establishing the programs and services to be offered, specifying the resources of each program, determining the student program assignments and student/teacher ratios can apply to other educational programs. Cost estimation in vocational education, compensatory education, and bilingual education can be conducted in the same manner, only substituting the appropriate student classifications, programs, and decision rules for those of special education. Regular education can be specified by elementary and secondary, by grade level, or even by subject, and the costs then estimated from student and program data and assumptions.[18] In each case, the RCM methodology is general enough to be appropriate for estimating the costs of the educational programs involved.

The RCM methodology can be used at all levels of government for planning and cost estimation purposes. At the federal level, it can serve as a macro-planning tool to estimate the general magnitude of costs involved in various education programs. For example, the cost effects of proposed federal regulations associated with PL 94-142 could be modeled nationally with this methodology. Possible applications would include the individual education program requirement, due process proceedings, and various related services. However, to develop reliable cost estimates it would be necessary to establish nationally applicable values of the programmatic and price variables in the model.

A brief example using psychotherapy services for emotionally disturbed students can serve to show both the process and the difficulties. First, it would be necessary to define what is meant by psychotherapy services (e.g., a single type of service provided by a specific professional, a range of different services provided by different types of personnel). Then, the resources for one unit of this (or these) psychotherapy service(s) must be specified along with their average national prices. Next, the numbers of emotionally disturbed students who will require psychotherapy services annually and the extent or duration of those services must be estimated. Also, the capacity of a unit of psychotherapy services (number of students which can be served by one unit) must be specified. These estimates and assumptions can then be combined through the RCM methodology to provide a projected national cost of the estimated type and level of psychotherapy services. The major problem faced in this process is establishing standard types of services, service levels, and service unit capacities that are valid across the nation. The variations in services (or lack of them) provided by school districts, in available resources and facilities, and in eligibility and placement practices may well limit the specification to the most general level. Nevertheless, the process does make it possible to develop national cost estimates. Further, it can identify areas where missing or incomplete data could be collected and the accuracy of the projections improved.

At the state level, the RCM methodology can also function as a planning tool to estimate educational program costs. However, since the state is a single jurisdiction with a single set of educational statutes and regulations uniformity in actual or desired program practices will be much more likely than on the national level. (In fact, the SEPM used in this study was originally developed as a state planning model.) The RCM methodology can serve as a basis for many state level analyses including program cost estimation, budget preparation, and special cost studies. State funding of categorical and/or regular educational programs can also be accomplished through this approach.[19] (The SEPM has been utilized to replicate the various special education funding formulas in use by states.)

Another important policy use of the methodology is to test the effects on costs, personnel, and students, of proposed new legislation or regulations that may cause changes in existing educational practices. Programmatic changes or changes in the methods or amounts of state aid to districts can be translated into terms of variables in the RCM methodology, and sensitivity analyses can be conducted to investigate the possible outcomes of the changes. The principal advantage of this procedure is that these activities can be carried out prior to passing legislation or finalizing regulations. If any undesirable effects are uncovered, it is possible to make appropriate modifications before statewide implementation. For example, a new bill to require annual psychiatric evaluation of all emotionally disturbed students may be motivated by the best intentions. However, if it would require twice as many psychiatrists as currently are in the state and if it would increase the total special education budget by 20 percent for this single service, perhaps the intent of the legislation could be accomplished in a more feasible manner (e.g., annual evaluations for only emotionally disturbed children in separate educational settings and/or allowing the evaluations also to be done by trained personnel other than psychiatrists). In this case, the modified programmatic changes would be utilized in the RCM, and new projections of costs and personnel obtained to examine their feasibility.

In a similar fashion, the ability to evaluate cost tradeoffs among different program practices is enhanced with the RCM methodology. Changes that would increase costs can be counterbalanced by other changes that would reduce costs, and the net effect of several related programmatic changes can be calculated. For example, a greater use of instructional aides (cost increase) in certain programs could be combined with higher numbers of students per unit (cost reduction) in those programs.

As an illustration, for two programs that have aides, resource room and special class, let us increase the use of aides from part-time to full-time in each program, while at the same time the number of students served by one unit of each program is increased by 10 students in the resource room and by five students in the special class. All other conditions remain constant. The impact of these changes on the most likely cost projections are shown in Table 9-16. Under these example conditions, the increase in aides alone would represent an additional cost of $650 million; however, the higher number of students per unit alone would reduce the costs by $939 million, and the interaction effect of the two variables (the fewer number of program units required due to the higher student/teacher ratios costed at the higher unit cost with aides) would cause a reduction of $186 million. The result would be a net cost reduction of $475 million for this example. Additionally, if the student outcomes (i.e., program effectiveness) of the original and alternative program practices were known or could be estimated, then the results of the RCM cost estimation could be used as the cost portion of a cost-effectiveness analysis.

Another type of tradeoff deals with establishing priorities among competing program proposals to meet budgetary limitations. By focusing on the programmatic aspects of the proposals and using the resource-cost model to translate program considerations into costs, this approach provides essential information to decision makers for choosing among different proposals and for making compromises among them. For example, would it be more important to lower the number of students per unit in special classes by an average of three students per class or to provide supplemental speech and language instruction to students in those classes? Both may be worthy objectives, but budget limitations may not permit both proposals. Analysis of such proposals through a resource-cost model will not answer the question of which proposal is more important, but it will provide an estimate of the costs of each proposal to aid in the decision. Further analysis can be conducted to determine programmatic compromises that could be made to achieve a portion of the objectives of each proposal and still remain within budget requirements. In the example above, this could mean lowering the average class size in special classes by one instead of three and providing speech and language instruction to only half of these students. In any such tradeoff analyses, however, care should be taken not to allow cost considerations to override good programming practices.

Uses of the RCM methodology at the local school district level are similar to those at the state level—program planning, analysis of program changes, comparison of alternatives, cost effectiveness. In fact, the RCM methodology can be applied at the school level or for a single program within a district. However, the more detail and precision would be required for district uses, such as budget preparation, than for state

Table 9-16. Example of Cost Tradeoffs between Program Changes: Greater Use of Instructional Aides and Higher Number of Students per Unit in Two Programs

Program	More Aides per Unit			More Students per Unit			Interaction Effect ($ million)	Net Cost Difference ($ million)
	Most Likely	High Alternative	Cost Difference ($ million)	Most Likely	Low Alternative	Cost Difference ($ million)		
Resource Room	0.33	1.00	+307	22	32	−390	−95	−178
Special Class	0.51	1.00	+343	11	16	−549	−91	−297
Total			+650			−939	−186	−475

planning purposes. Fortunately, it is often the case that district records can provide actual numbers of students, actual program placements, actual salary schedules, actual student/teacher ratios, instead of the estimated statewide averages that would be used at the state level.

One final aspect of the policy usefulness of the RCM approach is that it focuses attention on control points in the educational process. These are specific areas in which policymakers may intervene and have a direct influence on the programs' effects on students and on the program costs. For special education, the areas over which educational decision makers have some control or influence include broad or narrow definitions of handicapping conditions, resources utilized by various programs, placement of handicapped students in various instructional programs and related services, and numbers of students per unit of instructional programs. The degree of control will probably be greatest at the local level where the operating decisions are made; however, program standards and regulations promulgated at the state and federal levels can limit or direct local actions and provide the state and federal levels a means of controlling and/or influencing special education costs.

Summary and Conclusions

This study has used a particular cost estimation approach—a resource-cost model—to estimate the costs of serving all school-aged handicapped students in the United States in 1980/81. The results indicate that the most likely cost estimate is $9 billion, but the range of probable costs was from $7.3 billion to $12.4 billion. This substantial variation was the result of differing assumptions concerning the number of handicapped students to be served, the placement patterns of students in instructional programs, the student/teacher ratio, the use of related services, and the price levels for resources.

There were certain difficulties in developing these national cost estimates. They stem principally from the problems in establishing student and program measures that accurately reflect national averages. As a result, the cost projections should be understood to provide an indication of the magnitude of the costs involved, but clearly are not precise.

The RCM methodology, however, has broad applicability, not only in special education, but for other categorical programs and regular education as well. While this study has utilized the approach at the national level, it probably has greater usefulness at the state and local levels where a single set of laws, regulations, and standards are in force, where more uniformity in actual program practices exist, and where a greater level of detail is possible in student and program data. The methodology can be used for a variety of policy and analytical purposes including program planning, cost estimation, modeling of funding formulas, sensitivity analyses, testing of program or fiscal proposals before implementation, analysis of programmatic tradeoffs, and identification of critical control or intervention points for policymakers.

Notes

1. Fiscal concerns of the Congress related to PL 94-142 were related to placing a limit on the federal funding commitment rather than on estimating the cost impact of the legislation.

2. *Mills* v. *Board of Education of District of Columbia*, 348 F. Supp. 866 (D.D.C. 1972).

3. William T. Hartman, "Estimating the Costs of Educating Handicapped Children: A Resource-Cost Model Approach" (Ph.D. diss., Stanford University, 1979), p. 96.

4. For a comparison of different state laws and regulations governing special education, see *State Profiles in Special Education* (Washington, D.C.: National Association of State Directors of Special Education, 1977).

5. A standardized chart of accounts to record educational expenditures is provided by Charles T. Roberts and Allan R. Lichtenberger, National Center for Educational Statistics, *Financial Accounting: Classifications and Standard Terminology for Local and State School Systems*, State Educational Records and Reports Series, Handbook II, Revised (Washington, D.C.: Government Printing Office, 1973).

6. A. Metz, N. Ford, and L. Silverman, *Study of Excess Costs of Educating Handicapped Pupils*, National Center for Educational Statistics, Report 75-223 (Washington, D.C.: Government Printing Office, 1975).

7. Charles Bernstein, William T. Hartman, Michael W. Kirst, and Rudolph Marshall, *Financing Educational Services for the Handicapped: An Analysis of Current Research and Practices* (Reston, Va.: Council for Exceptional Children, 1976) provides a review of special education cost studies. Previous studies giving national cost estimates include: Richard A. Rossmiller, James A. Hale, and Lloyd E. Frohreich, *Educational Programs for Exceptional Children: Resource Configurations and Costs*, National Education Finance Project, Special Study No. 2 (Madison: Department of Educational Administration, University of Wisconsin, 1970); J. S. Kakalik, Garry D. Brewer, L. A. Dougherty, P. D. Fleichauer, and S. M. Genensky, *Services for Handicapped Youth: A Program Overview* (Santa Monica, Ca.: Rand Corporation, 1973); and James R. Stultz, "The Incidence of Educational Needs and the Cost of Meeting These Needs in the United States in 1980," *Journal of Education Finance* 1 (Winter 1976): 361–72.

8. William T. Hartman, "Estimating the Costs of Educating Handicapped Children: A Resource-Cost Model Approach—Summary Report," *Educational Evaluation and Policy Analysis* 3 (July/August 1981): 33–47.

9. For a description of SEPM and its uses, see Peggy L. Hartman, William T. Hartman, Charles D. Bernstein, and Carrie Levine, *Special Education Planning Model: User Guide* (Palo Alto, Ca.: Management Analysis Center, Inc., 1978).

10. W. V. Grant and C. G. Lund, *Digest of Educational Statistics*, 1975 ed., National Center for Educational Statistics, Report 76-211 (Washington, D.C.: Government Printing Office, 1976), p. 38.

11. W. T. Hartman, "Estimating the Costs of Educating Handicapped Children," p. 270.

12. Jean H. Mack, Josephine Barresi, and Joanne Bunte, "Special Education Class Sizes" (Reston, Va.: Council for Exceptional Children, 1980).

13. National Education Association, *Estimates of School Statistics 1979–80* (Washington, D.C.: National Education Association, 1980), p. 16.

14. Ibid.

15. P. Hartman, "User Guide," provides a thorough listing of related services.

16. W. T. Hartman, "Estimating the Costs of Educating Handicapped Children," p. 96.

17. *Progress Toward a Free Appropriate Public Education: A Report to Congress on the Implementation of Public Law 94-142: The Education for All Handicapped Children Act* (Washington, D.C.: U.S. Office of Education, Bureau of Education for the Handicapped, 1979), p. 162. The percentage of school-aged children served was adjusted for the total school-aged enrollments used in this study.

18. For examples of the resource-cost model approach applied in other educational settings, see Stephen M. Barro, "Modeling Resource Utilization in a School District," *Program Budgeting for School District Planning: Concepts and Applications*, ed. Sue A. Haggart (Santa Monica, Ca.: Rand Corporation, 1969); and W. Curtis, *Educational Resources Management System* (Chicago: Research Corporation of the Association of School Business Officials, 1971).

19. Jay G. Chambers and William T. Hartman, "A Resource-Cost-Based Approach to the Funding of Educational Programs: An Application to Special Education" (this volume, pp. 193–240).

Appendix: Supplemental Projections Students and Personnel *(Most Likely Case)*

Projected Number of Students by Handicapping Category (unduplicated count)

Classification Categories	Year				
	76–77	77–78	78–79	79–80	80–81
EMR					
Number Served	761,429	766,497	778,779	801,649	836,709
Percentage Served	85	87	90	94	100
Number Unserved	131,534	117,145	89,532	50,191	0
TMR					
Number Served*	202,405	199,791	195,339	190,184	184,908
Percentage Served	103	102	102	101	100
Number Unserved	−5,065	−4,511	−3,447	−1,932	0

Projected Number of Students by Handicapping Category (unduplicated count)

Classification Categories	Year				
	76–77	77–78	78–79	79–80	80–81
Hearing					
Number Served	91,366	95,529	103,927	116,753	134,058
Percentage Served	64	67	75	86	100
Number Unserved	51,705	46,049	35,195	19,730	0
Speech					
Number Served	1,341,152	1,368,235	1,425,240	1,517,020	1,645,680
Percentage Served	76	79	83	91	100
Number Unserved	415,173	369,756	282,598	158,422	0
Vision					
Number Served	40,166	40,654	41,732	43,564	46,227
Percentage Served	81	83	87	93	100
Number Unserved	9,169	8,166	6,241	3,499	0
SED					
Number Served	294,461	312,533	348,669	403,210	476,138
Percentage Served	58	62	71	83	100
Number Unserved	213,689	190,313	145,453	81,539	0
Ortho					
Number Served	88,623	88,692	89,107	90,292	92,454
Percentage Served	90	91	93	96	100
Number Unserved	10,047	8,948	6,839	3,834	0
OHI					
Number Served	134,173	137,070	143,139	152,854	166,417
Percentage Served	76	78	83	90	100
Number Unserved	43,433	38,682	29,564	16,573	0
SLD					
Number Served	818,206	853,678	925,365	1,035,097	1,183,411
Percentage Served	65	68	75	86	100
Number Unserved	444,769	396,114	302,743	169,715	0
Multiple					
Number Served	65,401	66,546	68,983	72,960	78,586
Percentage Served	78	80	85	91	100
Number Unserved	18,468	16,448	12,571	7,047	0
Total					
Number Served	3,837,382	3,929,225	4,120,280	4,423,583	4,844,588
Percentage Served	74	77	82	90	100
Number Unserved	1,333,159	1,187,343	907,517	508,842	0

*Negative numbers unserved represent overservice in this category, that is, greater than 100% of estimated incidence rate.

Projected Numbers of Students by Instructional Programs (duplicated count)

Type of Program	Year				
	76–77	77–78	78–79	79–80	80–81
Indirect Services	100,606	106,150	117,668	136,078	162,497
Speech & Language Instruction	1,421,400	1,455,248	1,526,295	1,640,548	1,801,715
Other Direct Services	138,553	149,353	172,449	210,947	269,181
Resource Room	1,025,540	1,069,657	1,161,052	1,306,247	1,511,980
Special Class	1,126,467	1,133,472	1,147,279	1,166,436	1,184,016
Other Agency Day School	74,141	78,439	87,477	102,171	123,707
Residential School	107,626	106,236	103,140	97,566	87,830
Hospital & Homebound	57,822	60,871	67,472	78,627	95,653
Total	4,052,155	4,159,426	4,382,832	4,738,620	5,236,579

Projected Number of Instructional Personnel Serving Each Handicapping Category

Classification	Year				
	76–77	77–78	78–79	79–80	80–81
EMR					
Certified	45,769	46,003	46,596	47,743	49,523
Noncertified	20,282	20,280	20,326	20,492	20,788
TMR					
Certified	15,523	15,372	15,129	14,872	14,645
Noncertified	7,582	7,503	7,372	7,231	7,100
Hearing					
Certified	6,419	6,606	6,957	7,433	7,946
Noncertified	2,266	2,310	2,385	2,465	2,501
Speech					
Certified	22,666	23,023	23,772	24,967	26,601
Noncertified	1,490	1,461	1,397	1,288	1,110
Vision					
Certified	3,119	3,158	3,249	3,400	3,620
Noncertified	954	968	999	1,051	1,127
SED					
Certified	21,702	22,957	25,436	29,111	33,901
Noncertified	9,436	9,873	10,699	11,824	13,099
Ortho					
Certified	7,031	7,059	7,135	7,294	7,557
Noncertified	1,647	1,646	1,649	1,662	1,692
OHI					
Certified	10,994	11,243	11,769	12,611	13,792
Noncertified	3,507	3,516	3,531	3,549	3,540

Financing

Projected Number of Instructional Personnel Serving Each Handicapping Category

Classification	Year				
	76–77	77–78	78–79	79–80	80–81
SLD					
Certified	39,809	41,567	45,124	50,589	58,011
Noncertified	14,459	15,030	16,171	17,885	20,140
Multiple					
Certified	6,178	6,363	6,759	7,404	8,344
Noncertified	3,032	3,119	3,303	3,604	4,042
Total					
Certified	179,210	183,351	191,926	205,424	223,940
Noncertified	64,655	65,706	67,832	71,051	75,139

Projected Number of Instructional Personnel by Instructional Program

Type of Program	Year				
	76–77	77–78	78–79	79–80	80–81
Indirect Services					
Certified	1,281	1,352	1,502	1,740	2,079
Noncertified	0	0	0	0	0
Speech & Language Inst.					
Certified	21,247	21,754	22,816	24,525	26,935
Noncertified	0	0	0	0	0
Other Direct Services					
Certified	5,435	5,828	6,673	8,088	10,235
Noncertified	0	0	0	0	0
Resource Room					
Certified	45,691	47,677	51,800	58,365	67,705
Noncertified	15,078	15,734	17,095	19,261	22,342
Special Class					
Certified	97,229	98,004	99,508	101,569	103,535
Noncertified	49,587	49,982	50,750	51,800	52,802
Other Agency Day School					
Certified	0	0	0	0	0
Noncertified	0	0	0	0	0
Residential School					
Certified	0	0	0	0	0
Noncertified	0	0	0	0	0
Hospital & Homebound					
Certified	8,327	8,736	9,627	11,137	13,451
Noncertified	0	0	0	0	0
Total					
Certified	179,210	183,351	191,926	205,424	223,940
Noncertified	64,665	65,716	67,845	71,061	75,144

Index